Leon C. Metz

EL PASO
CHRONICLES

BOOKS BY LEON C. METZ

John Selman: Gunfighter

Dallas Stoudenmire: El Paso Marshal

Pat Garrett: Story of a Western Lawman

The Shooters

City at the Pass

Fort Bliss: An Illustrated History

Turning Points of El Paso, Texas

Desert Army: Fort Bliss on the Texas Border

Border: The U.S.-Mexico Line

Southern New Mexico Empire

Roadside History of Texas

El Paso Chronicles

EL PASO CHRONICLES

A RECORD OF HISTORICAL EVENTS
IN EL PASO, TEXAS

LEON C. METZ

MANGAN BOOKS
El Paso, Texas

Published by Mangan Books
6245 Snowheights, El Paso, Texas 79912

Printed in the United States of America

Library of Congress Cataloging-in- Publication Data

Metz, Leon Claire.
    El Paso Chronicles: a record of historical events in El Paso,
Texas / Leon C. Metz.
        p. cm.
    Includes bibliographical references and index.
    ISBN 0-930208-32-3 (hard: alk. paper)
    1. El Paso (Tex.) – History – Chronology – Juvenile literature.
[1. El Paso (Tex.) – History – Chronology.] I. Title.
F394.E4M479 1993
976.4'96 — dc20
                                 93-29521
                                      CIP
                                        AC

To my brother, Charles
who once lived at the Pass.

RANDOM THOUGHTS
ABOUT
A CHRONOLOGICAL
DIG

A FEW YEARS AGO I was in the newspaper section of the El
Paso Public library and thumbing idly through a stack of
old newspapers. Quite by accident, I turned up a story about Harry
Houdini, the famous escape artist. He was in El Paso, in a strait
jacket and dangling from a cable between two telegraph poles in
Pioneer Plaza. As a paying crowd cheered, he freed himself and
dropped onto a net.

I took no notes as I had no thoughts about a chronology in
those days, but I remember the news story because of its human
interest. Ten years later I wrote a historical piece about Pioneer
Plaza for inclusion on a plaque sponsored by the Texas Historical
Commission. I included Houdini's feat, but the Commission
wanted more than just my word. It wanted evidence.

Well, I spent days in the library seeking that one elusive
newspaper column, and never found it. So I drew a line through
Harry Houdini's name, and Houdini vanished from the Texas
history plaque.

Except for this foreword, Harry Houdini doesn't appear in
this chronology either because I still haven't located the source of
that story. Still, I know that he visited this city. I know that he
awed a crowd.

So chronologies, even when as detailed as this one, do not include everything.

Nevertheless, I've been fortunate. During recent years an avalanche of local and regional books have reached the market. Researchers have explored and evaluated El Paso and its environs from practically every perspective. They and the newspapers, plus historical journals, plus thesis and dissertation copies, have furnished the hundreds of comments that go into this publication.

Yet, many possible events remain untouched. I either couldn't find them, didn't see them, or rejected them as unsuitable. But in all cases I took the research as far as I could.

If I had it all to do over, this chronological dig would be my first book instead of the twelfth. Chronologies offer a unique perspective regarding a city and its past. One can learn a lot from chronologies.

In this sense, I have striven to discuss El Paso and the El Paso Southwest from the context of balance, from the background of history as panorama instead of one-dimensional. To paraphrase an old movie title, I wanted to present the good, the bad, the ugly, the important, the inconsequential, and sometimes just the irreverent. I wanted history as intertwined tapestry. I wanted to demonstrate, however minutely, that ladies sponsoring a church supper had something in common with ladies calling out, "Company in the parlor, girls." I wanted to demonstrate that gamblers, gunmen, revolutionaries, politicians, editors and preachers had more in common than just their humanity.

A good chronology lists the details of lives and events that have rumbled down through history on separate but intertwining paths. It is the common fate of all, that people and events, in the end, are simply a patch on a quilt of many colors.

One cannot read a chronology without concluding that El Paso is and was such a richly interesting place. Nowhere in this country can one find 400 years of such colorful, diverse history. Where else can one encounter stagecoaches, old Spanish Trails, covered wagons, ox carts, forts, presidios, missions, mountains, deserts, rivers, swamps, dams, railroads and international airports. Where else would one identify Indians, Spaniards, Mexicans, Irishmen, Germans, blacks, Chinese, French, cavalrymen, farmers, stock raisers, gunfighters, revolutionaries, prostitutes, fur trappers, highwaymen, refugees, mercenaries, politicians, gamblers, builders, government men, cowboys, educators, laborers, professionals, leaders and followers, dreamers and oddballs? For whatever reason, they all came to the Pass. They all left their mark on what would become, and what is, a great city.

I'd like to thank my wife Cheryl who was patient as I piled books and papers all over the house. My thanks also go as usual to the El Paso Public Library and the UTEP Library. John McKinney was always there with whatever help I needed. My sister-in-law Morna Lee Fontaine spent days searching for elusive dates. My father-in-law, William Schilling, read every word of the manuscript and pointed out many shortcomings. Linda Harris, president of the Doña Ana County Historical Society, helped. Randy Lee Eickhoff lent me material relating to his research on a forthcoming Tigua Indian book. And Mark Bentley read and criticized portions of the manuscript. So did Martha Peterson.

Judy and Frank Mangan, publishers and editors (and good friends), as always, have been encouraging. What would I do without them?

Oddly, or perhaps not, a chronology of 60 to 100 pages would be thought complete if it hit the high points of El Paso's history. When the pages extend to several hundred, however, there is a tendency to notice omissions. Questions arise: Why aren't all the schools and city subdivisions included? How can one person or event be mentioned, and another just as important be ignored? My response is that no book is definitive. Even as I write, I think of subjects overlooked. Some I have gathered at the last minute.

And there comes a time in every manuscript when the author realizes he can't include (or even think of) everything, that things have to be wrapped up, that the time quickly comes to say "enough." The manuscript goes to press. The author crosses his fingers.

Every attempt has been made to be "right" in this chronology, but I have learned that broad disagreements often exist among historians in terms of what happened and when and where it happened. Nevertheless, the responsibility for errors falls where it should, on this author.

Leon C. Metz

EL PASO CHRONICLES

570 MILLION B.C.

Shallow seas cover El Paso Southwest.

140 MILLION B.C.

The land rises and the seas drain.

90 MILLION B.C.

The El Paso Southwest sinks again, and seas cover the land once more.

50 MILLION B.C.

Volcanos erupt. The Franklins and the Sierras de Juarez lift up from the plains. The Age of Reptiles begins. Tropics form. Dinosaurs inhabit the El Paso Southwest.

2 MILLION B.C.

Lake Cabeza de Vaca forms. It is as broad as Lake Superior. The last Ice Age moves in. So do mammoths and other wooly animals.

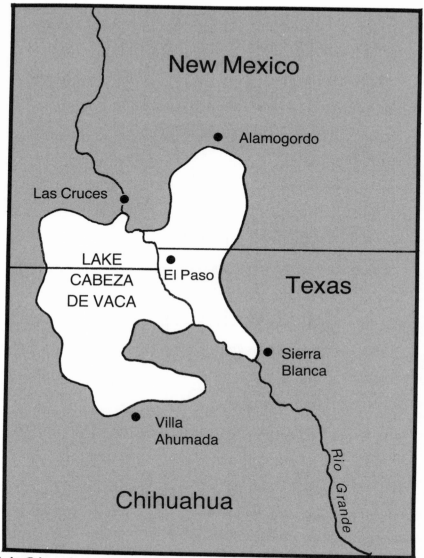

Lake Cabeza de Vaca is named for the European explorer, and this is the way the lake looked when mountain ranges blocked its way to the sea. It flooded natural basins in Texas, New Mexico and Chihuahua, and was roughly the same size as today's Lake Superior although much more shallow. Dry and wet eras caused the lake to recede and advance. With the melting of glaciers, the lake overflowed and cut its way through the Quitman Range near Sierra Blanca, Texas, took over the Rio Conchos and became through-flowing to the Gulf of Mexico.
(Map: Frank Mangan)

600,000 B.C.

The Rio Grande forms.

75,000 B.C.

Lake Cabeza de Vaca drains. The Rio Grande is established as a free-flowing stream to the Gulf of Mexico.

50,000 B.C.

The Rio Grande cuts the Pass of the North. El Paso Canyon forms.

35,000-28,000 B.C.

Early man crosses the land bridge between Asia and North America.

12,000-9500 B.C.

The rain stops falling, although the climate remains wetter than today.

10,000-6000 B.C.

Paleo-Indian Period. Clovis Culture arrives in the Southwest, to be followed by Folsom Man. The Clovis Fluted Point is frequently found in association with large game animals, especially the mammoth. Rainfall increases and so do expansive grasslands. The mountains contain pine and fir. The summers are cool and the winters relatively mild. The rain falls primarily in winter. Bones from wooly mammoths are laid down where Vista Hills Hospital is now.

10,000 B.C. TO 7000 B.C.

Large game animals become extinct in the El Paso region. Human occupants rely on small game, such as deer. Plants and vegetables become more important. The Chihuahuan Desert creeps north out of Mexico. Climate is likely similar to that of today.

1000 B.C. TO 1000 A.D.

Archaic Period. Desert culture flourishes near the Rio Grande. Pithouses become common. Maize, beans and squash are principal crops. Mogollon culture forms.
Hannibal crosses the Alps.

200 A.D. TO 1450

Formative Period. Ceramics are made. The Jornada branch of the Mogollon Culture occupies structures near present Northpark Shopping Center. This culture is also found throughout the desert valley and along the river. Some villages develop communal rooms. Natural and man-made reservoirs harness rain runoff from nearby mountains.
Charlemagne defeated by the Basques at Roncesvalles in the Pyrenees.

1150

The classic or Golden Age of Pueblo Culture begins. The tribes establish drama, formal religion and a system of government. The Mimbres people along the Mimbres River in New Mexico make the finest ceramic designs in the world. But by 1150, they have vanished.
Paris University is established, and Arabs in Spain manufacture paper.

1300

Moist climate prevails. Piñons and junipers likely cover the Franklin Mountains.
Trade fairs spring up at Bruges, Antwerp, Lyon and Geneva.

1325

The Aztecs of Mexico establish a capital (called Tenochtitlan) where Mexico City now stands.

1492

Christopher Columbus discovers the West Indies.

1498

Columbus discovers Trinidad and South America.

1520

Hernando Cortés conquers Mexico.

1536

Cabeza de Vaca claims to have seen Seven Cities of Gold. De Vaca may also have been the first European to make contact with the Tiguas. Although his route across Texas is debated, with as many as nine different approaches possible, one of these could have taken him through the Isleta Pueblo near present-day Albuquerque. With him are three other travelers: Alonzo Maldonado, Andres Dorantes, and a Moor, Estevan.
Queen Anne Boleyn is sent to the Tower of London and executed.

1540

Henry VIII creates professorships of Greek, Hebrew, divinity, civil law and physics at Oxford and Cambridge.

FEBRUARY 23: Francisco Coronado leaves Mexico City for today's American Southwest during a search for El Dorado. He traveled to the Great Plains before turning back. He found no gold, just Indians.

SEPTEMBER 7: Coronado crosses the Rio Grande near Albuquerque, and camps with the Tiguas at Isleta.

1543

The Spanish declare Indians living in Spanish provinces to be direct vassals of the Crown.

1550

Nueva Vizcaya, a huge, rambling district, began with the settlement of Zacatecas. It grew to include such diverse areas as Durango, Chihuahua, Sinaloa, Sonora and parts of Coahuila and New Mexico.

1565

St. Augustine, Florida founded.

1567

Santa Barbara, near Parral, Chihuahua, is founded by Rodrigo del Río de Losa. By the late 1570s, the village had a population of 35 Spanish families. When serious labor shortages occurred in the gold and silver mines, Spanish slavers pushed into the El Paso region and rounded up

Suma and Manso Indians to work in the Santa Barbara pits, after baptism, of course. Practically all Spanish expeditions into today's West Texas and New Mexico, including Oñate's in 1598, pushed off from Santa Barbara. The village, which is still active, is important in El Paso history.

Rio de Janeiro founded.

1580

The southern half of Nueva Vizcaya is occupied, and a slender arm of settlement is now poised for thrusting north into New Mexico.

It is uncertain if Indian occupation of the El Paso region(up until the arrival of the Spanish) are Puebloans, or Apaches, or who. Was this a transitional period? Researchers still aren't certain.

1581

Pope Gregory XIII attempts to reconcile Roman Catholic and Russian Orthodox Church.

AUGUST: The Chamuscado-Rodríguez Expedition passes through present-day El Paso. It describes the region as "a marshy valley extending 24 miles, an area suitable for ranches and for the cultivation of anything that might be desired." The Spanish named it *Los Valientes*. Three friars remained in New Mexico against military advice. Fray Santa María was slain by Tigua Indians near Isleta, while Friars Francisco López and Agustín Rodríguez were killed by the Tiguas at Puaray.

1582

NOVEMBER 10: Captain Antonio de Espejo leaves Santa Barbara for the north. His expedition hopes to rescue the Franciscan friars who traveled with Chamuscado.

1583

JANUARY 19: The Antonio de Espejo Expedition approaches the Pass while searching for the three priests. The name "New Mexico" appears for the first time in an expedition journal. The soldiers call the El Paso lower valley, *La Cienega Grande,* and describe the Manso Indians as having homes of straw. The group camps near present downtown El Paso, the Spanish referring to it as *Los Vueltos del Rio,* meaning "The Turns of the River." The area just west of the U.T. El Paso campus (the canyon) was called, *Barrancas de Los Vueltos del Rio,* "the Canyons of the Turns of the River."

1595

SEPTEMBER: Don Juan de Oñate is awarded a Spanish contract for the colonization of New Mexico at his own expense. Until this time, early travelers were interested only in the exploration of the land, not in the occupation of it.

1598

Shakespeare writes Much Ado about Nothing, *and* Henry V.

APRIL 20: An advance party of the Oñate Expedition reaches the Rio Grande 30 miles downstream from today's El Paso. Several horses drown in the water, and other horses drink until their bellies split. The expedition did not follow the conventional expressway of traveling down the Conchos River and up the Rio Grande, but had marched north across the Chihuahua Desert. Oñate party celebrates Thanksgiving near San Elizario.

APRIL 30: Oñate takes possession (La Toma) for God and King Philip of Spain of all lands watered by Rio Grande.

MAY 4: Oñate crosses the Rio Grande near the present-day Hacienda Cafe and names the ford, "El Paso del Rio del Norte." The name El Paso is now established.

1607

MAY 14: Colonists land at Jamestown.

1610

Santa Fe established.
Camino Real extends from Mexico City through El Paso to Santa Fe.
For three centuries it is the longest highway in NorthAmerica.

1620

Pilgrim Fathers land at Plymouth Rock.
A royal decree by the King of Spain requires each pueblo to choose a governor by popular vote, plus a lieutenant-governor and other officials to supervise the tribes. The decree stipulates that the inaugurations are to be held during the first week of the new year.

1621

A mission is built in the Isleta Pueblo (near Albuquerque) and dedicated to St. Anthony of Padua.

1629

Fray Alonso de Benavides recommends a mission at the Pass for Manso Indians.

1640

The pueblos of Jemez, Isleta, Alameda, San Felipe, and Cochiti conspire with the Navajos to revolt and expel the Spanish. Nine Indian ringleaders are hanged. Others are sold into slavery.

1644

Religious persecution of the Pueblo Indians results in the hanging of 40 Indians who refuse to become Catholic.

1659

Richard Cromwell resigns.

DECEMBER 6: At the Pass, Fray García de San Francisco y Zúñiga builds a little church of branches and mud, plus a monastery thatched with straw. He dedicates his work to the holy Virgin of Guadalupe. El Paso del Norte, Chihuahua (later Ciudad Juarez) dates its existence from this creation.

1660

Spaniards begin irrigated farming at El Paso. A stick and mud dam is constructed where the Sierra Madre diversion dam is today.

1662

APRIL 2: Fray García de San Francisco lays the first foundation stone for Nuestra Señora de Guadalupe Mission.

1668

The British East India Company obtains control of Bombay.

JANUARY 15: Construction completed on Our Lady of Guadalupe Mission in El Paso, Chihuahua.

1673

JANUARY 22: Fray García de San Francisco dies in the convent of Senecú where he is buried.

1678

NOVEMBER 29: First recorded Spanish marriage takes place in El Paso del Norte.

1680

AUGUST 10: Pueblo Revolt begins in northern New Mexico. Two thousand Spanish and Indian refugees flee south toward El Paso. Nearly 400 Spaniards are slain, including 21 missionaries. This becomes the greatest retreat from Indians in the history of North America.

AUGUST 21: The Spanish abandon Santa Fe.

AUGUST 24: The Spanish and their Indian allies are in Socorro, New Mexico. Many Piro Indians join them.

SEPTEMBER 18-OCTOBER 9: Spanish and Indian refugees camp at a site believed to be present-day Canutillo, Texas, an area called *La Salineta*. A muster roll lists 317 Christian Indians who are Tiguas, Piros and others.

OCTOBER 9: Refugees have been divided into three camps near El Paso del Norte: San Lorenzo for Spanish, San Pedro de Alcantara and Santisimo Sacramento. Sacramento later became Ysleta. All of the camps are destitute. Inhabitants consume wild herbs and mesquite beans. Many continue south toward the Mexican interior.

OCTOBER 12: Ysleta and Socorro are established in El Paso valley. The first Catholic Mass is said on soil that eventually becomes a part of the State of Texas.

1681

JANUARY: The jurisdiction of El Paso del Norte is passed from Nueva Vizcaya to New Mexico. El Paso is the capital of New Mexico, and will remain so until the province is recaptured from the Pueblo Indians in 1693.

JANUARY 17: A presidio (fort) will be constructed to protect the people of El Paso del Norte and to prevent hostile Indians from passing to Sonora and Parral. The presidio will have 50 men earning a yearly salary of 315 pesos.

NOVEMBER 5: Governor Antonio de Otermín seeks to recapture New Mexico.

NOVEMBER 5: William Penn settles Pennsylvania.

1682

Old Pueblo Road system extends from Ysleta to Socorro to Hueco Tanks.
Missions in Ysleta and Socorro are likely completed during this year. The original Ysleta mission (1680?) is said to have been built of logs.

JANUARY: Mescalero Apaches drive off 200 horses belonging to *Maestro de Campo* Alonso García of El Paso, Chihuahua. Pursuing soldiers kill several Indians and capture twenty.

FEBRUARY 11: Otermín returns to El Paso del Norte after burning the Isleta Pueblo near modern Albuquerque. He brings 385 Indian hostages with him. The Tiguas settle at the Ysleta del Sur location, and are impressed into building a new mission, Sacramento de los Tiguas de Ysleta. Tantos and Jemez Indians settled in Socorro.

1684

AUGUST 5: Ten Indians, most of them Mansos, are hanged in the El Paso del Norte mission plaza. They plotted against the Spanish and confessed. Their bodies hung several days from the gallows as a warning to others. Their heads are placed on stakes.

AUGUST 18: Permission is requested to abandon the El Paso valley because of hunger and Indian uprisings. Permission denied.

SEPTEMBER 19: A Manso Indian named Juan confesses to a plot hatched at El Ancon de Ximenes, downstream a few miles from El Paso. Indians from ten nations plan to attack and burn El Paso, killing everyone except one friar who will carry the news to Mexico City. As for Governor Domingo Jironza Petris de Cruzate, he will be captured, slain by the women, and his head cut off and placed on a stake facing the city in the manner Cruzate used for rebelling Indians. Cruzate strikes first, and a force of 70 soldiers and 100 friendly Indians immediately attack El Ancon de Ximenes, killing rebellious Mansos and burning the village.

NOVEMBER 11: Due to constant warfare between the Spanish and the natives of ten nations—Sumas, Mansos, Janos, Julimes, Conchos, Apaches, Jocomes, Chinaras, Salineros, and Dientes Negros—few crops have been harvested. Almost everybody in El Paso is starving. Great numbers of Spanish have fled south.

1685

NOVEMBER 28: After numerous petitions to abandon El Paso have bombarded Mexico City, the government decides that El Paso del Norte must become a permanent settlement.

1691

FEBRUARY 22: King Carlos II of Spain, through Governor Don Diego de Vargas, officially names two churches: Mision de Corpus

Christi de los Tiguas de Ysleta, and Mision de Nuestra Señora de la
Limpia Concepción de los Piros de Socorro.

FEBRUARY 22: Governor Diego de Vargas takes charge of New
Mexico province even though all he controls is El Paso del Norte.

MARCH 8: The Spanish discover salt flats near the Guadalupe
Mountains.

1692

*L'Archeveque, a Frenchman formerly with La Salle, is the first known
European other than Spaniards to arrive in the El Paso valley. He joins
the Governor Diego de Vargas expedition for the reconquest of New
Mexico.*

SEPTEMBER 13: De Vargas enters Santa Fe after burning and destroy-
ing numerous Indian pueblos.

1695

Spain essentially has reconquered New Mexico.

1702

*Santa Eulalia starts as a mining center. However, due to a lack of
water, the village became a forerunner of Chihuahua City.*

1706

Benjamin Franklin born.
*Albuquerque founded, and is named for the Duke of Alburquerque, the
Spanish viceroy in Mexico City.*

1707

Chihuahua City is chartered at the junction of the Chuviscar and Sacramento rivers. No one is exactly certain where the name "Chihuahua" originates, but it likely is a hybrid word coined from the Nahuatl and Tarahumara languages. It may refer to a place of two waters, or to a dry, sandy area.

England and Scotland unite under the name of Great Britain.

1730

The Hacienda de Tiburcios is the origin of today's San Elizario. The hacienda was founded sometime between 1730 and 1750. Little is known about it.

John and Charles Wesley found the Methodist sect at Oxford.

1740

Rio Grande flood waters wash away the Ysleta Mission.

1744

The Ysleta Mission is rebuilt on higher ground. The name is changed to Mision San Antonio de la Ysleta (St. Anthony's Mission). The mission has 70 families. These include 498 Indians and 54 Spaniards.

1751

Charles V, King of Spain, makes a land grant to the Pueblo de San Antonio de la Ysleta. The grant covers one league in each cardinal direction from the church, or approximately 17,712 acres.

Los Portales built during this period in San Elizario.

1756

French and Indian Wars begin.

1760

El Paso del Norte has over 350 Spanish families. Apple, pear and peach orchards flourish. Excellent wine and brandy are brewed.

1762

By some accounts the El Paso valley contains a quarter million grape vines.

1764

The Spanish government establishes several presidios in the northern provinces of Texas, New Mexico, Nayarit, Nueva Vizcaya, Coahuila, Nuevo Leon, California, and Nuevo Santander.

1765

AUGUST: The Marqués de Rubí, a man of influence in Spanish political and military circles, inspects the presidios on the northern frontier and makes recommendations concerning their reorganization.

1766

José de Urrutia, a Spanish engineer, draws the first map of El Paso del Norte.

Five thousand people, including Christian Indians, live in the El Paso valley.

1767

The estimated population of the El Paso valley, not counting Indians, is 2,000. Estimates fluctuate.

1772

SEPTEMBER 10: The Marqués de Rubí recommends, and Spain decrees, a chain of 15 presidios 100 miles apart on a line that roughly parallels the present international border. Rubí concluded that Spain could not hope to defend areas it had not effectively occupied. The El Paso del Norte garrison would be moved south to Carrizal. Since El Paso was the largest settlement north of Durango, it had sufficient population to defend itself.

Lieutenant Hugh O'Connor (Hugo Oconor), an Irishman with long experience in the Spanish Army, will supervise the presidios.

1773

An onslaught of smallpox leads to the extinction of the Manso Indians.

1774

There are 225 Spanish families and more than 510 families of Christian Indians living in the El Paso del Norte area.

The first San Elizario presidio (fort) is established near the Mexican town of Porvenir.

1776

MAY: The northern provinces are established as *Provincias Internas* (Interior Provinces), separated from the viceroyalty of New Spain, and placed under the command of Caballero Don Teodoro de Croix. He was given vast powers to solve problems.

JULY 4: The United States adopts the Declaration of Independence.

1777

DECEMBER 14: An Apache emissary comes to El Paso del Norte and requests peace for his people in the Sierra Blanca, Sacramento and Organ mountains.

1780

FEBRUARY 14: Teodoro de Croix reorganizes the presidial line. His order establishes a presidio at what is now San Elizario.

1781

During the 1780s, a massive smallpox epidemic rages in this region. The population dramatically drops.

1783

The territory of the United States extends to the Mississippi River, thanks to the Treaty of Paris. The new republic is now Spain's neighbor.

1784

Bernardo de Gálvez becomes viceroy of New Spain

1789

FEBRUARY 14: A presidio (ordered in 1780) is finally established at San Elizario.

1790

During this year, or prior to it, the lieutenant governor of Nueva Viscaya awarded a four-league tract of land to Francisco García, the military commandant of El Paso del Norte. The tract extended into what would become the Gadsden Purchase, and was called "Rancho de Santa Teresa."

San Elizario is a Spanish resettlement area for Apaches.

1798

JUNE 25: The Alien Act enables the United States to order the departure of any illegal immigrant deemed dangerous.

1800

MARCH 21: Construction begins on another bridge across the Rio Grande.

1803

OCTOBER 20: The United States Senate ratifies the Louisiana Purchase.

1804

MAY 14: The Lewis and Clark expedition leaves St. Louis.

1807

MARCH 21: Lieutenant Zebulon Pike becomes the first American to visit the Pass even though he is a Spanish prisoner. He was supposed to be surveying the headwaters of the Red River, but claimed he mistook the Rio Grande in New Mexico for the Red.

SEPTEMBER 1: Aaron Burr is acquitted on charges of treason. Burr had allegedly planned mercenary expeditions against the Spanish Southwest.

1810

SEPTEMBER 16: Hidalgo cites his famous *Grito de Dolores*, and calls for Mexican independence from Spain.

1811

Spanish laws prohibit the sale of Indian lands.

1812

The War of 1812 begins. Great Britain briefly occupies Washington.

1815

OCTOBER 15: Citizens of El Paso del Norte swear an oath of loyalty to the Spanish monarch.

1821

SEPTEMBER 27: Mexico gains independence from Spain. El Paso del Norte region proclaims its loyalty to Mexico. Mexico reaffirms the laws and protection of Indian rights and lands.

With Mexico's independence, Mexico decrees the Camino Real (Royal Road or King's Highway) shall henceforth be known as Camino Constitucional (Constitutional Highway or Road).

1822

The Santa Fe Trail opens between Santa Fe and Franklin, Missouri. William Bucknell, a Missouri Indian trader who became the "Father of the Santa Fe Trade," was hunting on the South Plains in the autumn of 1821 when he encountered Mexican soldiers and learned of Mexico's independence. American traders would be welcome in Santa Fe, the soldiers claimed. Bucknell returned to Franklin, Missouri, re-outfitted, and by the summer of 1822 he was in Santa Fe with trade goods.

1823

John G. Heath, a Missouri lawyer, receives permission from the Ayuntamiento of El Paso del Norte, to colonize 25 square leagues of the Mesilla Valley. The authority was later revoked.

MAY 30: The Canutillo Grant (one and one-half leagues of farm land) is awarded to 30 families. The grant was 16 miles northwest of El Paso del Norte—where Canutillo, Texas is today.

1824

A brisk commerce is flowing over the Santa Fe Trail.
Settlements in the El Paso del Norte area of the Rio Grande valley are incorporated into the state of Chihuahua. The total population is 3,000.

JANUARY 31: The provinces of Chihuahua, Durango and New Mexico, are combined to form *Estados Interno del Norte* (Internal States of the North).

MARCH 11: The United States Bureau of Indian Affairs is established.

JULY 6: Chihuahua becomes a Mexican state. El Paso del Norte, normally considered a part of New Mexico, is transferred to Chihuahua.

AUGUST: Trader Hugh Stephenson makes his first appearance in El Paso.

1825

The governor of Chihuahua creates a commission to settle the Ysleta-Socorro boundary dispute.

1826

James O. Pattie, a cultivated man as well as a fur trapper and explorer, visits the Pass. He praises the wine and quality of wheat.

1827

SEPTEMBER 20: Ponce de León, a prominent El Paso figure, acquires 211 acres north of the Rio Grande and builds a shack near today's northwest corner of Paisano and El Paso streets. Ponce began what we now call El Paso, Texas. He was a wealthy merchant who cultivated vineyards and wheat, and for a while was the *jefe político* of the El Paso district.

1828

AUGUST: Hugh Stephenson marries Juana María Ascarate. Her parents, aristocratic residents of El Paso, Chihuahua, have extensive land holdings at Janos and Corralitos. The Ascarate grant extended east of the present I-10 overpasses.

1829

The Socorro Mission is destroyed by a flood, and rebuilt a half-mile west. This same flood placed Ysleta, Socorro and San Elizario on the north bank of the main channel. The San Elizario chapel was destroyed.

The Mexican courts settle a boundary dispute between Ysleta and Senecú.

1830

Independence, Missouri has essentially replaced Franklin, Missouri as the primary outfitting point for the Santa Fe Trail.

MAY 4: A Rio Grande flood washes away the Ponce de León shack at today's El Paso and Paisano streets.

1832

Ponce de León acquires additional land, bringing his total holdings north of the river to nearly 600 acres. Ponce then builds a hacienda on the site of the present Plaza Theater. What is now downtown El Paso, Texas, was known in 1832 as Ponce's Rancho.

Apaches drive settlers off the Canutillo Grant.

The Chihuahua governor issues a decree recognizing and confirming the Ysleta grant. This resolves a dispute between the pueblos of Ysleta, Socorro and Senecú. The controversy occurred when the Rio Grande shifted its channel and placed the pueblo of Ysleta in a different location relative to the river.

1835

A Rio Grande flood destroys much of San Elizario and its church.

The Mexican government establishes a customs house in El Paso del Norte. The house will intercept and inspect trade goods along the Chihuahua Trail (the old Camino Real between Santa Fe and Chihuahua City).

The governor of Chihuahua reaffirms the grant of Ysleta and its protected status.

JUNE 24: The Chihuahua governor orders the El Paso District to burn its fields of tobacco. The Tiguas in Ysleta say they need to grow sufficient tobacco for scouting expeditions. Apparently the men like to smoke.

1836

An Apache chief demands that Paso del Norte release his wife and family. A battle occurs. The chief and 20 Indians are slain, as is the Mexican governor and several soldiers.

MARCH 6: Texas declares independence from Mexico. General Antonio López de Santa Ana marches north from Mexico with an army. The Alamo in San Antonio falls. Thirteen women and children, plus one Hispanic and one black slave, are the only survivors. Santa Ana is now pursuing General Sam Houston.

MARCH 27: Over 300 Texas prisoners shot on order of General Santa Ana at Goliad, Texas.

APRIL 21: General Sam Houston destroys General Santa Ana's army at the Battle of San Jacinto, near present-day Houston. Santa Ana is captured, and a disputed agreement is now reached. The Texans believe they are assured of the Rio Grande to its source as their southern and western border. General Santa Ana thinks differently, however, and once released, he returns to Mexico and still insists on the Nueces River as the southern, and historic, boundary. The Texas Republic is incomplete. What is now West Texas remains in Mexican hands until the Treaty of Guadalupe Hidalgo terminates the forthcoming Mexican War.

The Texas government recognizes all grants made by Spain and Mexico.

1837

The east side of the old San Elizario Chapel is rebuilt.
Texas claims Ponce's Rancho as a part of Bexar County, Texas.

1838

More than half the goods flowing down the Santa Fe Trail from Missouri are going through Santa Fe and heading down the Chihuahua Trail (old Camino Real or Constitutional Highway). Santa Fe has a paucity of money, the citizens and businessmen living mostly by barter. Chihuahua City has a mint. Money also exists in Durango and other Mexican cities. So American traders begin eyeing the Ponce Rancho area on the north bank of the Rio Grande as a suitable location for way-stations.

1839

A Kiowa war party is besieged at Hueco Tanks. Judging by which version of history one reads and believes, the attackers are either Mexican soldiers or Tigua Indians.

The governor of Chihuahua issues the The Doña Ana Bend Colony Grant to Don José María Costales and 116 colonists.

SEPTEMBER 12: Trader Josiah Gregg visits the Pass on his way to Chihuahua City. Gregg's *Commerce of the Prairies* is a classic.

An Apache-ravaged Chihuahua pays James Kirker, a scalp hunter, 100,000 pesos to bring the Indian troubles under control.

1840

Hugh Stephenson establishes his ranch on today's El Paso side of the Rio Grande. He calls it Stephensonville and, sometimes, Concordia, the latter being the name of his earlier home in Missouri, a jumping-off point for the Santa Fe Trail.

The Texas government adopts English Common Law except for issues affecting Spanish and Mexican land grants.

1841

JUNE 20: The Texas-Santa Fe Expedition leaves Austin for Santa Fe. Historians argue over whether it was a trading force or an armed invasion. Anyway, General Hugh McLeod commanded 300 Texans. Three Texas commissioners tagged along to carry out the political aims of the invading/trading caravan. However, the expedition lost its way and was starving near modern-day Tucumcari, New Mexico, when it surrendered in October to a

much smaller Mexican force. A death march then started toward
El Paso, Chihuahua. Texans who died along the road had their
ears cut off and strung on a piece of rawhide as proof that none
had escaped.

AUGUST 11: Fray Ramón Ortiz is confirmed *Cura Propio* for Paso del
Norte.

NOVEMBER 4: The Texas-Santa Fe Expedition prisoners have
reached El Paso. Cura Ortiz welcomes them into his home and
provides food, clothing, nursing and spiritual care. On November
9, the caravan starts south for Mexico City.

1843

JANUARY: The village of Doña Ana, New Mexico, is founded when
34 settlers dig an irrigation ditch five miles north of present Las
Cruces. Within a year nearly 300 residents lived in Doña Ana.

1845

*The Statue of St. Miguel is solemnly transferred to the new Socorro
Church.*

DECEMBER 29: Texas is admitted to the Union. The American government claims the Rio Grande as the southern and western
boundary.

1846

The Socorro Mission cemetery is established and blessed.

APRIL 23: A group of Mexican regulars cross the Rio Grande and
attack America forces south of the Nueces River near Brownsville.

MAY 13: The United States declares war on Mexico.

AUGUST 18: General Stephen Kearny, leads an Army of the West out of Fort Leavenworth, Kansas, captures Santa Fe without firing a shot. El Pasoan James Magoffin convinced Governor Manuel Armijo that resistance was futile.

AUTUMN (early): George Ruxton, an Englishman, visits El Paso del Norte. He describes the inhabited valley as extending between El Paso and San Elizario. Ruxton said the space between the villages contained a continuous line of adobe houses. Gardens and vineyards flourished.

SEPTEMBER 22: General Kearny establishes a code of laws (the Kearny Code) for New Mexico. It organizes a provisional government with a governor, three district judges and other territorial officials. The territory is divided into seven counties clustered along the Rio Grande in the northern and central portion of the present state. Arid stretches east and west of the river were unorganized. New Mexico also included present-day Arizona.

SEPTEMBER 25: General Stephen Kearny leaves Santa Fe and marches toward the Pacific. By December, California has fallen to American forces.

DECEMBER 14: Colonel Alexander Doniphan leaves Socorro, New Mexico, and marches south on the Camino Real (Chihuahua Trail) toward El Paso del Norte.

DECEMBER 25 (Christmas Day): Colonel Alexander Doniphan is victorious at the Battle of Brazito near modern-day Vado, New Mexico. Although the Mexican and American forces were roughly equal in numbers, the Mexicans were poorly led. The Americans took cover and simply shot the charging Mexican lancers to pieces.

DECEMBER 27: Colonel Alexander Doniphan and 800 Missouri Farm Boys walk through the mountain canyon past modern-day ASARCO, cross the Rio Grande at Hart's Mill, and bloodlessly capture El Paso, Chihuahua. Doniphan Drive in the Upper Valley marks the route of a conquering army.

1847

Lawrence Hubbell, who figured prominently in the Santa Fe trade, is briefly a collector of customs at Ponce's Station at what is now El Paso, Texas.

The Diocese of Galveston is established. Although it included all of Texas, El Paso is ignored apparently because it seems more in New Mexico.

JANUARY: Susan Magoffin, the young wife of Santa Fe trader Sam Magoffin, in her diary refers to a southern New Mexico site where Apaches in times past had attacked Mexican soldiers led by General Armijo. Fourteen soldiers were killed. Their graves were marked by rude crosses. The location became Las Cruces.

FEBRUARY 8: Doniphan's Missouri column leaves El Paso del Norte for Chihuahua City.

FEBRUARY 28: The climactic Battle of Sacramento is fought between Doniphan and Mexican forces outside the gates of Chihuahua City. Doniphan is triumphant.

MARCH 2: Doniphan's victorious army enters Chihuahua City. Northern Mexico has now fallen to the Americans.

1848

Hugh Stephenson opens silver mines in the Organ Mountains.

JANUARY 24: Gold is discovered in California. James Marshall finds particles of gold in the Sierra Nevada. A western movement without historical parallel begins, and it will have dramatic consequences for El Paso.

FEBRUARY 2: The Treaty of Guadalupe Hidalgo is signed. The war ends between Mexico and the United States. Mexico loses one-half of its territory. The treaty establishes the international boundary, and promises that United States Indians will be prevented from raiding Mexico. The agreement guarantees specific rights and protection for private property (including land grants) now in the United States.

FEBRUARY: General Sterling Price, commander of the American Army in New Mexico, not realizing the war has ended, occupies El Paso del Norte prior to capturing Chihuahua on March 1. He won the Battle of Santa Cruz de Rosales, outside Chihuahua City, 42 days after the signing of the Treaty of Guadalupe Hidalgo. Price occupied Chihuahua until July.

Major Benjamin Bell arrives in El Paso with a detachment of 1st Dragoons. Bell plans to curb Apache raids.

MARCH 15: On paper, the Texas Legislature creates Santa Fe County. It includes the Big Bend, Texas Panhandle, West Texas, a third of Oklahoma, most of New Mexico, half of Colorado, and chunks of Wyoming and Kansas. Santa Fe is the county seat.

JUNE 4: The Mexican government sets aside a special fund of 200,000 pesos for Mexicans needing repatriation expenses to return to their country of origin. The government offers 25 pesos for each adult and 12 for each child if they move to Mexico from territory ceded to the United States as a result of the Guadalupe Hidalgo treaty.

AUGUST: Frank White builds a trading post at Frontera (modern-day Sunland Park race track) near the intersection of Sunland Park and Doniphan.

AUGUST 19: The Mexican government organizes a commission to bring people into Mexico from territory newly acquired by the United States. Villages are created on the Mexican side of the international border with names like Mesilla, Guadalupe and Porvenir.

NOVEMBER 7: General Order No. 58 calls for the establishment of an army post at Ponce's Rancho.

DECEMBER: Texas sends a delegation from Austin, including a sheriff, to take possession of New Mexico east of the Rio Grande. This delegation will attempt to form a new county.

1849

Three routes open through El Paso to the California gold fields.
John S. Calhoun, Indian Agent for the Territory of New Mexico, refers in a report that Socorro and Ysleta (Texas) have landholdings of 72.25 square miles (46,240 acres).
The Mescalero Apaches raid Ysleta, Socorro, and San Elizario.

JANUARY: James Wiley Magoffin comes to El Paso and builds a hacienda known as Magoffinsville (modern corner of Magoffin and Willow streets).

APRIL: Sarah Bowman (Bourjette, Bouget, Borginnis, or Davis) the Great Western, arrives in the settlement of Ponce's Rancho. She was nicknamed after The Great Western, the largest steamship then afloat. She has been described as "an Amazon and a giantess," as well as the "greatest whore in the West." She changed husbands and partners frequently as she followed Taylor's army around Mexico. After the Mexican War, she owned a hotel and restaurant near Ponce's Rancho in El Paso, and likely ran a brothel out of it. She was a favorite of stage drivers, and in addition to her size she had charm, courage and good sense.

APRIL 12: A "Military" or "Lower Road" is established between San Antonio and El Paso. The route was blazed by William H. C. Whiting of the Army Engineering Corps and Lieutenant William F. Smith of the Topographical Engineers.

MAY 2: The "Ford-Neighbors Trail" (John S. "Rip" Ford and Robert S. Neighbors), often known as the "Immigrant" or "Upper Road," is established between Austin and El Paso.

JUNE: Benjamin Franklin Coons, a freighter and developer, arrives at the Pass.

Our Lady of Guadalupe Mission at El Paso del Norte, 1851. Drawn by Augustus A. Vauducourt of the American Boundary Commission. Scene probably drawn from where Juarez Avenue is today. The church was originally built of branches and mud in 1659. The mission is a brief walk from downtown El Paso. (Aultman Collection. El Paso Public Library)

SEPTEMBER 1: Captain Randolph B. Marcy passes through Doña Ana and Las Cruces. He thus blazed the Marcy Trail from Doña Ana to Fort Smith, Arkansas, a popular route for forty-niners heading for the California Gold Fields.

SEPTEMBER 8: Major Jefferson Van Horne and six companies of the Third Infantry arrive at Ponce's Rancho and take up quarters in adobe buildings. They called themselves the Post Opposite El Paso, New Mexico. The "El Paso" referred to El Paso del Norte, Chihuahua (modern day Juarez). The "New Mexico" referred to the rancho and the post as being in New Mexico, and not in Texas. These soldiers were infantry, and their primary duty was to walk east to the Pecos River and protect incoming immigrant wagon trains. The Post Opposite El Paso would evolve into Fort Bliss.

SEPTEMBER 15: The Post at San Elizario is occupied by companies I and K, plus a howitzer battery. It is in some respects a sub-post of the Post Opposite El Paso.

OCTOBER 13: Companies A and C and 120 wagons are dispatched to the Pecos River where they will escort a wagon train into Ponce's Rancho.

NOVEMBER: A wagon train belonging to Benjamin Franklin Coons is attacked by Apaches near the Guadalupe Mountains. One man is slain, and another wounded. Several head of livestock are taken.

NOVEMBER 10: Texas Judge Spruce M. Baird arrives in Santa Fe and declares Santa Fe part of Texas. The natives ignore him, so after a brief period he returns to Austin and argues that New Mexico is in rebellion.

DECEMBER: Simeon Hart marries Jesusita Siquieros of Santa Cruz de Rosales, Mexico. He is 41, she is 17. The couple come immediately to El Paso and construct Hart's (grist) Mill.

DECEMBER: Hugh Stephenson establishes Stephensonville, later known as Concordia. (The ranch was within a stone's throw of the modern-day Concordia Cemetery.)

1850

El Paso, Chihuahua has 4,000 residents. An estimated 10,000 people live on the south bank of the Rio Grande. The north side has about 200 people.

Sarah Bowman, the Great Western, leaves Ponce's Rancho for Yuma.

JANUARY: Charles A. Hopkin wrote Governor Peter Bell a report regarding political and lawless chaos in San Elizario. He claimed the alcalde still functioned under the laws of Chihuahua.

JANUARY 1: The Eleventh Judicial District is established. The district includes the counties of Worth, El Paso, Presidio and Santa Fe.

JANUARY 3: Texas Governor Peter Bell commissions Robert S. Neighbors to organize Worth, El Paso and Presidio counties.

JANUARY 16: Senatorial and representative districts are created in Worth, El Paso, Presidio and Santa Fe counties. (Of course, they are created but they have no legal responsibilities.)

JANUARY 23: The Third Regiment of the United States Army stationed at Ponce's Rancho forms a "Travelers' Home Lodge." It conducts the first known Masonic activities at the Pass.

FEBRUARY 18: El Paso County votes to joins Texas. San Elizario becomes the first county seat.

MARCH 1: Mesilla, Chihuahua, is founded by Don Rafael Ruelas and 60 settlers who formerly lived in Doña Ana. Several hundred persons eventually fled Doña Ana to avoid Anglo (mostly Texan) depredations.

MARCH 28: Simeon Hart signs a military contract to furnish flour to the military posts near Doña Ana, Ponce's Rancho and San Elizario.

AUGUST 9: The Compromise of 1850 establishes the Territory of New Mexico as well as the present boundaries of Texas. New Mexico's boundaries are defined as extending to the Staked Plains (*Llano*

Estacado) on the east, and on the west reaching to California, specifically the Colorado River. Today's Arizona was part of the Territory of New Mexico.

SEPTEMBER: A band of Mescalero Indians from the Guadalupe and Davis mountains, led by chiefs Simon Manuel and Simon Porode, visit San Elizario to see what they can expect from the Americans. They also visit El Paso, Chihuahua, and later negotiate with Major Jefferson Van Horne regarding a peace treaty.

SEPTEMBER 8: By an Act of the U.S. Congress, the middle of the Rio Grande becomes the boundary between Texas and New Mexico. The line will remain stationary even if the river changes its channel.

SEPTEMBER 15: Parker H. French, a confidence man with a fast gun, arrives at Ponce's Rancho with a wagon train of 200 gold seekers heading for California. French left a trail of worthless drafts scattered across the Southwest.

OCTOBER 12: George A. McCall, inspector general for the United States Army, reports that a strong garrison is not needed at Franklin. The post's primary purpose was to provide security to the Mexican town of El Paso, Chihuahua. Of the two posts (Franklin and San Elizario), McCall supported the latter as the most important, claiming the old presidio could be used as a depot. The inspector also noted that Mexico-bound wagon trains preferred crossing the Rio Grande at San Elizario rather than at Ponce's Rancho because the San Elizario ford permitted travelers to avoid the sandhills south of El Paso, Chihuahua.

NOVEMBER 13: John R. Bartlett, the American boundary commissioner, arrives at Magoffinsville. Bartlett, along with his Mexican counterpart, Pedro García Conde, is charged with determining the international line, then surveying and marking it.

NOVEMBER 19: A wagon train of 60 teams arrived in Ponce's Rancho today after being stranded for two months on the salt flats near the Guadalupe Mountains.

NOVEMBER 25: The final Texas-New Mexico boundary controversies are resolved when Texas accepts $10 million from the United States government to pay off debts incurred by the Republic. The de facto Texas counties of Santa Fe and Worth will hereafter be under the jurisdiction, and part of, the Territory of New Mexico.

DECEMBER: Major Van Horne convenes a Board of Inspectors to determine if three of his recruits are fit for duty. One has a missing thumb on his left hand, "lost during a drunken frolic." Another has "malformed" toes. The third has "intemperate and vicious habits, extreme physical disabilities and advanced age." (The last person died a month later.) All are dismissed from the army.

1851

JANUARY 8: Apaches raid the Magoffin ranch and drive off 40 mules.

FEBRUARY 12: John R. Bartlett, the American boundary commissioner, discharged several employees. Most of them moved to Socorro, Texas, 15 miles downstream, and caused trouble. Several innocent parties were slain, including Edward Clarke, son of a Rhode Island senator. By late January, the Socorro residents, including several boundary employees, had enough. The civilians deputized themselves, searched every building and captured three of the desperados. They were promptly tried for murder, found guilty, and hanged from a cottonwood tree in the mission plaza. The residents then placed a $400 reward on the head of Alexander Young, the ringleader. He was captured two weeks later, brought to Socorro, tried and hanged from the same tree on February 12. Socorro went back to being a peaceful community. Boundary Commissioner John R. Bartlett wrote a classic description of the trial.

APRIL 24: International Boundary Marker #1 is dedicated 42 miles north of El Paso, Chihuahua, on the west bank of the Rio Grande.

JULY 13: Businessman and developer Guadalupe Miranda receives a grant of land north of El Paso del Norte and embraced by hills and river bends known as *Muleros*. This would be the area in and around the present Sierra de Cristo Rey (Mt. Cristo Rey). Within several years, however, Miranda either misplaced or had lost most of his documents. He failed to prove his case to United States courts evaluating land grant claims after the property had become part of the Gadsden Purchase.

AUGUST 27: The American boundary commission caught Comancheros in the act of attempting to sell Inez Gonzáles, a young lady captured by Indians in Sonora and sold to the Comancheros. Boundary Commissioner John R. Bartlett ordered the Comancheros arrested and chained, and he decided to return Miss Gonzáles to her home in Santa Cruz, Sonora. The entire boundary commission disappeared into Mexico, and went financially broke in the process.

SEPTEMBER: The Post Opposite El Paso and the Post at San Elizario are closed due to budget cuts. The troops are reassigned, primarily to the new post of Fort Fillmore, near Mesilla.

NOVEMBER 1: Frontiersman Henry Skillman starts delivering mail from Santa Fe to Ponce's Rancho, Texas, and on to San Antonio.

DECEMBER 16: Passenger service starts on Henry Skillman's mail route.

1852

Juan María Ponce de León, the first known settler of El Paso, Texas, dies.

Benjamin Franklin Coons becomes the first postmaster, so he names the mail station after himself, Franklin. Thus Franklin becomes the name of the settlement which Coons leased from the heirs of Ponce de León. We also have the Franklin Mountains.

Presidio County is attached to El Paso County for jurisdictional purposes.

The Rio Grande channel, the legal boundary between Texas and

Mexico, has never been marked. Local residents note that the channel is shifting on a year-by-year basis.

JANUARY: Two thousand New Mexico emigrants (mostly Texans) are settling along the Rio Grande near Mesilla.

JANUARY 9: Doña Ana County is created by the Territorial Legislative Assembly of New Mexico, although the act did not become official for nearly a year. New Mexico included present-day Arizona. Doña Ana County stretched between such far-flung areas as Tucson and Roswell. Since the Mexican border had as yet not been completely surveyed, the southern boundary of Doña Ana County was "vague." Mesilla was the county seat.

JANUARY 19: Father Andres de Jesús Camacho hands over the Guadalupe, Ysleta and Socorro missions to the diocesan (Durango) representative, Father Ramon Ortíz. The ceremony ends a 172-year Franciscan administration.

FEBRUARY: The corrals of Captain Henry Skillman's residence in Franklin are broken into by Apaches, and several head of livestock are driven off. Furthermore, Skillman's mail wagons from San Antonio to Franklin are attacked several miles east of town.

MAY: Apaches raid portions of San Elizario and drive off 80 head of stock. Apaches also sawed through James Magoffin's corrals, and disappeared with 43 animals.

MAY 26: Pedro González, justice of the peace, wrote Texas Governor Peter H. Bell and complained of American outrages on Mexican citizens in Ysleta. González said the Ysleta inhabitants were "very much dissatisfied with the injuries and ravages they suffer from the Americans who reside there."

SUMMER: New Mexico Governor Carr Lane urges force to control the Mesilla Valley and protect American property rights from residents of Chihuahua.

JULY 28: Josiah Crosby, Archibald Hyde, Hugh Stephenson,

Charles Hopkin, Simeon Hart, James Magoffin and Juan Montello hold a meeting in the Magoffin Hacienda to determine how to respond to Indian attacks.

AUGUST 12: Majors Hopkin and Hubbell lost all of their horses and between 40 and 50 mules within sight of the army post.

AUGUST 17: Boundary Commissioner John R. Bartlett returns to El Paso. He is being recalled to Washington because he set the international boundary line north of Mesilla instead of near El Paso, Chihuahua. Bartlett travels to East Texas by way of Chihuahua City. The caravan is attacked by Apaches near Carrizal, 100 miles south of El Paso, and one man is killed.

1853

A cattle drive from Eagle Pass, Texas comes through El Paso on its way to San Diego.
A Masonic Lodge is established at San Elizario.

JANUARY: A detail of Mexican soldiers enter Socorro and Ysleta. They break into houses and assault residents as they search for Mexican military deserters. Mob action results, and the soldiers are driven back to Mexico.

FEBRUARY 2: The Texas Legislature assigns one senator and one representative each for El Paso and Presidio counties. The Legislature officially eliminated Santa Fe and Worth counties.

MARCH: Angel Trías overthrows the government of Chihuahua and assumes power as governor. Trías sends Colonel Emilio Langberg, a Mexican military officer of Swiss extraction, to imprison and properly indoctrinate the civil authorities at El Paso del Norte. Jailed are the mayor, the customs agent and the local priest. Other officials escape across the Rio Grande into Franklin, Texas, and seek the protection of Colonel Dixon Miles, commanding officer at Fort Fillmore, near Mesilla. The Post Opposite El Paso is still closed.

MARCH: Apaches drive off horse herds from San Elizario. Only a few are recovered.

MARCH: The mail delivery from San Antonio is attacked by Apaches, the carrier living just long enough to stagger into San Elizario.

MARCH 3: George H. Giddings gets a contract to deliver government mail from San Antonio to Santa Fe, via El Paso.

MARCH 8: Governor Peter H. Bell signs an act confirming the boundaries, and reconfirming the ownership of all the land claimed by the residents of San Elizario. The area occupied 12 square miles, and was bordered on the west by the Rio Grande, on the north by the Socorro boundary, on the east by the sand hills, and on the south by the old arm of the river.

MARCH 13: New Mexico Governor William Carr Lane issues a proclamation in El Paso calling for acquisition of what would become today's southern New Mexico-Arizona, and do so by force if necessary.

MARCH 23: The Ponce de León Grant is surveyed and contains 599 acres. The heirs of Ponce de León sold the land for $10,000 to William T. "Uncle Billy" Smith, a freighter who imagined he was also a developer. The community now becomes Smithville, although most residents still call it Franklin.

MAY: James Gadsden is appointed minister to Mexico by President Franklin Pierce. Gadsden will purchase sufficient land in northern Mexico to construct a railroad along the flat desert portion of southern New Mexico.

MAY: A herd of sheep belonging to Simeon Hart is slain by Apaches. The shepherd is also killed. The tragedy happened within a half-mile of the Hart residence.

JULY 4: Apaches drive off several herds of Ysleta livestock.

JULY 18: A group of California immigrants camped near Ysleta lose a herd of cattle to Mexican rustlers. James Magee, one of the party, followed the tracks to the Rio Grande, crossed over and recovered the livestock, in the process compensating himself with Mexican cattle that didn't belong to him. When Magee pushed his luck the following day, and went back for more Mexican livestock, the Mexican authorities arrested him. So, early in the morning and under cover of darkness on July 18, a group of armed Americans attempted a jail break. One was Esler Hendree, a Franklin district attorney. He was slain during the battle. Another man was seriously wounded before the attack ended.

JULY 31: Apaches in San Elizario are driven off before they can make a raid. They flee east with 13 well-armed San Elizario residents in pursuit. The Indians pause at Cornudas while the pursuers catch up. Ten of the 13 San Elizarians are killed.

DECEMBER 1: A military post is ordered reestablished opposite the Mexican town of El Paso.

DECEMBER 30: The Gadsden Purchase is agreed upon by Mexican President Antonio López de Santa Ana and American Minister James Gadsden. The price, if approved by congress, will be $15 million for Mexican land extending from western Arizona to West Texas.

1854

Caleb Sherman becomes the first El Paso County collector of customs. The U.S. government decides to build a string of army posts along the "lower road" from San Antonio to Franklin.

The Presidio of San Elizario is divided into 12 lots and sold. The ancient presidio apparently embraced the heart of modern San Elizario and included the church, plaza, jail, and today's Adobe Horseshoe and ballpark.

The State of Texas authorizes $2 million for public schools. None of these funds reach El Paso.

JANUARY: James Magoffin claims ownership of the salt lakes located on the modern-day White Sands Missile Range. He obtains a warrant to arrest New Mexicans taking his salt without permission. Thirty well-armed men, dragging a howitzer, leave Franklin and cross into New Mexico. A brief fight occurs, and 26 salt carts are captured. New Mexico warrants were subsequently issued for the arrest of James Magoffin, as well as the posse. The event becomes Magoffin's Salt War, and should not be confused with the later El Paso Salt War.

JANUARY 11: Four companies of the 8th Infantry Regiment garrison the "Post of El Paso" in Magoffinsville. The location was at modern day Magoffin and Willow streets.

JANUARY 31: The Relinquishment Act of the Texas Legislature grants the pueblo of Ysleta two leagues of land adjoining the original grant to replace property lost to Mexico in 1832 when the Rio Grande flooded and shifted the river's banks. Furthermore, the Texas Legislature confirms the original land grant made by Spain and authorizes the issuance of a patent title.

MARCH 8: The Post of El Paso becomes Fort Bliss, named after Colonel William Wallace Smith Bliss, a Mexican War veteran. He was "Perfect Bliss" at West Point, a brave and able officer, a chief of staff and son-in-law to General/President Zachary Taylor. Bliss died of yellow fever in New Orleans in 1853 without ever visiting the El Paso area.

APRIL 8: Masonic Lodge #130 holds its first meeting. Although it was referred to as the El Paso Lodge, its home base was San Elizario. It moved quickly to the Pass and initial meetings likely occurred at Hart's Mill.

JUNE: *El Sabio Sembrador* (The Wise Sower), El Paso's first newspaper, is published. Frederick Augustus Percy, an Englishman, hand-wrote it on 29 sheets of 8x12 inch paper. Volume 1, No. 3 is all that's extant. We don't know if there was a No. 1 and 2, or if there were additional issues.

JUNE 30: The Gadsden Purchase is proclaimed by the United States and Mexico. One-third of the agreed-upon $15 million was deleted by the United States, and one-third of the land was cut by Mexico. Arizona was thus deprived of a seaport. The southern boundary of Doña Ana County (New Mexico and Arizona) is established as the international border. Sierra del Cristo Rey marks the southeastern anchor of the Gadsden Purchase. Communities inside the purchase area include Yuma, Nogales, Douglas, Tucson, Wilcox, Lordsburg, Columbus, Deming and Mesilla.

JULY: Brevet Captain George E. Pickett has commanded Fort Bliss prior to the arrival of James Longstreet. Pickett and Longstreet will gain fame during the forthcoming Civil War.

JULY 9: The El Paso County seat moves from San Elizario to Magoffinsville. The courthouse is probably the Magoffin residence.

SEPTEMBER 13: The El Paso County seat moves from Magoffinsville back to San Elizario. The old presidio likely is the courthouse.

NOVEMBER 16: The United States takes full possession of Gadsden Purchase lands. Mexican forces pull down the Mexican flag in Mesilla, New Mexico, and Fort Bliss units march in and run up the United States flag.

1855

JANUARY: Mescalero Apaches in the White Mountains sue for peace after being battered by a succession of strikes by the military. The Indians are assigned to a reservation near Fort Stanton, New Mexico.

MAY: "Prince" John Bankhead Magruder, an artilleryman takes command at Fort Bliss for a brief period.

JUNE 4: Because of hostile Indians, it is unsafe to journey more than four miles from Franklin.

1856

AUGUST 22: The Texas legislature authorizes use of the Spanish language in justice of the peace courts west of the Guadalupe River, which includes Franklin.

DECEMBER 25: A group of Fort Bliss soldiers visit El Paso, Chihuahua, argue with a saloon owner and are arrested. Their friends make an effort to break them from jail the next day. Two soldiers are slain during the unsuccessful assault.

1857

JANUARY 9: Mescalero Apaches kidnap a drummer boy who wandered away from Fort Bliss. Although a detachment left immediately to rescue him, the youngster was never found.

FEBRUARY 5: María Juana Ascarate de Stephenson dies in El Paso and is buried at Concordia (Stephensonville). She was slain by a pet deer who gored her when she went to feed it.

MARCH 3: James Birch wins a government contract to deliver mail from San Antonio, Texas to San Diego, California via El Paso. Because mules pulled his wagons, the service becomes known as the Jackass Mail.

JUNE 28: Company K from Fort Bliss joins New Mexico soldiers in a campaign against the Gila Apaches. The battle commenced at 4:30 p.m. and broke off at dark. Twenty-four Indians are killed and 20 taken prisoner. Pueblo Indian guides (probably Tiguas) executed several Apache prisoners after the encounter.

JULY: The San Diego and San Antonio mail makes stage connections in El Paso.

JULY 7: A stage traveler recorded in his journal that "scarcely a mile of [the road] but has its story of Indian murder and plunder; in fact from El Paso to San Antonio [the road] is but one long battle ground."

JULY 27: Lieutenant Edward Beales brings the unique camel experiment to Franklin. Twenty-eight camels from Tripoli and Syria left East Texas to walk cross-country to California. Secretary of War Jefferson Davis wanted to know if camels could supplement the horse and mule in desert country. They do, but the Civil War caused the experiment to be abandoned.

OCTOBER 22: The Department of Interior is constructing the El Paso-Fort Yuma Wagon Road. An advance unit of workers reach Franklin.

1858

FEBRUARY 11: The Ponce de Leon grant, in the village of Franklin, is upheld by Texas courts.

MARCH 3: James Birch (later lost at sea), and George H. Giddings get the 1857 government contract for delivering mail from San Antonio to San Diego, via El Paso. The stage firm becomes the Giddings Line. The line ceased to function when the Civil War started.

MARCH 23: A gambler named Tom Smith killed Dr. Frank Giddings in the Ben Dowell Saloon. The first shot went through Giddings' thigh, and broke Billy Smith's leg. The second shot was fatal. Tom Smith fled to Mexico and was never tried. Giddings was the brother of George Giddings, operator of the Jackass Mail.

MAY 8: Anson Mills arrives in El Paso.

SEPTEMBER: Anson Mills constructs the Overland Stage offices on the southeast corner of El Paso and Overland streets. For 40 years it is the largest building in El Paso.

SEPTEMBER 30: The Butterfield Overland Mail rattles out of El Paso at 5:40 A.M., 14 days out of Tipton, Missouri. It was the first Overland Stage to reach the Pass. Waterman L. Ormsby, a reporter for the *New York Herald*, traveling all the way through, described Franklin as an adobe community with a few hundred residents. He wrote of passing many vineyards and comfortable ranches "looking extremely neat." He described the wines as "universally appreciated," and mentioned that the grapes and onions were "of world-wide celebrity."

OCTOBER 23: Chihuahua officials declare the Chihuahua/Texas/ New Mexico international border area as a Zona Libre (Free Zone). It means that goods sold will not be taxed.

DECEMBER: William Wallace Mills arrives in El Paso.

1859

Slaves crossing the Rio Grande into Mexico automatically achieve freedom, but one free Negro filed charges in a Mexican court and won back-wages from an Anglo-American living in Franklin, Texas. The man paid the sum, then rounded up eight friends and attempted to remove the Negro from Mexico to the United States. All were caught by Mexican authorities and jailed.

Ponce de León's ranch house is extended to Oregon Street.

JANUARY 30: William T. Smith, keeping a one-eighth interest in the township of Franklin (Smithsville), sells the remainder to John S. and Henry S. Gillett, Josiah F. Crosby, William J. Morton, Vincent St. Vrain and Anthony B. Rohman. The new owners form a syndicate known as the El Paso Company, and retain Anson Mills to survey a town plat.

FEBRUARY 8: The Battle of Dog Canyon near Alamogordo, New Mexico, takes place between Fort Bliss soldiers and Apache Indians. Lieutenant Henry Lazelle is seriously wounded as are six of his men. Three soldiers are killed during a fighting withdrawal.

FEBRUARY 28: The El Paso Company, with Anson Mills leading the way, changes the name of Franklin (Smithsville) to El Paso. In

An 1870s look down El Paso Street from Ponce's Rancho, which is today's Plaza Theater. In this photo, there are several "newspaper trees" but only the one at left remained for many years. The building on the other side of the barber pole would be Ben Dowell's Saloon, today's Camino Real Paso del Norte Hotel. The 1881 Four Dead in Five Seconds gunfight took place here, and this is where former City Marshal Dallas Stoudenmire died in 1882. (El Paso Public Library)

surveying and platting the village, Mills finds existing streets are neither parallel nor at right angles. The former owner, William T. Smith, had sold land and allowed homes to be built in random, disjointed fashion. Mills then attempts to lay out an orderly street plan, but few concessions are made by landowners. As a result, downtown El Paso still has streets that dead-end, or form triangles instead of squares. El Paso Street, for instance, dead-ended at the Ponce Rancho where the Plaza Theater is now. Otherwise, San Antonio Street went to San Antonio. Overland Street was where the Butterfield Overland Stage Company had its headquarters and corrals. The stage for San Francisco left town on San Francisco Street.

OCTOBER 15: Ysleta is incorporated as a town. H. L. Dexter is mayor.

1860

The first El Paso County census is taken. There were 428 residents from 26 states and five countries (Mexico, Ireland, Bavaria, Prussia and Saxony). Only eight of these people were 50 or older. The census listed four lawyers, one preacher and 45 laborers.

Chihuahua abolishes the Zona Libre along its international border.

JUNE: Gold mining in the Pinos Altos area of New Mexico expands.

AUGUST 6: Anson Mills pinned a message to the Plaza Newspaper Tree. The missive was the first of several:

"I have just been informed that J. S. Gillett, W. J. Morton, and J. R. Sipes stated last night to R. Doane and F. Remy that I was an abolitionist, for the purpose of injuring my character. As I have never cast any other than a Democratic vote or expressed other than Democratic sentiments, I denounce these three above-named persons as wilful and malicious lying scoundrels. Sipes and Morton owe me borrowed money for the last two years. I would like to have a settlement. I have never asked any one to vote for me as surveyor and I now withdraw my name as a candidate and will not serve if elected."

The response followed:

"A certain contemptible 'pup,' signing himself A. Mills, having publicly published the undersigned as scoundrels, we have only to say that he is so notoriously known throughout the entire county as a damned black Republican scoundrel, we deem him unworthy of further notice. However, we hereby notify this fellow that his insignificance shall not protect him in the future."

DECEMBER 8: Fort Bliss leaves the Department of New Mexico and is reassigned to the Department of Texas.

1861

FEBRUARY 1: The state convention in Austin votes for secession, subject to ratification by the counties.

FEBRUARY 23: El Paso votes for secession. The ballot box was in Ben Dowell's Saloon, and only two individuals supported the Union.

FEBRUARY 18: General David Twiggs orders Union posts in Texas to surrender. State appointed commissioners, James Magoffin and Simeon Hart, handle the orderly transfer of military stores and currency.

MARCH: Texas joins the Confederacy. Tucson and Mesilla hold separate conventions and vote also to join the Confederacy. The Territory of New Mexico remained loyal.

MARCH 31: Colonel Isaac V.D. Reeve lowers the stars and stripes at Fort Bliss, and marches his troops under parole down the Rio Grande toward Fort Quitman. Quitman evacuates on April 5 and Fort Davis on April 13.

APRIL 1: The Butterfield Overland Mail discontinues operations.

APRIL 12: The Civil War commences when Southern artillery falls on Fort Sumter in the harbor at Charleston, South Carolina.

MAY 9: Six companies of the Fort Bliss 8th Infantry are met at San

Lucas Spring, near San Antonio, by Brigadier General Earl Van Dorn of Texas and forced to surrender unconditionally. Most of these troops are held in confinement and not paroled until February 1863.

JUNE 8: Texas Governor Edward Clark issues a proclamation announcing a state of civil war.

JULY 1: (probable) Colonel John R. Baylor and five companies (300 men) of the Texas 2nd Mounted Rifles occupy Fort Bliss.

JULY: W. W. Mills is kidnapped off the streets of El Paso, Chihuahua, and locked in a Confederate jail in El Paso, Texas.

JULY 11: The San Elizario Spy Company is organized to scout for the Confederacy.

JULY 23: The last stage from El Paso, carrying Union men fleeing to California, is ambushed by Apaches led by Mangas Coloradas near Cook's Peak in New Mexico (near present-day Deming). All seven men are slain. A monument to their memory stands behind the present downtown Public Library.

JULY 27: Colonel John R. Baylor attacks Fort Fillmore near Mesilla. Major Isacc Lynde, in command, sets fire to the military stores and retreats toward Fort Stanton. The Union surrenders at San Augustine Ranch, roughly one mile from the modern-day headquarters complex at White Sands Missile Range.

AUGUST 1: Colonel John R. Baylor issues a proclamation creating the Territory of Arizona, and himself as governor. The Territory of Arizona included Doña Ana County, New Mexico roughly the southern one-third of today's Arizona and New Mexico.

AUGUST 16: The War Department orders Brigadier General E. V. Sumner, stationed at San Francisco, to depart with volunteers to Mazatlan, Mexico, and from there march across Mexico and attack West Texas. This plan was abandoned before it got underway.

SEPTEMBER 27: Mangas Coloradas leads a large group of Apaches during an attack on Pinos Altos, New Mexico.

OCTOBER 24: John R. Baylor warns Simeon Hart that the Union is moving south in New Mexico, and while the situation was not yet alarming, it would be best for Hart to transfer belongings into El Paso, Chihuahua. Hart, who was a Confederacy quartermaster, moved 50,000 pounds of flour across the Rio Grande.

NOVEMBER: Confederate General Henry Hopkins Sibley departs from San Antonio and heads for El Paso with three regiments of Texas Volunteers.

DECEMBER 12: General Henry Sibley arrives at Fort Bliss with a force he designates as the Army of New Mexico.

DECEMBER 12: Colonel John R. Baylor shoots Robert P. Kelley, editor of the *Mesilla Times*. The altercation takes place in the Mesilla square. Kelley died of his wounds.

1862

The Homestead Act is approved. The American West is opened to 160 acre farms.

Tularosa, New Mexico is settled. The residents arrive primarily from tiny settlements near Las Cruces.

JANUARY 18: John Lemon, Jacob Appelzoller and Crittenden Marshall are arrested at Mesilla and charged with being Union men. A party of Southern sympathizers removed them from the military guard house, took them to the Rio Grande and lynched Marshall. Appelzoller was dangling from a tree limb when, for whatever reason, he was cut down. He and Lemon survived, although Lemon was killed later at Mesilla when he was clubbed to death during a riot between political factions.

JANUARY 18: Confederate President Jefferson Davis officially creates the Territory of Arizona. Mesilla is selected as the capital.

FEBRUARY: A special unit of Sibley's army is formed and called the Brigands. Others call them the Company of Santa Fe Gamblers. They were scouts, freebooters living off the land.

FEBRUARY 2: The Confederate invasion of New Mexico begins. General Sibley takes Socorro and Albuquerque.

MARCH: The Confederacy occupies Santa Fe.

MARCH 28: Sibley suffers a standoff at Battle of Glorieta Pass. His wagon train is destroyed by Union cavalry. He retreats back into El Paso, and then into the Texas interior after burning Fort Bliss.

APRIL: Confederate New Mexico/West Texas has ceased to exist.

APRIL 18: General Sibley bitterly writes his superiors stating, among other things, that "The grand aim and object of the leading men of Western Texas, [Simeon] Hart, of El Paso, [Josiah] Crosby and others, is to annex Chihuahua and Sonora to Texas...."

MAY 5: Cinco de Mayo, a national Mexican holiday. On May 5, 1862, the Mexican Army fought the French to a blistering standstill at Puebla, Mexico. As victories go, this was a minor one. But it gave the Mexicans sufficient self-confidence to carry them through three more despairing years until final and ultimate victory.

MAY 21: The Brigands are paid off and discharged by the Confederacy. They immediately reorganize as "mounted spies and guides" operating initially out of San Elizario. Led by Captain George Madison, the group waged a brief, ineffective guerilla campaign against the Federals in New Mexico.

JULY 17: The United States Congress passes a law calling for confiscation of Confederate property.

JULY 6: The last of the Confederates who invaded New Mexico have now crossed back into Texas, and are departing for the interior.

AUGUST 20: The Union's California Column arrives and assumes command of Fort Bliss, although the troops station themselves at Hart's Mill.

SEPTEMBER 27: Colonel Christopher Carson's regiment of New Mexico Volunteers reoccupies Fort Stanton, and Carson has orders to kill all the male Mescalero Apaches he finds. Women and children will be fed and guarded.

1863

JANUARY 24-28: The famed Apache leader Mangas Coloradas, who turned himself over to American soldiers near Santa Rita, is slain by guards when he tries to escape.

JANUARY 29: The New Mexico Assembly, under Union control, restores Doña Ana County to New Mexico.

FEBRUARY 20: The Territory of New Mexico is divided on a north-south line. New Mexico is shrunk in half as the Territory of Arizona is created.

MARCH: General James H. Carleton, Union commander of New Mexico, subdues the Navajos and Mescalero Apaches, forcing them onto the Bosque Redondo Reservation on the Pecos River north of Roswell.

1864

APRIL 15: Captain Henry Skillman, called by some the "Viking of the Southwest," was a man of magnificent physique. He stood over six feet tall, and had long sandy hair and beard. He was likely the best known El Pasoan of the 1850s. He lived near Concordia, and was at times a stage driver and mail contractor. Although Skillman had Union leanings, he went with his state and became a dispatch rider for the Confederacy. He was ambushed and slain while sleeping near Presidio, Texas.

JUNE: Don Luis Terrazas, governor of Chihuahua, flees the French who are occupying Mexico. He and his family take refuge in El Paso, Chihuahua.

NOVEMBER: President Abraham Lincoln issues land patents to all the pueblos except Ysleta del Sur. Since Ysleta was in the Confederacy, it was out of United States jurisdiction.

1865

APRIL 9: General Robert E. Lee surrenders. The Civil War ends.

SPRING: The Rio Grande undergoes massive flooding. Mesilla, which had always been west of the river, is now east of it.

MAY 8: Fort Selden, north of Las Cruces, is established.

JULY 4: General James Carleton lifts martial law in New Mexico.

AUGUST 14: Mexican President Benito Juárez arrives in El Paso, Chihuahua, to continue his struggle against the French. El Paso, Chihuahua, becomes the provisional capital of Mexico.

OCTOBER 15: Fort Bliss is officially re-established at Magoffinsville, two miles west of El Paso (Magoffin and Willow streets). The Headquarters, Band and Companies G and K of the 5th Infantry Regiment take up quarters. The 5th Infantry remains in New Mexico during the Civil War, it being the only regular regiment not called east.

NOVEMBER 3: Conditions are so horrible at the Bosque Redondo Reservation on the Pecos River in New Mexico, that the Mescalero Apaches quietly vanish during the night.

DECEMBER 2: The property of Confederate sympathizers is auctioned from the El Paso Pioneer Plaza.

DECEMBER 19: A decision has been made to sell Fort Bliss at Magoffinsville. The property is purchased by Captain Albert French.

DECEMBER 28: The writ of habeas corpus, suspended during the war, is again in effect. Through 1865, the army had been the law at the Pass. Now the law reverts to civilian control.

1866

JUNE 17: The French are defeated in Mexico. President Benito Juárez leaves El Paso del Norte for the south.

AUGUST 12: The 5th Infantry is relieved at Fort Bliss and replaced by Companies G and H of the 125th United States Colored Troops. This unit performed garrison and escort duty.

AUGUST 21: Fort Bayard is established eight miles southeast of Pinos Altos, New Mexico.

DECEMBER 23: Sarah Bowman, the Great Western, dies in Yuma, Arizona. She receives a full military funeral.

1867

Congress abolishes the peonage system in New Mexico. The territory had 3,000 Indian slaves and an unknown number of indebted peons.

M. A. Jones, a lawyer, had an office at the corner of Main and Mesa. As the legal business slowed, he turned his office into a school and taught children to read and write. His office was the first non-church non-public school in the county. Jones was the second mayor of El Paso.

The Texas Almanac *describes Ysleta as being inhabited by a semi-civilized tribe known as Pueblos.*

FEBRUARY 18: The county seat moves from San Elizario to Ysleta.

MAY 18: A Rio Grande flood destroys much of Magoffinsville and Fort Bliss.

JULY 27: The colored troops at Bliss are transferred to Santa Fe, and are relieved by Companies A and K of the 35th Infantry Regiment. The Fort Bliss troops were only remotely involved in fighting Indians. As infantry, they could not pursue mounted Indians. The infantry's job was to establish a semblance of order along a turbulent border.

OCTOBER 11: Fort Bliss receives permission to move the garrison to higher ground, specifically to the Concordia Ranch.

NOVEMBER: Mrs. Arabella Reed, during a long El Paso stopover on her way to California, opened a private school at the intersection of San Francisco and Santa Fe streets.

NOVEMBER 21: The garrison at Fort Bliss (7 officers and 150 enlisted men) moves to the Concordia Rancho.

1868

Benjamin Williams and William M. Pierson, two attorneys, assume ownership of the ferry service operating between El Paso, Texas and El Paso, Chihuahua.

Captain Albert H. French publishes a small, four page, hand-written newspaper called El Paso Montezuma Weekly Times. *The masthead stated that it would accept any article, no matter how abusive. It once printed a bawdy song entitled, "I Met Her in A Hogpen." The newspaper soon folded.*

A political salt ring is organized in El Paso to monopolize the salt trade near the Guadalupe Mountains.

JANUARY 2: Masonic Lodge #130 buries Moses Carson, who died at the age of 76. Moses was the older half-brother of Kit Carson, the famous frontiersman. The coffin cost the lodge $17. Carson's grave is either under the downtown Popular Dry Goods Company, or beneath one of the houses fronting on Stevens Street across from Concordia Cemetery.

FEBRUARY: Fort Bliss becomes Camp Concordia. The post is astride several major roads. One (the Lower Road) went to Hueco Tanks and through forts Quitman and Davis to San Antonio. Another road cut north toward Tularosa and forts Stanton, Sumner and Union in New Mexico.

MARCH 11: Mescalero Apache raiders sweep through the Tularosa country killing eleven men and two women. They run off thousands of sheep.

SPRING: Mrs. Frances Helen Corey Clarke assumes control of Arabella Reed's school in order to teach her own daughter as well as neighboring children. This is the largest school yet.

APRIL 7: The Battle of Round Mountain takes place near Tularosa. Mescalero Apaches attack a military supply wagon, but the military is reinforced by settlers from Tularosa. The fight continued for hours until the Indians broke off. The Hispanics were so excited about the victory that they erected a church which sits alongside the main street today. The names of Indian fighters are inscribed on the back wall.

JUNE: The Navajo Indians are sent home from the Bosque Redondo Reservation north of Fort Sumner. A miserable, cruel experiment in human relations had failed.

JUNE: W. W. Mills, as part of the El Paso delegation in Austin, calls for the secession of West Texas and the creation of the Territory of Montezuma. It would include the counties of El Paso and Doña Ana (New Mexico).

AUGUST: The county seat moves from Ysleta back to San Elizario.

SEPTEMBER 27: James Magoffin dies of dropsy in San Antonio, Texas.

1869

FEBRUARY 10-12: Second Lieutenant Bernard H. Harkness and 35 infantrymen pursue Mescalero Apaches who stole cattle from within the limits of the post. The soldiers marched 80 miles and never fired a shot.

MARCH 23: The Camp Concordia name is discontinued and Fort Bliss is re-established even though the post remains at Concordia (Stephensonville).

APRIL: Four soldiers desert Fort Bliss and blend in with the drifter population at Ysleta. When Lieutenant Harkness tries to arrest them, he is slain by privates Hugh Anthony and Jessie Ree. The men are apprehended in Mexico, returned to Bliss, tried and executed.

OCTOBER: Fort Bliss is partially staffed by the 24th Infantry, black troops called Buffalo Soldiers by the Indians.

NOVEMBER 12: Albert Jennings Fountain is elected from El Paso to the Texas legislature, beating W. W. Mills in a bitterly-contested election. Fountain eventually becomes president of the Senate and chairman of the Indian Affairs Committee, all within four years, the only term he serves.

1870

A stately ash Newspaper Tree stands in the middle of the Little Plaza (Pioneer Plaza).

JUNE 24: The Texas legislature passes a Militia Bill providing for the organization and drilling of two classes of militia: the State Guard and the Reserve.

AUGUST 26: Company N, a frontier force led by Captain Gregorio García is mustered in under the Militia Bill law. The force numbered 60, and all but two had Spanish surnames.

The Central Hotel where the Plaza Theater is today at the head of El Paso Street. Ponce's Rancho is on the right, and portions or all of the hacienda may have been converted into the hotel. This is perhaps El Paso's oldest picture. 1870s. (Cleofas Calleros Collection)

OCTOBER 9: Parson Joseph W. Tays conducts the first Protestant church service in El Paso when the St. Clement Church opens. The church was on the north side of the public square.

OCTOBER 11: Hugh Stephenson dies at La Mesa, New Mexico and is buried at Las Cruces. His body presently lies somewhere under the Western Bank parking lot.

NOVEMBER: Felix Burton, a miner, discovers silver-bearing ore near a New Mexico village called San Vicente de La Cienaga. As a town grew, Anglos changed the name to Silver City.

NOVEMBER 1: Parson Joseph Wilkin Tays opens a mission school for ten El Paso students.

DECEMBER 7: The Salt War explodes as politicians begin killing each other on the streets of El Paso. Attorney Ben Williams is drinking and ranting in Ben Dowell's Saloon when Colonel Albert Jennings Fountain walks in. Fountain is shot twice, his life saved by a pocket watch stopping one of the bullets. Fountain alerts District Judge Gaylord Clarke and State Police Captain Albert French who pursue Williams into his residence. The door is broken down, and the confrontation moved to the street where Williams kills Judge Clarke with a shotgun. Williams was then slain by Captain French who shot him twice.

1871

Presidio County is divided to form Pecos County.
A company of 24th Infantry is relieved at Fort Bliss by a company of 25th Infantry, all Buffalo Soldiers.

SEPTEMBER 26: The Texas legislature passes "An Act to Incorporate the Town of Ysleta in El Paso County." The bill is introduced by Albert J. Fountain. Authorization is given for the incorporation commission, consisting of Fountain's friends, including Ben Dowell, El Paso's soon-to-be first mayor, to sell land to any individual willing to become a citizen of Ysleta. Indians are excluded since they are considered wards of the government even though the patents issued earlier give the Tiguas sole title to their lands. (The town incorporated on October 15, 1859, but had not operated under a charter.)

MARCH 4: Roswell, New Mexico is established. The town is named for Roswell Smith, a professional gambler.

APRIL 5: San Elizario incorporates.

AUGUST 21: Company N, the 60-man frontier force headed by Captain Gregorio García is mustered out of service.

AUGUST 7: The Mesilla riot occurs. As the liquor flowed, Democrats and Republicans paraded in opposite directions around the Mesilla, New Mexico, plaza. A collision took place, and that sparked the fighting. When it ended, nine men lay dead and between 40 and 50 were wounded. No charges were brought.

OCTOBER: A trespass suit filed by Senecú against Ysleta reaffirms the original Spanish grants made to the Indians.

1872

El Paso, Chihuahua, has 10,000 residents.
Two miners claim to have discovered diamonds near Ralston,New Mexico. Ralston had formerly been known as Mexican Springs and Grant (after General U. S. Grant). However, the diamond hoax embarrassed the community, so Colonel John Boyle, who owned the Shakespeare Mining Company, suggested that the town change its name to Shakespeare. Shakespeare is two miles from Lordsburg, New Mexico.

JANUARY 6: West Overland is a three-fourth mile straightaway, and scene of numerous horse races. The races generally end at El Paso Street. On this day a famous horse race occurred when Fly and Kit competed against each other. Fly was owned by Lucien Maxwell, owner of the huge New Mexico Maxwell land grant, and Kit by Ben Dowell, the first El Paso mayor. Great local excitement prevailed, and people came from miles away to watch. At least $25,000 changed hands when Kit won by 15 feet. Kit, the fastest horse in the Southwest, died in El Paso in 1875.

AUGUST 8: The southern portion of the Santa Teresa grant (which is in Mexico) is sold to Pablo Miranda, who in turn sold the grant to Jesús María Escobar. Escobar and his brother, Jesús Escobar y Armendaris then acquired most of the north half inside the Gadsden Purchase from the heirs of Francisco and Josefina García. They asked United States courts to validate the grant.

DECEMBER 22: Bishop John B. Salpointe of Tucson takes possession of the Ysleta and Socorro Missions.

DECEMBER 25: The *El Paso Sentinel* begins operation.

1873

A transept is added to the Socorro Mission.

APRIL 8: General George Crook, in Arizona, issues his famous Order No. 13. He urged whites to treat the Apaches as "children in ignorance, not in innocence."

MAY 17: El Paso incorporates.

MAY 29: Washington establishes a Mescalero Apache Indian Reservation near Fort Stanton in New Mexico.

AUGUST 12: The first city elections are held. The 105 qualified voters selected saloon owner Ben Dowell as mayor. Council meetings were held in his saloon. Since the city took its water from irrigation ditches, the council made it a crime to bathe or water animals in the ditches.

AUGUST 25: The City Council passes an ordinance requiring all persons who use water from the *acequias* (irrigation ditches) to perform a prescribed amount of labor for the amount of water used. Anyone over 18 who was not a landowner had to provide one day's labor each year on the acequias.

DECEMBER 6: The *El Paso Sentinel* ceases to operate.

DECEMBER 7: The county seat moves from San Elizario to Ysleta.

1874

JANUARY 21: Simeon Hart dies at his home in El Paso. His body was interred at El Molino (Hart's Mill). In 1911, his son Juan, erected a columned tomb which held both his father and mother.

MARCH 1: Bishop John B. Salpointe, over vigorous Tigua protests, removes Saint Anthony as the patron saint of Ysleta and installs Our Lady of Mt. Carmel. Salpointe also grants confirmation to 300 children and adults.

MAY 9: The Texas legislature passes a bill introduced by Albert J.Fountain called "An Act to Repeal an Act to Incorporate the Town of Ysleta in El Paso County." The bill has six months before it goes into effect, and over 500 conveyances of Tigua property are made. The Tiguas lose almost all their land.

MAY 27: An El Paso County Frontiersmen Minute Company (Texas Rangers) is organized under the command of Lieutenant Telésfero Montes. Like the previous company of Texas Rangers, they were stationed primarily at San Elizario and spent most of their time fighting Indians.

SEPTEMBER 5: A block of land bounded by Franklin, Missouri, Mesa and Oregon streets is allocated as a Masonic Cemetery.

1875

JANUARY: Mescalero Apaches flee the reservation near Fort Stanton, New Mexico, when soldiers do not protect them from white marauders.

MARCH 2: The United States Supreme Court places immigration under the jurisdiction of the federal government. Congress quickly passed a law barring Chinese prostitutes and contract labor.

SEPTEMBER 25: The City of El Paso goes out of business as an incorporation.

SEPTEMBER 25: The present (Joseph) Magoffin Home is constructed. The outside adobe walls are four feet thick, and inside walls are two feet. Ceilings are 14 feet high. Wood work (beams, flooring, etc.) is hand-hewn and was brought by wagon from Mescalero.

OCTOBER 20: An executive order extends the Mescalero Reservation of New Mexico into the Sacramento Mountains.

NOVEMBER 27: The El Paso County Frontiersmen Minute Company is mustered out. Just a week prior to dismissal, the Company followed the trail of three Indians driving stolen livestock. They killed one Indian, recovered seven horses and a mule, and captured three Indian ponies.

1876

JANUARY: Three Mormon missionaries enter El Paso, Chihuahua. They are treated well, so they move deeper into Chihuahua and investigate settlement opportunities before returning to Salt Lake City.

MARCH 20: The El Paso County Frontiersmen Minute Company (Texas Rangers) are again mustered in.

APRIL 16: The El Paso Rangers follow an Indian trail for two days and nights, and track it into Dog Canyon, near Alamogordo. However, the company claimed to have been fired on by 200 Indians. The Rangers barely escaped.

JUNE 25: George Custer and parts of the 7th Cavalry are annihilated at Little Big Horn, Montana.

El Paso Street looking north from Mexico toward Ponce's Rancho (Central Hotel) in 1870s. Photo taken roughly at present intersection of El Paso and Paisano streets. The second large building on the right would be the Butterfield Overland Stage Building. (Author's Collection)

SEPTEMBER: Billy the Kid rides through El Paso on his way to break a friend out of the San Elizario jail. He briefly stops at the Ben Dowell Saloon in El Paso.

1877

Construction begins on the present San Elizario Church, but it will not be completed for 10 years. Evidence indicates that the old presidio chapel was on the north side of the present church, and a door from the old chapel opened into the present chapel.

JANUARY 17: Fort Bliss at Concordia (Stephensonville) is abandoned. The site was too far from most Indian activity.

MARCH 28: Mexican President Porfirio Díaz has reinforced El Paso, Chihuahua with 100 cavalrymen. The soldiers are a group of cut-throats, according to German businessman Ernst Kohlberg. To meet expenses, the cavalry extracted forced loans of $160 each from the business people. A few weeks later, the cavalry suddenly abandoned the city and the town was occupied by Colonel Paulino Z. Machorro and the 2nd Regiment of Mexican Infantry. Machorro had declared allegiance to Don Sebastian Lerdo de Tejada, who wants to be president.

JUNE: Mogollon, New Mexico has the Copper Queen, the Copper King, the Silver Twig and the War Cloud mines. The village sits on fabulous gold and silver wealth.

JUNE 1: The Order of June 1 goes into effect. Mexican authorities are on notice that along the Texas/Mexico border, the United States Army reserves for itself the right to cross the Mexican border without permission when in hot pursuit of Indians or marauders.

JUNE 11: Colonel Paulino Machorro makes a forced loan demand on the Paso del Norte merchants and learns the merchants have no money left. So Machorro demands forced loans from the peasants. This leads to a bloody fight ending with the bodies of Machorro's men scattered over the Mexican hillsides. Machorro himself nearly drowns swimming the river into El Paso, Texas and accepting refuge.

AUGUST: Hillsboro, New Mexico established. The miners drew names from a hat, and Hillsboro was selected. The surrounding hills produced $6 million in gold and silver.

OCTOBER 10: The El Paso Salt War flares as Judge Charles Howard kills Hispanic factional leader, Luis Cardis, in El Paso with a shotgun.

NOVEMBER: The El Paso Weather Bureau opens.

NOVEMBER 12: Major John B. Jones, chief of rangers, comes to El Paso as a result of the Salt War and organizes a 20-man detachment of Texas Rangers known as Company C. John B. Tays, brother to Parson Tays, is placed in command.

DECEMBER 13: Judge Charles Howard and Company C of the Texas Rangers enter San Elizario determined to resolve the salt problems. The Rangers take refuge in an adobe building and remain under siege for three days. Sergeant C. E. Mortimer is killed, as is Charles Ellis, a local storekeeper. The Rangers surrender, the only such Ranger outrage in history. Howard and two San Elizario residents, John McBride and John Atkinson, are brutally executed by the mob.

DECEMBER 22: Another group of Texas Rangers, these being desperados recruited from Silver City, New Mexico, ride through the El Paso lower valley with a buckboard of coffins. Rapes and murders became common.

DECEMBER 22: Colonel Edward Hatch arrives in San Elizario with a mixed force of 9th Cavalry (Buffalo Soldiers) and 15th Infantry from forts Bayard, Davis and Stanton. The Army restores order.

DECEMBER 22: The Masonic Lodge #130 described 1877 as such a bad year, that even though the Lodge had rented a meeting room "for safety, security, privacy and comfort, [the members] would frequently meet in the bedroom of Solomon C. Schutz at 177 San Francisco Street."

1878

Hatch, New Mexico, a farming and ranching community, is established. The village is named for General Edward Hatch, local military commander.

JANUARY 1: Fort Bliss is reestablished but the Concordia site is in a shambles. The troops then occupy empty buildings in El Paso, and drill in the public square (San Jacinto Plaza).

JANUARY 22: A four-man congressional investigation takes place in El Paso as a result of the Salt War. Reams of testimony are taken, and numerous indictments are handed down. But no one is ever brought to trial.

APRIL 1: At nine o'clock in the morning, Sheriff William Brady and three deputies walk down the main street of Lincoln, New Mexico. Brady and Deputy George Hindman are shot dead by Billy the Kid and six other assassins hiding behind a corral gate.

APRIL 4: The gunfight at Blazer's Mill near Mescalero, New Mexico, takes place. Billy the Kid, Dick Brewer, George Coe and others tangle with Andrew L. "Buckshot" Roberts, one of several suspected slayers of Englishman John Tunstall. Roberts is seriously wounded, but holds off his attackers, in the process killing Dick Brewer with a remarkably long shot from across the canyon. Roberts dies from his wound and he and Brewer are buried side by side on a nearby hill.

JULY 14-19: The Five Day Battle occurs in Lincoln. When it finally ends, the Lincoln County War is over. Only Billy the Kid and a few outlaw friends are still loose and running.

1879

Sisters of Loretto establish the valley's first parochial school at San Elizario.

JANUARY 4: District Judge Allen Blacker visits Austin and confers with incoming Governor Oran Roberts. The two men discuss lawlessness in El Paso, Blacker claiming the county has been invaded by desperados from Lincoln, New Mexico, where virtual civil war has been raging.

JUNE 28: Victorio and his Apache Indian band surrender to the military in New Mexico.

AUGUST 21: Victorio and his warriors bolt from Fort Stanton, New Mexico and travel west across into the Black Range near Silver City. He recrosses the international border several times while fighting successful skirmishes. This will be Victorio's last series of raids.

AUGUST 30: El Paso Masonic Lodge #130 begins construction of a one-story adobe meeting room on the northeast corner of San Antonio and Mesa streets (present Popular Dry Goods).

SEPTEMBER 12: Captain George Baylor and a company of Texas Rangers are stationed at Ysleta. They are primarily Indian fighters, and the Tiguas serve as scouts. James Gillett is the first sergeant, and he will write the famous book, *Six Years With the Texas Rangers*.

DECEMBER 31: The Ysleta Volunteer Guard is organized as state militia known as Company F, 1st Regiment of Cavalry.

1880

The City of El Paso has a population of 736. El Paso County has 3,845. The railroads reach Lamy (near Santa Fe), New Mexico. The Santa Fe Trail, as a wagon road, ceases to exist.

A group of 23 El Paso citizens petition for the establishment of free city schools. Nothing comes of it.

Twelve and fourteen horse teams are hauling ore and bullion into Silver City, and bricks of gold and silver are stacked on the sidewalks outside of shipping offices.

Chamberino, New Mexico is founded. The name could be an Indian word meaning "deep ford."

JANUARY: Victorio returns from old Mexico to raid in New Mexico and West Texas. Three Tiguas serve as scouts for General Ben H. Grierson.

MARCH 20: The Southern Pacific reaches Tucson.

JUNE 11: Sergeant Simon Olguin, a Tigua Indian scout living in Ysleta, and several 10th Cavalry troopers are slain by Apaches in Presidio County. Only one soldier escapes.

JULY 3: El Paso re-incorporates. Solomon Schutz is elected mayor.

JULY 26: John B. Tays becomes the first city marshal.

AUGUST 3: The City Council places a tax of $2 on all city *bailes* (dances).

AUGUST 5: Ysleta is again incorporated. Twenty-eight votes went for incorporation, 11 against.

OCTOBER 14: The great Apache war chief, Victorio, and his followers are slain at Tres Castillos, Chihuahua, 70 miles south of El Paso. Lieutenant Colonel Joaquin Terrazas achieves a striking victory. The Mexican militia suffered three killed and ten wounded. Seventy-eight Apaches were slain, and 68 taken prisoner, all of them women and children. Terrazas, later promoted to full colonel, reportedly earned $17,250 for the scalps and $10,200 for the prisoners who were sold into slavery.

OCTOBER 18: Lordsburg, New Mexico, is founded as a railroad stop for the Southern Pacific. It was named for an engineer in charge of the construction crew.

OCTOBER 25: John Tays is removed as city marshal. No details given. A. I. Stevens, a carriage maker, is appointed to the position. His deputy is Bill Johnson, who has problems with liquor.

NOVEMBER 26: A. I. Stevens is removed as city marshal for "neglect and dereliction of duty." No details. Johnson remains as deputy.

DECEMBER 1: George Campbell is appointed city marshal. The 30-year-old Ohioan had previously been a deputy sheriff in Henrietta, Texas. Johnson is still deputy.

DECEMBER 6: The people of Ysleta (Tiguas) are said to have bad reputations as *brujos* (witches).

DECEMBER 15: The Southern Pacific Railroad establishes Deming, New Mexico, and names it for Mary Ann Deming, wife of Charles Crocker, one of four Southern Pacific directors. Deming was initially a railroad stop.

DECEMBER 23: The marshal and City Council ask Governor O. M. Roberts to assign the Texas Rangers, currently stationed at Ysleta, to move to El Paso and protect the public. The letter claims the city has "hordes of vagabonds, gamblers, burglars, thieves, and particularly murderers thrust upon us."

DECEMBER 23: Fort Bliss moves to Hart's Mill. This gets the post out of town, and permits military construction for barracks and supply buildings.

DECEMBER 24: A. M. Conklin, editor of the *Socorro New Mexico Sun* is slain in Socorro as he leaves church services.

1881

Jesuits take control of the Ysleta Mission. Father Lossaigne places the statue of Our Lady of Mt. Carmel on the main altar and the Statue of St. Anthony on the side altar. The Jesuits rename the church, Misión de Nuesta Señora del Monte Carmelo (Our Lady of Mt. Carmel). The church is officially still called that even though the Tiguas refer to it as the Church of St. Anthony.

The Southern Pacific builds a wooden railroad bridge across the Rio Grande near today's ASARCO.

Lightbody and James, two cousins, erect a two-story frame structure (a grocery store) on the northwest corner of El Paso and Overland streets. It becomes the Davis Block.

The Central Hotel is razed.

Zach White builds a permanent bridge for the Mexican Central Railroad. The railroad will build south from El Paso, Chihuahua to Mexico City, the only rail line hooking the nation's capital with the border.

Mesa Gardens is built at Yandell and Rio Grande streets. The gardens are something of an outdoor restaurant and beer garden.

The Pierson Hotel opens, to be razed in 1929-30. Today, this site holds the Newspaper Printing Corporation Building (not the editorial office building).

Organ, New Mexico is founded. The mining town is named for the Organ Mountains, but the community was originally called San Augustine.

JANUARY: Las Cruces, New Mexico, hires a four-man police force.

JANUARY 1: A mob of toughs terrorize El Paso. Gunmen roam the streets firing randomly into buildings, especially those owned by El Paso politicians.

JANUARY 6: Captain George Baylor and the Texas Rangers are ordered to El Paso from Ysleta to restore order.

JANUARY 14: The El Paso Street Railway Company gets a franchise for a streetcar line.

JANUARY 14: Charges of inciting a riot are dropped against Marshal George Campbell, and he is allowed to resign. Ed Copeland is sworn in as the new marshal. Copeland owns and operates the Occidental Saloon. Bill Johnson is still the deputy marshal.

JANUARY 28: Mexican police jail every American in El Paso, Chihuahua.

Prior to bridges, a ferry had operated back and forth across the Rio Grande for years during periods of high water. The ferry connected what is now Juarez Avenue with El Paso or Santa Fe streets. (Aultman Collection. El Paso Public Library)

JANUARY 29: Captain George Baylor, his Rangers, and three Tigua scouts (Bernardo and Domingo Olguin, and Aniceto Duran) trail and attack a group of Apaches in the Diablo Mountains west of Guadalupe Peak. The Rangers surprised the Indians and killed four braves, two women and two children. When the battle ended, Rangers took breakfast on the ground, Baylor writing, "We had almost a boundless view from our breakfast table. The beauty of the scenery was only marred by man's inhumanity to man, the ghostly forms of the Indians lying around."

FEBRUARY: The State National Bank opens.

FEBRUARY 14: The City Council rules that Ed Copeland is not fully qualified to be marshal, and he is dismissed. Bill Johnson is elevated from deputy to marshal.

FEBRUARY 17: Congress authorizes the Southern Pacific to lay tracks directly across the Fort Bliss parade ground.

FEBRUARY 18: Six Americans break jail in El Paso, Chihuahua. Three are recaptured, and three are slain while crossing an irrigation ditch.

FEBRUARY 28: The Las Vegas, New Mexico *Optic* describes El Paso as "equal to the orthodox church belief in hell."

MARCH 31: The City Council grants a franchise to establish the El Paso Water Company.

APRIL: Las Cruces dismisses its four-man police force because the railroad crews have moved to El Paso.

APRIL: James Gillett and George Lloyd, Rangers stationed at Ysleta, cross the Rio Grande into Zaragoza, Chihuahua, and kidnap Onofre Baca, one of the accused murderers of *Socorro Sun* editor A. M. Conklin. The Rangers and their captive outrun pursuit and make it to Texas. Gillett then takes Baca by train to Socorro, turns the man over to a mob, collects his $500 reward, and notes later as he leaves on the southbound train, that Baca's body was hanging from a gate crossbar.

APRIL 1: Wells Fargo opens for business.

APRIL 2: The *El Paso Morning Times* and *El Paso Herald* begin operation on substantially the same day.

APRIL 2: Eugene O'Connell is shot and dies in the street. His body lies there three days before merchant Ben Schuster is moved to buy a coffin. The *Lone Star* praises this generous act.

APRIL 2: Newspapers report that coaches, lumbering wagons, and the odds and ends of all sorts of vehicles are running almost hourly to the end of the approaching railroad track, bringing in crowds of new residents and visitors.

APRIL 11: Dallas Stoudenmire, a 36-year-old Alabaman, is hired as the new city marshal. He then dismisses Deputy Marshal Bill Johnson. Stoudenmire is over six foot tall, and carries a revolver in each of two leather-lined hip pockets. One weapon is a "belly gun," meaning the barrel is sawed-off and has to be in an opponent's belly before the trigger is pulled. Otherwise, one might miss.

APRIL 12: Two Mexican vaqueros are killed in the bosque near Canutillo.

APRIL 13: At Mesilla, Billy the Kid is tried for the murder of Sheriff William Brady. Judge Warren Bristol sentenced the Kid to be hanged in Lincoln on May 13 between the hours of nine and three.

APRIL 14: The El Paso Water Company gets a franchise.

APRIL 14: The bodies of two bushwhacked Mexican vaqueros are brought into El Paso. An inquest is held where the Camino Real Paso del Norte Hotel is today. Seventy-five riders from Mexico storm up and down El Paso Street. When the inquest is terminated, the bodies and the vaqueros go to Mexico. Marshal Stoudenmire crosses the street for a bite to eat. In the middle of El Paso Street, former City Marshal George Campbell argues with Gus Krempkau, constable and former Texas Ranger. Campbell turns to mount his horse as his friend, Johnny Hale, screams "I'll take care

A subdivision of El Paso following arrival of the railroads during the 1880s. Corner of present Montana and Oregon streets. Rio Grande Street is hardly a dirt path on the left. (U.T. El Paso Archives)

of this for you, George." Hale shoots Krempkau. Stoudenmire comes on the run, kills an innocent bystander, and then shoots John Hale as well as George Campbell. The famous Four Dead in Five Seconds gunfight is history.

APRIL 17: City Marshal Dallas Stoudenmire kills Bill Johnson, former deputy marshal. At the intersection of El Paso and East San Antonio streets, Johnson tried to assassinate Stoudenmire with a shotgun, and missed. Stoudenmire put nine bullets in Johnson, and the former deputy died on a pile of bricks. The Rangers restore order.

APRIL 20: Vigilantes organize as the Law and Order League. They disband within a month.

APRIL 23: The State National Bank receives permission from the state comptroller to open.

APRIL 28: Billy the Kid makes a dramatic break from the Lincoln County Courthouse jail, killing his two guards James Bell and Robert Olinger.

MAY: El Paso has a terrible housing shortage. Tents line the streets. People sleep in saloons.

MAY 19: Five hundred Chinese arrive in El Paso. They are construction workers for the Southern Pacific.

MAY 13 (or thereabout): The Southern Pacific arrives in El Paso.

JUNE 2: The Atchison Topeka and Santa Fe arrives in El Paso.

JUNE 6: The First National Bank gets permission to open for business.

JULY 14: Billy the Kid is shot dead by Sheriff Pat Garrett in Fort Sumner, New Mexico. The dramatic incident took place inside the bedroom of local landowner, Pete Maxwell.

AUGUST: The *El Paso Daily Independent* starts publication.

The Southern Pacific built this depot at the present-day southeast corner of Franklin and Stanton streets. The Central Hotel (Ponce de León Hacienda) is in the background. (Aultman Collection. El Paso Public Library)

SEPTEMBER: Miss Ella Nunn opens a county school for 42 pupils. However, no public space is provided, and the students move from building to building until the project fades away.

SEPTEMBER 1: Silvester Watts builds the city's first water plant.

OCTOBER: The El Paso Literary Group organizes.

OCTOBER: The Reverend Father Carlos Persone arrives in El Paso. He takes charge of the Ysleta Mission.

OCTOBER 12: Simeon Harrison Newman establishes the *El Paso Lone Star*. He had recently published the *Las Vegas Mail* and the *Las Cruces Thirty-Four*.

OCTOBER 26: The Gunfight at the OK Corral occurs in Tombstone, Arizona. Wyatt Earp and his brothers Virgil and Morgan, plus gambler and tubercular John H. "Doc" Holliday meet Ike and Billy Clanton, Tom and Frank McLowery, and Billy Claiborne. When the smoke clears 30 seconds later, Ike and Claiborne have fled, and Billy Clanton, Tom and Frank McLowery are dead. Their tombstones read, "Murdered on the Streets of Tombstone."

NOVEMBER 7: Construction starts out of Juarez on the Mexican Central Railroad.

NOVEMBER 16: The Nellie Boyd Dramatic Company performs *Fanchon the Cricket* and *A Case for Divorce*.

NOVEMBER 19: Hills Hall opens on San Antonio Street. Built of adobe and resembling a barn, the theater was constructed in less than one week. The Nellie Boyd Troupe and others played to appreciative audiences.

NOVEMBER 24: The cornerstone is laid for the Trinity Methodist Church.

NOVEMBER 25: James Manning leases the Manning Saloon where Ben Dowell's Saloon used to be.

DECEMBER 1: When the White Oaks Railroad reaches ten miles east of the city, someone suggested this location for a townsite. Since the railroad had drilled two wells, the first on the mesa east of the Franklins, Mrs. Joseph Magoffin suggested the name of LaNoria, meaning "the well." Fort Bliss would make its home at LaNoria some twelve years in the future.

DECEMBER 1: The Southern Pacific and the Texas & Pacific meet at Sierra Blanca, Texas. This was a major east-west connection worthy of national recognition, but the only ceremony was an ordinary spike driven into a drilled hole in a railroad tie. Since then, historians can't even agree on which day in December the event occurred.

DECEMBER 3: Within three weeks of its opening, Hills Hall has become a restaurant. After this it became a boarding house, and even later a home for the Cactus Club.

DECEMBER 10: James B. Gillett is appointed assistant city marshal of El Paso.

DECEMBER 22: The El Paso Social Club forms and holds a ball at Hills' Hall. Only the best people belong, and only invited guests attend.

DECEMBER 25: Parson Tays lays the cornerstone on Christmas for "The Watch Tower on the Rio Grande," St. Clement's Episcopal Church on Mesa Street.

1882

El Paso gets gas street lights.

The city buys two acres of land and establishes a pauper burial ground at Concordia Cemetery.

A series of heliograph stations link Fort Bliss, Texas, and Fort Stanton and Robledo Mountain (Fort Selden) in New Mexico. These light signals were supposed to pinpoint hostile Apache locations, but since the Indian wars were substantially over, the heliograph never had an opportunity to display its strength.

El Paso church women install a hospital in a long wooden building at
South Santa Fe and West 5th Street. It was staffed by church volunteers
since no professional nurses were available. Consumptives filled the
majority of its 20 beds.

Ruidoso, New Mexico, is established, although it was formerly known
as Dowlin's Mill. The village was named for the Ruidoso River, which
means "noisy."

JANUARY 2: The Texas & Pacific Railroad arrives in El Paso. It made
the trip from St. Louis in 66 hours.

JANUARY 4: The *Daily El Paso International Link*, after undergoing
several name changes during the last few years, devoted special
attention to Mexican and American news. Editor Juan Hart kept it
going only one month before consolidating it with the *El Paso
Times*.

JANUARY 25: The Southwestern Ice Company opens.

JANUARY 29: This is dedication day for Trinity Methodist Church
at the corner of Texas and Stanton streets.

FEBRUARY 7: El Paso's first mule drawn streetcar company is organized by Anson Mills, Joseph Magoffin and a Floyd Bates. The
wooden cars seat 12 persons and run on four wheels. Mandy was a
generic name for working mules.

FEBRUARY 11: The *El Paso Lone Star* reported "four of the five smallpox patients who were sent to the miserable hovel [Pest House or
City Eruptive Hospital] at old Fort Bliss have died. The one who
did not die got up and walked back to town. It is nothing less than
murder to send patients to such a place."

FEBRUARY 14: Samuel M. "Doc" Cummings, brother-in-law of City
Marshal Dallas Stoudenmire, is murdered by James Manning. The
shootout took place in the Manning Saloon, although Cummings
stumbled out onto El Paso Street to die. An autopsy showed
Cummings also had a fractured skull.

MARCH 25: The *El Paso Lone Star* prints a Law and Order editorial. It refers to the feud between City Marshal Dallas Stoudenmire and the Manning brothers, James, Frank and George (Doc). The newspaper said the city was "standing on a volcano," and that the "streets may be deluged with blood at any moment."

MARCH 28: Twenty-five votes are cast in favor of the city assuming control of the El Paso Public Schools, none of which exist.

MARCH 29: City Marshal Dallas Stoudenmire drafts a letter to Adjutant General King in Austin. He accuses the Rangers of siding with the lawless rather than the law-abiding, and requests that the Rangers keep out of El Paso.

MARCH 29: The City Council passes an ordinance prohibiting the excessive use of opium.

APRIL 6: The First Presbyterian Church opens.

APRIL 16: City Marshal Dallas Stoudenmire and the Manning brothers sign a peace treaty claiming to have "settled all differences and unfriendly feelings," and that all parties will "thereafter meet and pass each other on friendly terms." The treaty was published in the *El Paso Herald*.

APRIL 20: Belle Branton, a prostitute, is permanently crippled when struck by a run-away carriage. Since she is unable to work, she is also unable to pay the city's $5 monthly fine (fee), but she does pay $4.70, which was all the money she had. She was jailed for not paying the entire amount. After several days, she is released by Mayor Joseph Magoffin, who ordered her money returned.

APRIL 29: The city water franchise is transferred to Sylvester Watts of St. Louis.

MAY 5: The Chinese Exclusion Act goes into effect. El Paso will become a center of the Chinese smuggling trade.

MAY 22: Company K of the 1st Regiment is a volunteer guard of infantry raised at El Paso and known as the Stonewall Greys. By August, the group has changed its name to the El Paso Rifles, and in 1883 to the El Paso Light Guards.

MAY 27: El Paso City Marshal Dallas Stoudenmire meets with the city council to discuss his dismissal. The big marshal walks into the conference room twirling his six shooter and saying, "I can straddle every goddamned alderman here." The meeting was adjourned.

MAY 29: Stoudenmire sobers up and resigns. Deputy Marshal James Gillett is appointed to replace him.

JUNE (or thereabout): The Coliseum Variety Theater is built at the rear of the El Paso House hotel on El Paso Street. Publicity dubbed it the largest theater between San Francisco and New Orleans. The notorious Manning brothers (Doc, Frank and James) owned it, and the theater bragged of seating 500 people. The 25 boxes reportedly held six people each, but that meant three men with girls on their laps.

JULY 13: Former City Marshal Stoudenmire accepts a government job as United States deputy marshal with headquarters in El Paso.

JULY 19: The Cactus Club organizes. It began as a debating club, but switched over when a majority of members were more interested in good fellowship and social activities.

AUGUST 16: Kingston, New Mexico is established and named for the Iron King Mine. The town becomes known as much for its rustlers and desperados as for its mines and silver.

AUGUST 23: Twenty-two out of 46 volunteer firemen organize the El Paso Fire Department and set up Hook and Ladder Company No. 1.

AUGUST 26: The First Baptist Church is organized. A week later the Reverend George W. Baines, Jr., was named pastor.

SEPTEMBER 1: The City Council officially recognizes the El Paso

Volunteer Fire Department. It approved the selection of officers, and took under advisement the department's request for three carts and reels and a thousand feet of the best rubber hose.

SEPTEMBER 8: A banquet in the old Central Hotel honors the Watts water system. It has been tested and accepted. However, the pipes soon leaked, and the water pressure flowed by gravity out of the Sunset Reservoir. For the next 25 years, people still obtained much of their drinking and cooking water from Deming, New Mexico.

SEPTEMBER 18: Former City Marshal Dallas Stoudenmire is slain on El Paso Street by the Manning Brothers. The gunfight started with Stoudenmire and Doc Manning inside the Manning Saloon (present Camino Real Paso del Norte Hotel) and ended on the sidewalk with James Manning shooting the ex-city marshal in the head. Masonic Lodge No. 130 paid funeral costs: burial suit $11.55. Lumber for coffin, $4.50. The Mannings were tried for murder and acquitted.

NOVEMBER: Bill Thompson, brother of the notorious gunman, Ben Thompson, was captured in El Paso and extradited to East Texas. Bill escaped en route.

NOVEMBER 15: The El Paso Volunteer Fire Department reorganizes into Hose Company No. 1, Hose Company No. 2, and Hook and Ladder Company, No. 1

NOVEMBER 18: The first street lamp erected in El Paso is in front of Masonic Lodge #130.

NOVEMBER 23: Pinos Altos, New Mexico erected a large Cross on a high hill just north of town. The citizens and Apaches agreed that no killing would be done for as long as the Cross stood. There were no murders between Indians and whites for nearly 20 years.

DECEMBER 14: The first Fireman's Ball is held.

DECEMBER 25: The Reverend Father Joseph Montanarelli celebrates the first Mass in St. Mary's Chapel on Christmas morning. The church was located at the intersection of North Oregon and Wyoming.

1883

Rincon, New Mexico, founded. Named because of a mountain corner. It marked the southern end of the dreaded Jornada del Muerto (Journey of Death, or Dead Man's Journey). In the 1880s it was home to a particularly murderous group of desperados and cattle rustlers led by John Kinney.

JANUARY: The progressive citizens of El Paso are ashamed because El Paso still has no free public schools.

JANUARY 12: The G.H. & S.A. Railroad comes to town.

JANUARY 15: This is a traditional date for the arrival of alligators in the Public Square (San Jacinto Plaza).

JANUARY 24: The *El Paso Lone Star* reports that an irate husband dashed into a saloon brandishing a revolver and screaming "he had just discovered his wife in close proximity with a neighbor inside a privy." The gunman was arrested.

FEBRUARY: A two-wheeled hose cart arrives in the city and becomes the first piece of apparatus owned by the fire department.

FEBRUARY 16: The El Paso Board of Trade organizes and becomes a forerunner of the Chamber of Commerce.

MARCH 5: The first public school opens and is called the "Public School." A Mr. McKay is employed as a teacher, and he enrolls 53 pupils on the first day.

MARCH 7: The First Presbyterian Church is dedicated. It was built of stone from Mt. Franklin and fronted on Myrtle Street across from the Courthouse.

MARCH 24: City Marshal James Gillett resigns after threatening to shoot Mayor pro tem Paul Keating. Keating had questioned Gillett's financial records, and Gillett had referred to Keating as intoxicated while on city business. The two men argued, and Gillett banged his six-shooter off Keating's head.

APRIL: A block of El Paso Street on the west side is wiped out by fire. The firemen never heard the alarm because of the wind.

APRIL: Since firemen are frequently exhausted by towing heavy and awkward apparatus carts to a fire scene, the city offered $3 ($5 for an out of town blaze) to a driver of any team of horses willing to pull the hose carts and hook and ladder vehicles. Unfortunately, some horse drivers got into fist fights over who was first.

APRIL 1: The first issue of the *Bullion* (a mining newspaper) is published in Socorro, New Mexico.

APRIL 18: Frank Manning replaces James Gillett as city marshal of El Paso.

MAY 4: The *El Paso Times* starts a campaign to get the railroad tracks removed from Main Street. Sixty-five years later, the job gets done.

MAY 19: The old Coliseum and Variety Theater is reopened as the National Theater. The newspapers said nothing complimentary.

MAY 26: City Marshal Frank Manning resigns after beating a merchant with a cane.

JUNE: The Bell Telephone Company installs a telephone exchange over the Lightbody Dry Goods Store on El Paso Street.

JUNE 29: A herd of 100 horses are driven through El Paso on their way to Silver City, New Mexico.

JULY 1: Lieutenant Thomas W. Symons will lead an American team along the international land border to inspect the condition of boundary markers.

City Marshal Frank Manning standing in background. Seated in front is his brother, James Manning, slayer of Dallas Stoudenmire, Mrs. James Manning, and son, William. (Author's Collection)

JULY 5: Joseph Brinster is legally hanged at the county seat of Ysleta for rape. He was convicted of raping the wife of a non-commissioned officer at Fort Davis. He was the first man ever legally hanged in El Paso County, and he had to be dropped twice because the first drop did not produce death.

JULY 6: Tom Mode becomes the first city policeman killed in the line of duty in El Paso. He had gone to investigate a brothel disturbance and was shot.

JULY 12: The Fashion Saloon opens with electric lights.

JULY 23: The Schutz Opera House opens at 123 San Francisco Street.

AUGUST 15: Masonic Lodge No. 130 buys two acres of land for a Masonic Cemetery at Concordia.

AUGUST 15: The El Paso Republicans begin publication of *The Rescue,* a newspaper with a Republican point of view. It ran eight issues, then went out of business.

AUGUST 15: Union soldiers buried in the Fort Bliss cemetery (Cleveland Square) will be removed and taken to Fort Snelling, Minnesota.

AUGUST 18: Concordia Cemetery has been selected as the burial place of the Free Masons, the Roman Catholics and the City. The area is described as "entirely above water and free from quicksand."

AUGUST 20: The adobe wall that surrounds the cathedral plaza in El Paso del Norte is being torn down. The ground has been plowed, and will be planted with trees. Sidewalks are going in.

AUGUST 28: There is a Chinese laundry for every two families in El Paso.

SEPTEMBER 20: Telephone service starts with forty subscribers, thirteen in El Paso, Chihuahua. The telephone company was next door to the Parlor Saloon in El Paso, and the saloon had a couple of cables dangling from the ceiling with rings about eight feet off the floor. Unbeknown to most people, those cables were attached to a wire extending from the telephone company. When a visitor wandered in from the train station, the local saloon hangers-on would ply him with drinks, then challenge him to catch hold of those rings and pull himself up and down a few times, showing the crowd how strong he was. Someone then signaled the telephone girl who threw a switch sending electricity through the cables. While the inebriated man thrashed about and couldn't let go, the saloon patrons rolled on the floor holding their bellies. The fun stopped when a visitor sued both the saloon and the telephone company.

NOVEMBER 3: One hundred and ten residents of El Paso County sign a petition calling for an election to determine the county seat.

NOVEMBER 18: Five different time zones are adopted in the United States. El Paso is in the Mountain Time Zone. It had been on "Sun Time."

NOVEMBER 20: Ground is broken for a streetcar line on San Antonio Street.

NOVEMBER 25: A group of six cowboys, all masked but one, derail a Southern Pacific train 14 miles west of Deming. They killed the engineer and robbed the express car, getting about $200 and a gold watch.

DECEMBER: El Paso's Volunteer Hook and Ladder Company No. 1 is in operation.

DECEMBER: The El Paso Stonewall Greys (Light Guards, El Paso Rifles), is decommissioned.

DECEMBER 3: The village of El Paso has about 300 voting residents, but somehow it musters 2,252 votes to transfer the county seat from Ysleta to El Paso. The only explanation is that voters from Juarez (El Paso, Chihuahua), came across and cast their votes

Mandy the Mule pulling a streetcar east on Mills Street at the corner of Stanton. The O.T. Bassett Lumberyard in the background is the present site of the State National Bank. (Aultman Collection. El Paso Public Library)

illegally in large numbers. At any rate, El Paso has the county seat, and it will remain here.

DECEMBER 14: The El Paso county seat officially moves from Ysleta to El Paso. For the first time, El Paso has more lawyers than Ysleta. The first courthouse in El Paso is the Lessor Building in the Monarch Block at today's corner of South El Paso and Paisano Drive.

DECEMBER 29: J. Fisher Satterthwaite is paid $600 to clean up San Jacinto Plaza.

1884

While El Paso must have had baseball teams prior to this year, we know only that in 1884 the city fielded the Reds, named for the red socks the players wore. (In 1885, the team apparently switched socks because they were known as the Blues.) Their chief competition came from Fort Bliss.

Commissioners Court orders a road built from Ysleta, through Socorro, San Elizario, Fabens, Fort Hancock, Fort Quitman, Sierra Blanca, Van Horn, and on to the Presidio County line.

The Second Baptist and the Methodist church for blacks is organized. There were only 25 blacks in El Paso.

The Satterthwaite Addition begins. Later it is called Sunset Heights because of an El Paso Herald contest. As the elite section of El Paso, it appealed to wealthy families.

JANUARY 19: Organ, New Mexico, has a smelter of 40 tons daily capacity.

FEBRUARY 9: Several buildings around the city are lighted with electricity. The lights appear brightest and steadiest at one (unnamed) saloon and gambling house.

FEBRUARY 13: The Grand Central Hotel opens on the site of the old Central Hotel. The hotel has three stories and is the showplace of the region.

FEBRUARY 14: El Paso has an ordinance against carrying a gun, which is rarely enforced. However, J. Fisher Satterthwaite, who had recently been beaten by a Mr. Fernandez, thereafter carried a six-shooter for protection . . . and was fined $25 by the courts. *Lone Star* editor Simeon Newman, wryly editorialized that it would have been cheaper for Satterthwaite to kill Fernandez. Satterthwaite then could have gone scot-free.

FEBRUARY 23: Gas service comes to the Pass when the first jet in the city is lit in Pioneer Plaza.

FEBRUARY 23: Anthony, Texas/New Mexico gets a post office. The AT&SF Railroad called the village La Tuna. The town has even been called Half Way House. The Anthony name may stem from an outline on the nearby Franklin Mountains called St. Anthony's Nose.

MARCH: Central School opens. It is the first "genuine" school in El Paso. The Bell Telephone Company Building eventually will be constructed on the Central School site.

MARCH 8: The Mexican Central Railroad now extends from Juarez to Mexico City.

MARCH 25: John L. Sullivan, heavyweight champion of the world, arrives in El Paso and holds exhibitions in the National Theater. Seats sell for $1 to $5. Boxes go to $30.

APRIL: The Pictorial Theater, sometimes called the Peoples Theater, opens. It does not receive rave reviews.

MAY 7: The *El Paso Lone Star* suggests that ladies of El Paso who have pure daughters to train and educate begin the task by not allowing copies of the *El Paso Herald* into their home.

JUNE 4: Speeding carriages are becoming a threat on the streets.

JUNE 4: Because of their "brazen effrontery," the French women in the Overland Building should be forced to move somewhere else in the city.

JUNE 8: The streetcar bridge into Juarez washes away during a flood.

JULY 1: Camp Rice, 53 miles southeast of El Paso and along the Rio Grande, becomes a permanent post. Its origins are obscure although it had been a sub post of Fort Davis since September 1882.

JULY 29: *Acequias,* where El Pasoans draw most of their water, are full of sand. The town is experiencing a severe water shortage.

AUGUST 25: The county signs a contract calling for a new courthouse (on the modern-day site of the present courthouse), to be constructed within 15 months.

SEPTEMBER 2: A festive cowboy rode his horse into the Fashion Saloon today and ordered a drink brought outside to him. When it wasn't forthcoming, he rode back into the saloon and ordered again, this time in an impatient voice. A judge fined him $15 and costs, and he is now in jail.

SEPTEMBER 24: The so-called Cardiff Giant is brought into town by hoaxers.

OCTOBER 4: The Shalam Colony becomes a model agricultural development in Doña Ana County. John Ballou Newbrough, its founder, was guided by *Oahspe,* a strange bible he claimed was written under the guidance of spirits. The book directed him to establish the colony, and to populate it with orphan children, plus adults, called Faithists, who would educate them.

OCTOBER 7: Governor John Ireland visits El Paso and makes a speech in Schutz's Hall.

NOVEMBER: The Stanton Street International Bridge is rebuilt.

NOVEMBER: Several new buildings are constructed at Fort Bliss, among them a guard house, hospital and officers quarters.

NOVEMBER: The $2,614.42 bid for a new Pest House and Hospital is accepted by the county.

NOVEMBER 12: A treaty is signed between the United States and Mexico. It declares that, except for avulsive (rapid) changes, the middle of the Rio Grande, or its deepest channel is to be the international boundary.

NOVEMBER 21: The Reverend Joseph Wilkin Tays, better known as Parson Tays, dies in El Paso. He had officiated at the funeral of a smallpox victim, and a few days later came down with the black smallpox himself. He died after a week of suffering and being tended to only by his wife and son. That night about nine o'clock, two men from the city came to the house, wrapped Parson Tays in a sheet and rushed the body to Concordia Cemetery where it was hastily buried during a furious thunderstorm. Parson Tays, who had ministered to so many sick and dying, was himself laid away with only two drenched, grave digging strangers to say a kind and final word.

DECEMBER 14: Charlie Utter, golden-haired gambler of the Rockies and friend of Wild Bill Hickok, is in town again.

1885

Calvin Easterly becomes the first El Paso superintendent of schools. He serves until 1890. The Mexican Preparatory School, later Aoy School, opens.

The Center Block Building is finished. It was so named because it was in the center of town on Pioneer Plaza. For a while it was the El Paso Herald Building. It became an Oasis Restaurant during the 1950s and '60s.

A group calling themselves The Howlers Club, organized and gave burlesque and musical performances in order to raise sufficient money to buy a clock for the courthouse.

JANUARY 14: The *El Paso Lone Star* says the city has not had a natural death in some time.

JANUARY 17: The City Council orders mud puddles filled on San Antonio Street. Hunting parties will now have to leave the city to find duck ponds.

Looking south on El Paso Street in 1885; taken from site of today's Plaza Theater. "Newspaper tree" remains at left. (Aultman Collection. El Paso Public Library)

JANUARY 24: Mexico establishes a free trade zone along its entire international border with the United States. The zone extends 20 kilometers south of the boundary. Juarez prospers as businesses flourish.

JANUARY 28: Work begins on the foundation of a new El Paso county courthouse.

MARCH: Midland County is created as Midland because it is halfway between Fort Worth and El Paso.

MARCH 1: The First Baptist Church is dedicated.

MARCH 1: Prostitute fines (license fees) will now cost $10 monthly instead of $5. The council also restricts prostitution to specific areas of town.

MARCH 14: El Paso has the only international streetcar line in the world. Travelers can ride to Juarez for 10 cents.

MARCH 21: Seven or eight prairie schooners (covered wagons) pass through the city each day.

SPRING: The entire 10th Cavalry (Buffalo Soldiers), commanded by Major General Benjamin Grierson, pauses at Fort Bliss while in route to join General George Crook in Arizona during his pursuit of Geronimo.

APRIL 6: The 34th United States District Court is established, the first in El Paso.

APRIL 8: The (Joseph) Magoffin Home (today's historic site) is surrounded by a forest of fruit trees in bloom.

APRIL 14: A gunfight erupts in the Gem Saloon. Buck Linn is mortally wounded by a man named Renic. Bill Raynor tries to avenge Linn, and is shot dead by Robert Cahill.

APRIL 19: El Paso's water reservoirs have more mud and fish than water.

APRIL 19: An iron bridge over the Rio Grande connects the Mexican Central with the Santa Fe Railroad.

MAY 15: Over 400 Mormon colonists are camped on the bank of the Casas Grandes River waiting to move onto land their elders are purchasing. This is the beginning of a massive Mormon immigration into Mexico. Although most Mormons did not practice polygamy, they believed in it and thus considered Mexico a place of religious refuge.

MAY 20: Lieutenant General Phil Sheridan visits El Paso accompanied by his family and staff.

JUNE – JULY: Massive fraud seeps into construction of the El Paso County Courthouse. During the trial, attorney James P. Hague said he was given $2,500 to testify on behalf of the accused. Hague produced the money in court, and stated, "I want the court to know that Hague and [attorney] Coldwell are not for sale." Then, to the cheers of spectators, Hague donated the money to charity.

JULY: Captain Arthur MacArthur, the father of Douglas MacArthur, arrives from Fort Selden to sit on a general court martial at Fort Bliss.

JULY 15: Mrs. Joseph Magoffin and Mrs. Dieter sponsor a grand benefit ball for wounded Confederate soldiers.

SUMMER: A Negro school opens in the colored Methodist Church opposite the Post Office. About 15 students are in attendance.

AUGUST 5: W. H. Austin, cashier at the State National Bank, blacks both eyes of City Councilman James P. Hague when Hague makes insulting remarks about Austin's potential abilities as city treasurer.

SEPTEMBER: The Gem Theater opens at 201 South El Paso Street. Not much happened there except for variety shows, dog fights and boxing matches. The Gem finally became nothing more than a saloon, and was later torn down for the construction of Sonora Street, later renamed West San Antonio Street.

The El Paso County Courthouse in 1896. The present courthouse sits on this exact spot. This is the fourth courthouse at this site. (Aultman Collection. El Paso Public Library)

SEPTEMBER: The first high school opens in El Paso on the second floor of the Central School. The principal was Miss Emma Seabaugh.

SEPTEMBER: City Council declares war on opium joints in El Paso. The joints can be fined up to $10.

SEPTEMBER 5: Second Lieutenant Britton Davis of the 3rd Cavalry, plus Chief of Scouts Al Sieber, plus packers and interpreter, plus 26 Apache scouts arrive at Fort Bliss. They remained for seven days, then departed by Southern Pacific for Bowie Station, Arizona Territory.

OCTOBER 30: Hubert Howe Bancroft, the celebrated historian, is in town.

NOVEMBER 28: Silver City, New Mexico, asks all non-property-owning Chinese to leave town at once. Most come to El Paso.

NOVEMBER 15: A new county road between El Paso and Ysleta is on the verge of completion.

DECEMBER 8: A huge meeting is called in the Schutz Opera House to discuss building the El Paso and White Oaks Railroad.

DECEMBER 19: Sam Schutz, who owned Schutz Opera House, published the following: "Owing to the fact that the State Board of Insurance has raised my rate to such an extent to make it onerous, I hereby notify the public that my hall is now closed and will not be used any more for any kind of amusement or performance." The building burned a few years later.

1886

The million acre Corralitos Ranch between Casas Grandes and Janos, Chihuahua is established.

Baseball fever is sweeping the town, and El Paso's team is now the

Browns apparently because they wear brown shirts and brown stockings. The pants are white and the caps are striped. However, it is also possible that the team is named after the St. Louis Browns who won what amounted to the World Series.

The International Cigar Factory opens in El Paso.

Another floor is added to the Grand Central Hotel, making it four stories.

JANUARY 20: Commissioners Court certifies the El Paso County Courthouse as complete and acceptable. The structure is insured for $50,000. All records will be transferred from the Lessor Building.

FEBRUARY 7: More than 150 prostitutes march on city hall and demand that the monthly fees of $10 be reduced to $5. The City Council broke the rebellion by threatening to check the books and arrest those girls who had neglected to pay an occasional fee in times past.

MARCH 27: For the fourth and last time, Geronimo and roughly 40 Apaches, including women and children, break away from the San Carlos Reservation in eastern Arizona. They flee across the international line into the Sierra Madre Mountains of Sonora, Mexico.

APRIL 6: Federal court trials are now taking place in El Paso. Federal cases had previously been handled in San Antonio.

APRIL 18: Etta Clark and Big Alice Abbot, two parlor house madams, argue in Etta's Parlor. Big Alice struck Etta several times, but Etta found a six-shooter and started firing, shooting Big Alice in what the newspapers should have said was the pubic arch, but instead said was the public arch. Big Alice survived.

APRIL 18: Camp Rice will hereafter be known as Fort Hancock.

MAY 12: Etta Clark found not guilty of the attempted murder of Big Alice Abbot.

JUNE 8: A crazed Chinaman has been parading nude in front of the courthouse and in front of the mayor's residence.

JUNE 8: Horse thieves steal 40 head of stock from a ranch near Socorro. The thieves are likely hiding in the nearby bosque.

JUNE 15: Utah Street (today's South Mesa) has become Bloody Utah because of so many shootings.

JUNE 30: A. K. Cutting worked for the *El Paso Times*, but he also published separate newspapers, one being *The Bulletin* and the other a Spanish language sheet called *El Centinela*. Unfortunately, another *El Centinela* newspaper was already functioning in El Paso across the river. That angered Cutting and he called his Mexican counterpart a fraud. Cutting was arrested in Mexico, and a Mexican judge ordered Cutting to print a retraction in his Spanish language newspaper, and Cutting did. Cutting returned to El Paso and inserted a notice in the Herald whereby he retracted the retraction. If Cutting had remained in El Paso, that would have ended the matter. But Cutting hurried into El Paso del Norte to gloat, and was re-arrested and sentenced to a year of hard labor and a fine of $500. The silly episode caused an international furor, mob actions, Mexican and American military alerts and rumored invasions of Mexico. Mexico finally bowed to United States pressure and reduced Cutting's sentence to the two controversial, uncomfortable and unnecessary months he had already spent in a Mexican jail.

SEPTEMBER: Douglass School for blacks opens in a church building on 7th Street.

SEPTEMBER 3: Apache leader Geronimo surrenders to General Nelson Miles at Skeleton Canyon in Arizona. The American government had sent the San Carlos Reservation families of Geronimo and his band into Florida exile, and Geronimo had to surrender if he wished to see his wives and children again.

SEPTEMBER 9: Geronimo and approximately 40 Apaches come

through Fort Bliss and El Paso by way of the Southern Pacific. As prisoners of war, they are on their way into exile at Fort Marion, Florida. On April 23, 1887, they are sent to Mount Vernon Barracks, Alabama. On October 4, 1894, the prisoners (numbering over 200, including wives and children), are shipped to Fort Sill, Oklahoma.

SEPTEMBER 26: Captain Lawton, who convinced Geronimo to surrender, is in town.

OCTOBER 1: The El Paso Post Office will hereafter handle special mail. There is a charge of ten cents, eight of which goes to the delivery boy.

OCTOBER 9: El Paso has a saloon for every 232 inhabitants, including women and children. The chances of dying of thirst are not alarming.

OCTOBER 20: Newspapers demand that the city spend more than $2 a day to clean up the public square (San Jacinto Plaza). It is woefully neglected.

OCTOBER 26: The Reverend S. W. Thornton of the Methodist Episcopal Church gave a sermon at the courthouse, a favored place for lectures. The good reverend denounced Mormons as disloyal to the United States, and called them a race of people unable to think for themselves.

OCTOBER 28: El Pasoans mail out 800 letters per day, and receive 440 on average.

OCTOBER 30: School children in El Paso number 775, of which 14 are colored.

DECEMBER 2: The whole town is cleaning the public square.

DECEMBER 19: Bat Masterson, the renowned gunman, is in town today.

1887

El Paso, Chihuahua, has 12,000 residents.
El Paso lays its first sewer, a twelve-inch line on Second Street.

JANUARY 1: The El Paso National Bank opens its doors.

JANUARY 6: The *El Paso Lone Star* publishes its last issue and goes out of business. Editor and Publisher Simeon Newman said the newspaper "has not attempted to secure popularity by sacrifice of principles, or to obtain patronage by pampering to the depraved public tastes." Newman lived another 40 years and earned his living as an insurance agent.

FEBRUARY 2: Cowboy Jack, a woman masquerading as a man, attempted suicide today.

FEBRUARY 9: Congress is considering an Act to grant the Rio Grande & El Paso Railroad a 100-foot right of way across the Fort Bliss military reservation (at Hart's Mill).

FEBRUARY 22: Two companies of the 16th Infantry arrive at Fort Bliss from San Angelo.

FEBRUARY 24: Sarah Bernhardt arrived today from Mexico. She complained that she had more problems getting her belongings through El Paso customs than from all other international customhouses put together.

MARCH: El Paso is under a cholera quarantine. Travelers from infected areas in Mexico and South America cannot visit the town.

MARCH 8: Hoodlums throw stones and kill one of two alligators in the plaza.

APRIL 7: Pedro García, editor of the *Observador Fronterizo* is in jail at El Paso del Norte and charged with libeling Mayor Provincio.

APRIL 7: The *Bullion* newspaper transfers from Socorro, New Mexico, to El Paso. Professor Charles Longuemare edits the weekly which appeals to mining interests throughout the Southwest and northern Mexico.

MAY 10: A late night fire at Fort Bliss kills 23 mules, three Indian ponies and two private horses.

MAY 13: El Paso has a one minute, twelve second earthquake. It is barely noticed, and no damage is done.

MAY 20: Miss Kate Moore, age 16, and George Prentiss Robinson, 20, become the first El Paso High School graduates. Ceremonies are held in the 34th District Courtroom.

JUNE 20: The El Paso Ice and Refrigerator Company begins operation.

JULY 1: Free mail delivery starts house to house in El Paso. The city marshal is charged with seeing that all houses are numbered. However, the marshal doesn't admit that his math is faulty, so the numbers get mixed up. The event becomes a minor scandal.

JULY: The National Theater, often called the Holland, closes after several unsuccessful seasons. It had finally been reduced to holding cock fights.

AUGUST 27: The Mt. Sinai Association becomes the first organized charity group in El Paso.

AUGUST 29: Today's ASARCO begins operation. In 1887 it was both the Towne Smelter and/or the El Paso Smelter. It opened with 250 workers. Other than the railroad and Fort Bliss, the smelter was the area's largest employer. The El Paso Smelter was several miles from the city, and no one suspected the fumes would eventually become a nuisance.

SEPTEMBER: Olivas Aoy arrives in El Paso. Since children who could not speak English were refused admittance to public schools, Aoy rented an upstairs room on San Francisco Street and, after buying equipment out of his own pocket, started teaching Mexican children. Upon breaking his leg in December 1890, he came to the attention of the El Paso School Board, and the Board began meeting some of his expenses.

SEPTEMBER 20: The *El Paso Times* becomes the first *daily* newspaper ever published in El Paso. It made full use of the Associated Press services.

OCTOBER: The City Council orders one-dozen ball-and-chains to be used for tramps. Hobos will serve their jail time by working on rock piles and street improvements.

OCTOBER 14: Three train robbers stop the Galveston, Harrisburg and San Antonio Railroad. J. E. Smith, Wells Fargo Express messenger, kills two bandits with a shotgun.

OCTOBER 14: The City Council orders all policemen to wear uniforms when on duty. The city furnishes only a badge. El Paso police will shortly begin dressing like New York policemen.

OCTOBER 30: General B. H. Grierson, commander of the District of New Mexico, recommends the abandonment of forts Bliss and Hancock.

OCTOBER 28: Dr. A. L. Nichols, in a fit of spite, fills in the *acequia* where it crosses his land. The action shuts off all water for irrigation and drinking. Townspeople are demanding immediate and tough action.

NOVEMBER 1: The Merrick Building at 301 South El Paso Street is constructed. It remains an outstanding example of El Paso's unique architectural heritage.

NOVEMBER 16: El Pasoans are treated to professional baseball when St. Louis plays Chicago and wins 14 to 7 in a dull game.

NOVEMBER 17: The El Paso Browns play Chicago and win 14 to 3. The town goes wild.

NOVEMBER 18: Ysleta angrily protests El Paso's practice of dumping raw sewage into the Rio Grande. It makes the water taste funny.

NOVEMBER 30: Between 15 and 30 stray dogs are shot each week by policemen.

DECEMBER 15: The Myar Opera House opens with *Monte Cristo*, starring James O'Neill. Seats cost $1.50, $2.00 and $2.50. The Myar opened on the site of the old Coliseum Variety Theater, also known as the National and the Holland theaters.

DECEMBER 29: Two men are fined in Mayor's Court (Corporation Court) for riding on the public streets with prostitutes.

DECEMBER 30: Edwin Biggs, age 13, dies of hydrophobia after extreme suffering.

1888

The Grand Army of the Republic forms in El Paso.

JANUARY 2: El Paso has its first football game. Hart's team beats Harper's, 18 to 12.

JANUARY: Sportsman's Park, the city's first athletic field, is opened in the Campbell Addition near the river.

JANUARY 10: Commissioners Court orders all taxes paid in cash and not in script. (The city and county pay its employees in script, which is discounted by banks and businessmen to about 75 cents on the dollar.)

JANUARY 10: An attempt falls through to create an El Paso Baseball Association.

FEBRUARY 24: The Edwin Booth and Lawrence Barrett Company arrive in El Paso by special train. They put on a tremendous performance of *Julius Caesar*.

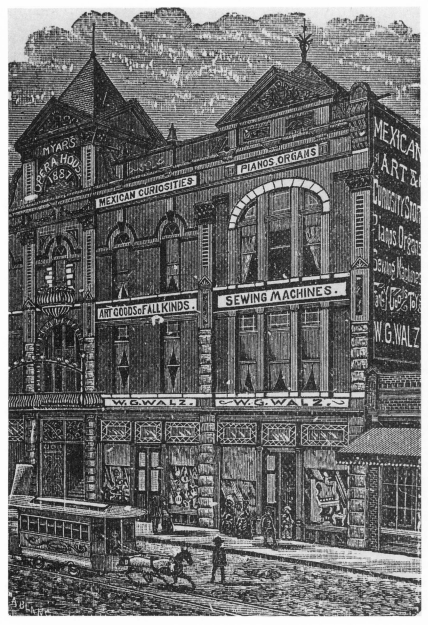

Myar Opera House in 1888. (Frank Mangan Collection)

PRIL 4: A. F. Bandelier, a noted historian, visits Our Lady of Guadalupe across the river and copies the records.

1AY 9: Five students graduate from El Paso High School. Exercises take place in the Myar Opera House.

JNE 27: The El Paso, Kansas City and Mexican Railroad is chartered by a group of El Pasoans. The company is going out of business after laying 8.19 miles of track.

JLY 1: El Paso del Norte is quarantined because of diphtheria. Traffic back and forth across the river is halted.

JLY 4: An electrical storm kills 52 goats that sought shelter under a tree near Major Noyes Rand's house.

JLY 6: Myar Opera House, prize showplace of the Southwest, is in ruins. The first floor fell into the basement due to the storage of 15 tons of beans. But all was repaired, after a fashion, and the Myar continued as "the" opera house in the Southwest. The Mexican National Grand Opera Company played there, as did the Grand Spanish Opera from Madrid, the Tovany Grand English Opera Company, the Grand Opera Dior, and the Judie French Opera Company. The last recorded major performance was *Lucia di Lammermoor* on May 19, 1905.

JLY 12: Etta Clark's Parlor House on South Mesa burns. Arson suspected. No one is hurt.

UGUST 14: Alice Abbot, whose parlor house is across from Etta's, is arrested. Also arrested are two Negroes, Ben Johnson and Will Ragland, better known as "Stuttering Will." All are charged with arson in the burning of Etta Clark's place.

UGUST 16: The cornerstone is laid for the First Methodist Church at the corner of Myrtle and Campbell.

UGUST 23: A modern, concrete Santa Fe Street Bridge is constructed.

SEPTEMBER: Franklin, the black grade school, is renamed Douglass School for Frederick Douglass. The El Paso School Board did not recognize any of the classes taken by older students, so all students started again at the primary level.

SEPTEMBER 15: The Las Cruces College opens in a two-room adobe building. It is the forerunner of New Mexico State University.

SEPTEMBER 16: El Paso del Norte becomes Ciudad Juarez. A statue of Benito Juárez is unveiled during elaborate ceremonies.

SEPTEMBER 19: C. C. Fitzgerald sells the El Paso Smelter for $100 and stock to the International Smelting Company.

SEPTEMBER 25: Major Anson Mills suggests a dam on the Rio Grande near the Southern Pacific Bridge at ASARCO.

OCTOBER 19: The Myar Opera House has been rebuilt and will reopen tonight.

NOVEMBER 19: The El Paso Irrigation Company is formed to build what will become known as the Franklin Canal.

DECEMBER 18: A committee reports that county records are in an awful mess.

DECEMBER 18: Patrick Sheedy was in El Paso and Juarez yesterday seeking a potential site for the forthcoming John L. Sullivan-Jake Kilrain championship fight.

1889

The city has 18 laundries, all operated by Chinese.
Mesa School is opened.
The McGinty Club, El Paso's loudest, drinkingest and most fun-loving organization, is created.
The El Paso Daily Democrat *becomes the first newspaper to print a weather report.*

The El Paso kindergarten is opened. First in Texas.

FEBRUARY 11: Five people die in Ysleta quicksand near the river.

MARCH: Democrat and Republican parties conduct primaries for the first time in the history of the city.

MARCH 1: The International Boundary Commission is re-established to avoid future problems with Rio Grande channel changes. The commission will determine if the channel movements are caused by erosion (slow) or avulsive (rapid) adjustments.

MARCH 5: Workers are no longer soaping the rails at the street corners, so El Paso streetcars are regularly jumping the track.

MARCH 20: A band of Holiness Evangelists gathered on a dry goods box today at the corner of El Paso and Overland, and claimed that people who wear fine clothes are going to hell.

APRIL 2: The County Convict Camp, six miles east of El Paso, keeps the county road in good condition by working prisoners whose terms range from 15 days to one year.

APRIL 9: Adolf Krakauer and C. R. Morehead run for mayor and Krakauer wins by 37 votes. It is the dirtiest election in local history. Both sides claim fraud, arguing that too many Juarez voters were "naturalized." Nevertheless, Krakauer and the Republicans take over city hall, barricade it and move in with boxes of Winchester rifles, water and food. Sheriff James White has to tell them they can't do that. Finally Krakauer is declared the mayoral winner by five votes, and then it is learned that he is a German citizen and ineligible to be mayor. The election results are thrown out, and two different opponents run for office.

APRIL 21: Professor LeRoy rode a hot-air balloon out of the Little Plaza and reached 4,000 feet into the blue El Paso sky. Thousands watched as he then parachuted out. Both he and the balloon landed in Mexico.

APRIL 29: The Texas Press Association is meeting in El Paso for the first time.

MAY 3: Some ladies of easy virtue have refused to pay their monthly fines, and warrants have been issued for their arrest.

MAY 3: The *El Paso Times* publishes a list of advertisers whom it claims have boycotted its newspaper because of political stands.

MAY 17: A huge dog named "Pittsburg Pat" fought a mountain lion in front of a paying crowd in the Gem Saloon today. Pat finally killed the lion and was on his feet at the finish although both eyes were scratched out and he was completely disemboweled.

MAY 24: Three dead, unidentified horse thieves are found near Anthony. One was lying on the ground, shot to death. The other two were hanging from the limb of a riverbank cottonwood.

MAY 30: Memorial Day. A special train takes El Pasoans from town to Fort Bliss (Hart's Mill) where flowers are scattered on graves of 17 Union soldiers. The train then goes to Concordia Cemetery where additional services are held.

MAY 31: Newspaper Editorial: "Does someone have to get killed before arrests are made for buggy speeding in the streets?"

JUNE 19: The colored people celebrate Texas Emancipation Day with a grand ball in the courthouse. A number of men wear full evening dress.

JUNE 28: Two city police officers, in uniform and carrying weapons, are charged with restraining a large group of persons and compelling them to vote for a certain candidate.

JULY 6: The El Paso Irrigation Company is chartered. The company hopes to construct a wing dam 200 yards south of the old Mexican Dam. The Franklin Canal will then follow Eighth Street for 19 blocks before swinging around Cordova Island. The canal will end just north of Fabens.

AUGUST 2: The Rio Grande has practically stopped flowing, and a group of El Pasoans is offering the city 20 acres of free land east of the Franklins if the city will erect, own and operate an underground water system.

AUGUST 2: Any home within 100 feet of a sewer must make a connection.

AUGUST 8: A number of nude men showed their disrespect for common decency by bathing in a freshly dug water hole under the international bridge. Several ladies passed in carriages during this time.

AUGUST 10: A town council (once again) incorporates Ysleta as a city.

AUGUST 12: The El Paso Board of Trade becomes the Merchants and Shippers of El Paso.

AUGUST 16: T. C. Lyons has been appointed chief of police. Until now, all such persons have been called city marshals.

AUGUST 22: About 3,000 persons attend a mass meeting in Little Plaza to protest proposed new duties on lead ore.

SEPTEMBER: A right-of-way has been granted for the Franklin Canal.

SEPTEMBER 6: The police should arrest and fine bicycle riders who race on the main streets after dark.

SEPTEMBER 6: The City Council passed the following ordinance: "If anyone shall relieve the calls of nature in any place exposed to the public sight or gaze, or do so upon any public street or plaza, such person shall be deemed guilty of an offense."

SEPTEMBER 6: The Senate Irrigation Committee has arrived in El Paso to take testimony relating to damming the Rio Grande.

SEPTEMBER 9: The tents on San Antonio Street are a fire hazard.

SEPTEMBER 12: International boundary commissioners are convinced that the recurring dryness of the Rio Grande is a result of water diversions in Colorado and New Mexico.

SEPTEMBER 14: Good colored cooks are in demand. Salaries range from $14 to $40 a month.

OCTOBER 24: Editor George Speck of the *El Paso Tribune* has been severely beaten in his newspaper office because he accused a local citizen of forgery.

OCTOBER 26: The El Paso National Bank has established a branch office in Juarez.

OCTOBER 28: A lion and a bear fought to a dull draw today before a large, but disappointed Juarez audience.

NOVEMBER 1: The first cast iron pipe is laid in El Paso.

NOVEMBER 8: The Law and Order League has served notice that it will no longer tolerate public gambling.

NOVEMBER 13: Over 300 El Pasoans gather to denounce the proposed prosecution of saloon men by the Law and Order League.

NOVEMBER 17: A large gold find was reportedly made across the Rio Grande from Ysleta. About half the Ysleta population is out looking for it.

NOVEMBER 28: Two unsavory brothels known as Hudson Dive and Cuckoo Dive are ordered closed.

NOVEMBER 30: The El Paso Bar Association is taking steps to organize.

DECEMBER: The International Light and Power Company will operate a generating plant for El Paso and adjoining communities, including Juarez.

DECEMBER 3: The Chinese claim a paid Chinese assassin, a "highbinder," is here to kill them. One man has been arrested.

DECEMBER 6: About 50 leading citizens and ex-Confederates sign a resolution lamenting the death of Jefferson Davis. Memorial services are conducted in Trinity Methodist Church.

DECEMBER 13: Editor Carl Longuemare of the *Bullion* has been bitten by a tarantula and is suffering intensely.

DECEMBER 18: The St. Louis Browns defeat the El Paso Browns 10 to 3 and 14 to 5. A large crowd gathered in spite of the cold and admission prices doubled to fifty cents. A disappointed *Herald* reporter wrote that "The St. Louis Browns could have worn crutches and won the game."

DECEMBER 23: The El Paso Light Infantry sponsored the town's first "civilian" military ball last night.

DECEMBER 30: The El Paso City Council passes an ordinance to restrain gambling. A license fee will be paid quarterly and in advance. The newspapers figure that the Wigwam, Gem and Mint—the most patronized saloons in town—have expenses of $4,000 a month. So figuring a profit of 25 percent, that means the saloons must average $5,000 a month "from the hard earnings of our mechanics, clerks and businessmen."

1890

The City of El Paso has a population of 10,338, an increase of 1,305 percent in ten years. El Paso county has 15,678, a 308 percent increase.

El Paso is the largest Chinese smuggling center on the border.

Kate Moore Brown introduces music teaching in the El Paso schools. She also organized the first Music Teachers Association.

A group of squatters settle near modern-day Rim Road and form a community called La Mesa.

A bicycle craze strikes the country, and nowhere is it more admired and practiced than in El Paso.

JANUARY 1: Gamblers pay $800 in taxes each year to stay in business.

JANUARY 7: El Pasoans vote on whether to have a municipal water company. In spite of terrible water, however, nobody seems interested in the issue, and the vote fails to pass.

FEBRUARY 20: Fort Bliss at Hart's Mill is to be sold.

FEBRUARY 21: A bond issue passes to fund the city's water company.

MARCH 1: Congress authorizes Fort Bliss on the mesa, and appropriates $150,000 for land and buildings.

MARCH 3: Jay Gould, the railroad magnate, is in town.

APRIL: Lightweight Champion Charles Herald puts on a boxing exhibition with local pugilists in the Gem Saloon.

APRIL: The El Paso Progressive Association is formed, a forerunner of a Chamber of Commerce.

APRIL 1: I. G. Gaal and Benigno Alderete both claim to have won the race for mayor of Ysleta. Neither will concede.

APRIL 17: Texas Ranger Charles Fusselman is slain in a canyon near north Mt. Franklin. He and El Paso lawmen were pursuing horse thieves.

APRIL 23: The Juarez lottery begins operations. Colonel John Mosby, famous Confederate cavalry leader, is master of ceremonies. Mosby is a frequent visitor to El Paso.

MAY 8: Juan S. Hart, editor of the *El Paso Times*, is elected president of the Texas State Press Association.

MAY 13: The first of a series of summer concerts opens at San Jacinto

Plaza. The Fort Bliss band plays as five or six hundred people watch.

MAY 31: W. H. Wheat, the city dog catcher, has shot 410 dogs this month.

SUMMER: The first Mexican Baptist Church opened at Fourth and Kansas streets. Days later, 22 Spanish-speaking converts are baptized in the Rio Grande.

JUNE: A Grass Widowers Protective Association is formed. The Bachelors Protective Association is not far behind. Both groups survived for roughly 15 years.

JUNE 11: A pitched battle is raging in Ysleta. Mayor Benigno Alderete and his supporters were cleaning an *acequia* when I. G. Gaal, who claims he is the legitimate mayor, ran everyone off and put his own men to work. Alderete swore out a warrant, and shooting started between the two factions. Fifteen to twenty men were involved on each side. One man dead and several wounded. Fortunately, more horses were slain than people, and the sheriff restored order.

JUNE 13: Alderman Joseph Magoffin recommends the discharge of the entire police department. Only 50 percent are dismissed, primarily because of their ties with gambling and prostitution.

JUNE 26: The entire front page of the *El Paso Times* is devoted to Juarez lottery winners. Colonel John S. Mosby, the famous Confederate cavalryman, turned the wheel and read the numbers.

JULY 4: A chartered train takes hundreds of El Pasoans to Ora's Grove in Ysleta where the Bachelors' Club holds a picnic. Barbecued pork and mutton, ice cream and lemonade are on hand. Elders danced, engaged in card games or played croquet while small boys sneaked into the nearby apple orchard. Upon returning to El Paso, the tired but happy picnickers were greeted by a rousing band concert and fireworks.

JULY 19: A gold strike has been made on the east slope of Mt. Franklin, two-and-one-half miles from the City Pest House.

AUGUST 14: El Pasoans drill a well on Fort Bliss land, and plentiful supplies of underground water are confirmed.

AUGUST 25: Heavy rains cause flooding in El Paso and Juarez. Juarez is under three feet of water and numerous homes are destroyed.

AUGUST 28: The Senecú Indian village opposite Ysleta in Mexico suffered terribly from the rains. Pueblo Indians are repairing the damage.

SEPTEMBER 8: El Paso establishes its first mounted police patrol. Officer T. C. Lutterloh furnishes and feeds his own horse, but he is provided $20 a month in expenses.

SEPTEMBER 15: The Federal Building (courthouse) is constructed at the southeast corner of Oregon and Mills streets. The courthouse was also the Custom House, Post Office and Weather Bureau.

SEPTEMBER 22: Professor Savage has decreed that henceforth school-boys are forbidden to write obscenities on fences. They cannot smoke during recess, and they cannot play ball in the street.

SEPTEMBER 27: El Paso citizens have donated more than $11,000 in cash to help finance Fort Bliss on the mesa.

NOVEMBER: An El Paso County Collector of Taxes is elected. Until the county reached a population of 10,000 people, by law the sheriff was the collector.

NOVEMBER: Henry Henderson, a black United States citizen, shot a Mexican national in Juarez. A Mexican judge fined him $20 and sentenced him to jail when he couldn't pay. However, on his way to jail, Henderson broke loose and raced nearly a mile to the Santa Fe Street Bridge, which he crossed. At a point 200 yards north of the border, he collapsed of exhaustion, and the pursuing officer caught up with him. Henderson was dragged back through

American customs and across the river to the Juarez jail. The United States protested, and Henderson was released. The valiant Mexican police officer, who was only doing his duty, was thrown into jail by his superiors.

NOVEMBER 17: Four bandits attempt to rob the Texas and Pacific train at Kent, Texas, after it left El Paso. Two of the holdup men were wounded and are recovering in the El Paso County Jail.

NOVEMBER 24: Bishop Peter Bourgade, of Tucson, expels the Jesuits from Ysleta.

DECEMBER 6: Company B of the 23rd Infantry from Fort Davis will garrison Fort Bliss while Bliss units leave for the Platte River. This is a buildup for the Battle of Wounded Knee.

DECEMBER 16: The famous war chief, Sitting Bull, is killed.

DECEMBER 29: The Battle of Wounded Knee takes place. The Messiah Craze among the Indians has been crushed.

1891

Fresh water costs 30 cents a barrel.
Franklin School is built at 215 Leon Street.
Columbus, New Mexico, gets a post office. Several of the first settlers are from Columbus, Ohio.
The city purchases its first horse to pull fire equipment.

JANUARY 24: Muldoon, world champion wrestler, passed through El Paso today on his way to the West Coast.

MARCH 1: The Immigration and Naturalization Service is established.

MARCH 3: An Act of Congress provides for the deportation of all undocumented aliens who enter the country illegally.

MARCH 4: Schoolboys find a large number of cannonballs and bombs in a cave slightly north of the city.

MARCH 15: Captain George Ruhlen has arrived in El Paso and has commenced surveying the new site of Fort Bliss.

MARCH 18: The Emma Juch Grand English Opera is playing at the Myar Opera House.

MARCH 25: General Nelson A. Miles arrived in town on his way to Mexico City.

MARCH 26: W. D. Malone, champion pool player of the United States, is in El Paso and engaging in a pool tournament at Bronson's Billiard Hall.

APRIL 21: Benjamin Harrison is the first U.S. president to visit El Paso, and he meets briefly with local and Mexican officials. While Mrs. Harrison slipped off for shopping in Juarez, President Harrison spoke for 15 minutes in front of the courthouse. His subject dwelled on a Good Neighbor Policy as he described El Paso as a gateway to trade as well as friendship. In a pointed reminder about El Paso's notoriety, he reminded the residents that foreign capital as well as foreign visitors could never be attracted "unless you have a reputation for social order."

APRIL 24: General Nelson A. Miles, accompanied by his wife and son, will remain in the city until his son recovers from an illness contracted in Mexico.

AUGUST 1: A 44½ pound fish was caught today in the Rio Grande. The type of fish was not mentioned.

AUGUST 27: General R. G. Dyrenforth promises to bring his rainmakers to El Paso from Midland, Texas, where they have had success in making it rain. Mayor Richard Caples and his aldermen are delighted, and promise free transportation. *El Paso Times* editor Juan Hart and Professor Charles Longuemare are in charge of arrangements.

SEPTEMBER 17: Explosions rock the city as government rainmakers struggle to make it rain. While the town received no rain, the report stated that a heavy dew fell, and a heavy dew was practically unknown in El Paso.

OCTOBER 15: Co. B of the 23rd Infantry at Fort Bliss marched into town today and camped near the present library.

OCTOBER 22: John Gilam, better known as French John, a hermit who lived at Hueco Tanks, is fished out of the Rio Grande. He had been badly beaten. One ear was missing.

NOVEMBER 3: John Selman, a Texas gunman and soon to be El Paso constable, is stabbed while walking on the street. He believes his assailants were involved in the death of French John on October 22.

NOVEMBER 12: The Child Culture Study Club, a woman's organization, is organized.

DECEMBER 1: The largest crowd ever to visit Juarez watched a woman balloonist go up and parachute back to earth. She broke her arm when she landed.

DECEMBER 8: This is the traditional date of establishment for the McGinty Club. It flourished in El Paso for decades.

DECEMBER 15: El Paso hosts its first mining convention with emphasis on silver. Hundreds of visitors flock to the city.

1892

The El Paso Irrigation Company goes into receivership.
An iron railroad bridge replaces the old Southern Pacific wooden structure that crosses the Rio Grande near ASARCO.

JANUARY 24: A new stage line leaves the Little Plaza every morning at 9:30, and at 2 and 5 P.M. for the (ASARCO) smelter and Fort Bliss at Hart's Mill.

FEBRUARY: The International Boundary Commissioners leave El Paso. They will resurvey the land border, install new monuments and repair the old ones. As a result, the number of monuments increased from an original 52 to 258. Until now, Boundary Marker No. 1 had been on the Pacific shore south of San Diego. Now, Boundary Marker No. 1 is in El Paso. By 1993 there are 276 monuments varying from 0.14 to 4.91 miles apart.

FEBRUARY: Fort Selden, New Mexico, is closed. The land reverts to the public domain.

FEBRUARY 2: Four Sisters of Charity from Detroit, Michigan, arrive and open St. Mary's Hospital of the Sisters of Charity (usually called Sisters Hospital) at the corner of East Overland and Ochoa.

FEBRUARY 6: The *El Paso Tribune* begins publication, and quickly becomes the "official" newspaper of Commissioners Court. Within a brief period, the *Tribune* is a leading El Paso newspaper.

FEBRUARY 12: The Grand Central Hotel is destroyed by fire because firemen could not get water to the fourth floor. When a watching crowd jeered, the frustrated firemen turned hoses on the bystanders, causing lawsuits.

FEBRUARY 14: The John C. Brown Camp of the United Confederate Veterans has organized in El Paso.

MARCH 6: Sisters Hospital has moved from 1015 Overland Street to the Dieter House, 415 Upson. The Sisters are ready for patients.

MARCH 22: The Grand Army of the Republic holds its convention in El Paso.

MARCH 22: Captain Jack Crawford, the Poet Scout, and his daughter arrive in the city.

MARCH 28: *The Bullion* runs its last newspaper issue.

APRIL 4: Governor John Ireland addresses the Grand Army of the Republic in El Paso.

APRIL 17: The *El Paso Herald* complained that people who attend concerts and other entertainment for the purpose of talking and giggling and making it generally unpleasant for those who go to hear the music, should stay home.

APRIL 28: Jay Gould is in town and buys the El Paso and White Oaks Railroad for an estimated $50,000. Then Gould decided he couldn't afford further construction, so he accepted his loss and left town.

MAY 6: A phonograph provided a sensation today. It reproduced "Dixie" as played by a band in New Orleans.

MAY 15: General Ruíz Sandoval, the implacable enemy of Mexican President Porfirio Díaz, is in the city.

MAY 28: Gentleman Jim Corbett, who will fight John L. Sullivan on September 7 for the heavyweight boxing championship, is in town and boxing a few public exhibitions at the Myar Opera House.

JULY 7: The Right Reverend Thomas F. Brennan, bishop of Dallas, annexes the Catholic churches of El Paso to the diocese of Dallas.

OCTOBER 10: The Sisters of Loretto moved their academy at San Elizario to the Sacred Heart School at Fourth and South El Paso. It becomes the new St. Joseph's Academy, the first parochial school to open in El Paso.

NOVEMBER 8: John Selman is elected constable in El Paso.

DECEMBER 11: The Sacred Heart Church is dedicated.

DECEMBER 25: The Church of St. Rosalia and St. Joseph opened on Christmas morning in Smeltertown.

1893

Rose Gregory Houchen creates the Houchen Settlement House, today's Houchen Community Center.

An Act of Congress awards the old Fort Bliss Cemetery, at Cleveland and Library squares, to the City of El Paso.

The Sisters of Charity purchase the entire block between Arizona and Montana streets, and plan to open a hospital called Hotel Dieu.

FEBRUARY 12: The Dog Canyon rancher Oliver Lee kills Mat Coffelt and Charley Rhodius where the El Paso International Airport is today. Rhodius was a good-looking, red-headed, thirty-three year old unattached cowboy. His girlfriend placed the following inscription on his Concordia Cemetery headstone:

She stoops and gently plants a flower of sweet perfume
To blossom forth in beauty upon a cowboy's tomb.

MARCH: A chimney spark burns the old Pest House to the ground.

MARCH 4: Washington Park is dedicated. It was intended to be George Washington Park, but the name George was dropped.

MARCH 15: A movement is afoot to establish a Lodge of Eastern Star in El Paso.

MARCH 15: Dr. Burrow says he can cure cancer. No cure, no pay.

JUNE 9: The construction of Sacred Heart Church is completed, and the structure is blessed by Bishop Edward Fitzgerald of Little Rock, Arkansas.

JUNE 11: The Immaculate Conception Church is blessed by Bishop Fitzgerald, even though construction is incomplete.

JULY 3: The McGinty Club plants its cannon on top of McGinty Hill where the Civic Center or City Hall is today, and fires it to "usher in the glorious Fourth."

JUNE 30: Texas Ranger Captain Frank Jones is slain on Pirate Island, a huge patch of bosque in the Lower Valley, while in pursuit of outlaws. The rangers cross the international line without realizing it, and fight a brief battle at *Tres Jacales* (Three Shacks) in Chihuahua, where Jones is killed.

AUGUST 2: The El Paso National Bank fails to open its doors.

SEPTEMBER: The first public kindergarten in Texas opens at Central School.

OCTOBER: The first units of Fort Bliss troops begin arriving at LaNoria Mesa, five miles east of El Paso. This would be the sixth and presumably final location of Fort Bliss.

OCTOBER 5: A brass band of Juarez bullfighters marches up and down El Paso streets during Sunday mornings. Churches are complaining that the noise disturbs religious services.

DECEMBER: Professor Frederick R. Koch organizes the first El Paso Symphony Orchestra.

DECEMBER: The *El Paso Tribune* goes out of business.

1894

Miss Mary I. Stanton, a teacher, single-handedly becomes founder of the El Paso Public Library system when she moves her personal collection of 1,000 volumes to a room in the Sheldon Block and makes the books available to young boys.

The city spends $2,600 on a new 65-foot hook and ladder truck. Three horses are required to pull it. The city retains two full time drivers and a tillerman for the truck, these men becoming the nucleus of a forthcoming professional fire department.

JANUARY 25: St. Mary's Hospital formally becomes Hotel Dieu. The 80 room hospital, operated by the Sisters of Charity, has a chapel on the second floor and an operating room in the basement. The hospital is bound by Kansas, Stanton, Arizona and Rio Grande.

MARCH 25: A "General Fry" informs city council that he is bringing 800 men (a portion of Coxey's Army) to El Paso, and they will be hungry and in a bad mood. The city wires Governor James Hogg for assistance, but meanwhile a group of businessmen cooperate and feed the unfortunates. Only about 400 appear. They will become Sierra Blanca's worry as they move east.

APRIL 5: A wild gunfight occurs at Tillie Howard's Parlor House. Constable John Selman, U.S. Deputy Marshal Baz Outlaw and Englishman Frank Collinson visit the brothel. Baz fires a weapon in the bathroom, Tillie runs into the backyard and blows a police whistle, Baz pursues her, and Texas Ranger Joe McKidrick, in town and chatting with a friend in a print shop, jumps the brothel fence and interrupts the confrontation. At that point, Baz kills the ranger. He then fires at John Selman who had reached the back porch. The bullet zips past Selman's ear. The powder blinds Selman who gets off a lucky shot that hits Outlaw squarely over the heart. Outlaw reels to the fence, fires again, and the bullet strikes Selman in the leg and severs an artery. Selman now stumbles off to bleed while Outlaw falls over the fence and onto Utah Street. Two bystanders carry him inside the Boss Saloon and lay him on the bar where a doctor shakes his head. Baz is then transferred to a back room prostitute's bed where he dies four hours later, screaming, "where are my friends?"

MAY 25: A city ordinance forbids all prostitutes from walking, riding, or being seen on any other street in town except Utah (South Mesa) Street.

MAY 26: A city ordinance is passed restricting "the riding of ladies with case-hardened spiritual natures" in an area bounded by Seventh, Stanton, Oregon and the river. It also forbids any woman, "good or bad," from riding astraddle a horse inside the city limits. Fines range from $10 to $100.

AUGUST 4: Mayor Robert F. Johnson issues a proclamation barring open gambling.

AUGUST 10: Jeff Milton, well known Wild West gunman, becomes chief of police in El Paso. He starts running the gamblers out of town. The exodus lasted about two months, but it also sent business into a depression. Open gambling is again tacitly tolerated.

DECEMBER 26: Frank Rochas, better known as "Frenchy," who lived in Dog Canyon, near Alamogordo, New Mexico, is mysteriously slain.

1895

Ciudad Juarez has 6,917 residents. This represents a 42 percent drop from published figures of 1887.

The Jolly Girls Bachelor Club is formed by the town's elite young ladies trying to create additional entertainment for themselves.

JANUARY 6: The Tiguas adopt a constitution and by-laws to insure survival. A tribal government is established.

FEBRUARY 1: Secretary of Interior Hoke Smith grants an English firm permission to build a dam on the Rio Grande at Engle, New Mexico. This is the forerunner of Elephant Butte.

MARCH 14-16: The El Paso Cycling Association announces three days of racing.

APRIL 9: R. F. Campbell is elected mayor. He will be the last "admitted" Republican mayor in the city's history.

APRIL 12: Martin Mroz is arrested at Magdalena, Chihuahua, and returned to the Juarez jail. With him is his wife, Beulah Mroz. She hires John Wesley Hardin as an El Paso attorney for her husband.

APRIL 21: John Wesley Hardin, Chief of Police Jeff Milton, and U.S. Deputy Marshal George Scarborough are in Juarez and meet several Mroz friends in the Deiter and Saur Saloon. An argument follows, and Hardin waves a six-shooter in Tom Finnessey's face. Milton prevents what would have been a killing, although Hardin then turns and slaps a man named Lightfoot, the sound of which

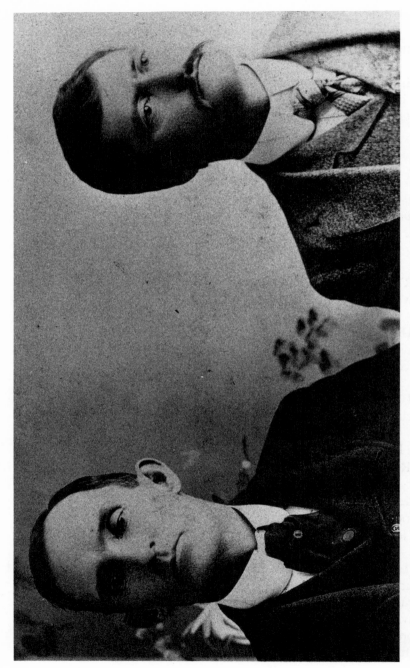

"Killin'" Jim Miller (left) and his shirttail relative, attorney John Wesley Hardin, in El Paso in April 1895. Miller and Hardin were two of the West's most notorious man-slayers. (Mary Curry & Nita Neveu Collection)

is heard out into the street. Hardin, Milton and Scarborough then back out of the saloon and return to El Paso.

APRIL 27: Olivas Aoy dies in El Paso and is buried in Evergreen Cemetery. Aoy School is named in his honor.

MAY 1: .A number of women meet in County Commissioners Court to organize the Current Topics Club and to elect Mrs. W. W. Mills as the first president. This is the beginning of what will eventually become the Woman's Club.

MAY 1: Mayor Robert Campbell discharges Jeff Milton as chief of police, and replaces him with Campbell's political supporter, Ed Fink—a former police officer who had been fired by Milton.

MAY 1: John Wesley Hardin scoops up a pot in the Acme Saloon and walks off. No one objects, and Hardin does not find it necessary to pull a gun.

MAY 2: While engaged in a crap game upstairs in the Gem Saloon, John Wesley Hardin accuses the dealer of "hurrahing" him. Hardin put a six-shooter in the dealer's face and recovers the $97 Hardin claims he lost.

MAY 4: Hardin is arrested and charged with "unlawfully carrying a pistol."

MAY 16: John Wesley Hardin is found guilty of carrying a revolver, and fined $25. During the trial, a witness stated that as Hardin was going downstairs in the Gem Saloon with the $97, one of the players complained about his sportsmanship. Apparently there was nothing wrong with Hardin's ears, for he dashed back and challenged anyone to step out into the street and "show their manhood" if they didn't like the sportsmanship. The witness finished by saying, "since nobody stepped out in the street, I guess we really did like his sportsmanship."

JUNE 3: The Army band, struggling to become the finest in the country, presents a great performance at Myar Opera House. However, not a person claimed the 25 and 50 cent seats. Colonel Daingerfield Parker, Fort Bliss commander, vowed that the band would never again perform in El Paso except for military functions.

JUNE 29: Martin Mroz is lured across the Mexican Central Railroad bridge at night by U.S. Deputy Marshal George Scarborough. On the El Paso side, Mroz is shot and killed by Scarborough, former Chief of Police Jeff Milton, Texas Ranger and former deputy marshal, Frank M. McMahon, and, by some accounts, Constable John Selman. Mroz was buried the following day in Concordia Cemetery. Besides the burial crew, only two witnesses were present: the Mroz widow, Helen Beulah Mroz, and her lover and Martin's attorney, John Wesley Hardin.

JULY: The speed limit of horses and bicycles inside the city limits is raised from six to ten miles per hour.

JULY 4: Annie Londonderry is giving a series of lectures at the Vendome Hotel (later the Cortez) on the subject of physical development. She has been bicycling around the world and earning her expenses by lecturing. She then left El Paso on July 4 and reached New York on September 24, arriving 14 days ahead of the 15 months set for herself. Miss Londonderry collected $10,000, and earned $5,000 in lecture fees.

JULY 4: During the Independence Day parade, the Fire Department volunteers showed their competitive spirit. They dragged hose from the carts to the water faucets and squirted water in a marvelously fast time.

AUGUST 2: Beulah Mroz is arrested for carrying a revolver.

AUGUST 11: John Wesley Hardin publishes a public apology in the *El Paso Times*: "I have been informed that on the night of the 6th while under the influence of liquor, I made a talk against George Scarborough, stating that I had hired Scarborough to kill M'Rose [sic]. I do not recollect making any such statement and if I did the statement was absolutely false, and it was superinduced by drink and frenzy."

AUGUST 15: The *El Paso Times* reported that "Mrs. M'rose [sic] went west yesterday to grow up with the country." She got as far as Deming and wired Hardin, saying, "I feel you are in trouble and I'm coming back." She did return but left shortly thereafter for Phoenix, Arizona.

AUGUST 19: John Wesley Hardin was shot dead by Constable John Selman in the Acme Saloon on the northwest corner of San Antonio and Utah streets. Hardin walked into the saloon after dark, stepped up to the bar, rolled the dice, turned to grocer H. S. Brown, and said, "Brown, you have four sixes to beat." At that moment Constable John Selman stepped through the door and shot Hardin three times: once in the head, once in the chest, and once in the arm. Hardin fell dead, lay on the floor four hours while much of the town filed by to look at him, and then was hauled off to the undertakers where he was washed and photographed. The newspapers said that except for being dead he was in good shape. Hardin was buried in Concordia Cemetery within fifty feet of the Chinese section, and only a grave or two away from Martin Mroz.

SEPTEMBER: Douglass School, the only school in town for blacks, now becomes a high school as well as a grammar school. The school was named for Frederick Douglass, ex-slave, abolitionist and orator.

OCTOBER 14: The El Paso County Commissioners Court abolishes the Ysleta incorporation.

OCTOBER 22: Chopin Hall offers excellent musical entertainment by the Torbett Company of New York City. Professor Ferdinand Dewey, who came to El Paso from Boston for asthmatic relief, has built a New Lyceum Theater, as Chopin Hall is often called. The building sits between Campbell and Kansas streets where the Federal Courthouse is now.

NOVEMBER 13: Fort Hancock, 60 miles southeast of El Paso and near the Rio Grande, is abandoned. The last frontier post has ceased to exist.

NOVEMBER 14: The Chamizal controversy gets its start when Pedro I. García files suit in the Juarez Primary Court of Claims for the return of 7.82 acres of El Paso. The Rio Grande had for years gradually eroded south into Mexico and transferred portions of García's land north to El Paso.

DECEMBER 27: Bob Fitzsimmons, a challenger for the heavyweight boxing championship, comes to El Paso and sets up his training headquarters in Juarez. He uses a bicycle for exercise, and keeps a full-grown lion on a leash.

1896

El Paso is divided into four political wards. Chihuahuita is designated the First Ward. South El Paso is the Second.
A Chinese Baptist Mission opens at 412 San Antonio.

JANUARY 4: Herren Schott and Fickinscher present a classical music program at Chopin Music Hall. Schott is a Wagnerian singer.

JANUARY 8: The Woman's Christian Temperance Union is organized.

JANUARY 11: Peter Maher, who will fight Fitzsimmons for the heavyweight championship, arrives in El Paso. Maher trains in Las Cruces.

FEBRUARY 1: Colonel Albert Jennings Fountain and his eight-year-old son, Henry, are murdered in the eastern foothills of the San Andres Mountains in New Mexico. A century later, the case remains one of New Mexico's greatest murder mysteries.

FEBRUARY 10: James H. Mabry, adjutant general of Texas, arrives in El Paso with ten grim and well-armed rangers. The rangers say there will be no prizefight.

FEBRUARY 14: The boxing championship purse between Fitzsimmons and Maher has reached $10,000. An arena for 20,000 people is considered in El Paso. Other fights would be held, three of them for world championships. John L. Sullivan would make an appearance.

FEBRUARY 15: Arizona Governor Hughes turns out the National Guard to prevent the heavyweight championship fight from transferring to Arizona.

FEBRUARY 15: Famed gunman and sportsman, Bat Masterson, is in town to see the big fight.

FEBRUARY 21: Judge Roy Bean comes to El Paso and moves the heavyweight championship fight to Langtry, Texas, where it takes place across the Rio Grande in Coahuila with Texas Rangers watching from the hillside. Fitzsimmons knocked out Maher in less than two minutes of the first round.

APRIL: The Chamizal question is removed from the Juarez Primary Court of Claims, and transferred to the International Boundary Commission for a solution.

APRIL 1: Police officer John Selman Jr., son of Constable John Selman, pedals a bicycle across the Rio Grande with a 15-year-old-girl. They plan to marry, but the girl's mother has John jailed in Juarez.

APRIL 5: Deputy Marshal George Scarborough puts four bullets into Constable John Selman, and Selman dies on the operating table the next day. The fight took place in an alley alongside the Wigwam Saloon.

APRIL 7: "Big Alice" Abbott, famed El Paso madam, dies of a heart attack. She is buried in Evergreen Cemetery.

APRIL 11: George Scarborough resigns as United States deputy marshal.

JUNE 20: George Scarborough is acquitted of murder charges in the death of Constable John Selman.

AUGUST 4: The International Boundary Commission is unable to make a decision on the Chamizal controversy.

OCTOBER 29: Lieutenant William Jefferson Glasgow marries Josephine Richardson Magoffin, daughter of Joseph and granddaughter of James Magoffin. The wedding takes place in the Immaculate Conception Church, and it is the social event of the 1890s.

NOVEMBER 11: Cura Ramón Ortiz, a beloved Catholic priest, dies in Juarez at age 82. There is a tremendous turnout for his funeral. Hundreds of businesses close on both sides of the border.

1897

FEBRUARY 1: Under the leadership of promoter Charles B. Eddy, the El Paso and Northeastern Railroad (formerly the El Paso and White Oaks Railroad) lays track to the Texas-New Mexico line.

MAY 8: Floods sweeping down the Rio Grande turn Smeltertown into a lake.

MAY 24: Floods stun El Paso. Water over a foot high covers El Paso Street to Overland. One dike after another crumbles around the city as water enters the jail and courthouse. Adobe houses in South El Paso are melting, and residents are taking refuge in a string of empty Texas & Pacific boxcars. Over 200 families take refuge at Old Fort Bliss at Hart's Mill. A raging dust storm compounds the misery.

JUNE 3: The flood level drops in El Paso. Over 500 homes are now just soggy piles of mud. Two thousand people are homeless. Many trek up on the mesa where Rim Road is today and start a community called Stormsville. It was named for the owner D. Storms, and not for the flood.

JUNE 7: The El Paso Bar Association formally organizes. The initiation fee is one dollar. Monthly dues are 25 cents.

SEPTEMBER 20: The Ysleta Mission is fitted with a large and handsome dome.

OCTOBER 1: W. W. Mills is appointed as United States consul to Chihuahua, Mexico.

OCTOBER 16: A German First Lutheran Church opens on Myrtle Avenue.

1898

After years of frustration and receivership, the El Paso Irrigation Company is reorganized as the Franklin Irrigation Company.

MARCH 12: James A. Harden-Hickey, better known as Baron Harden-Hickey, a Frenchman and one of the world's great eccentrics, is found dead by his own hand in the Pierson Hotel. The *El Paso Times* printed this for an obituary: "There was something incomplete about him. He was out of plumb, unevenly balanced and could not adjust himself to the practical age in which he lived. He was born a dreamer and died one."

MARCH 17: The Hotel Dieu School of Nursing opens.

MARCH 18: The Current Topics Club brings Miss Will Allen Droomgoole to El Paso. She is a brilliant Tennessee writer of dialect stories, and she will speak in Chopin Hall during a fundraising benefit for the library.

MAY 25: Juan Hart recruits a company of El Paso soldiers for the Spanish American War. Within three days he has signed up 115 men. They report to Galveston.

JUNE 15: The El Paso and Northeastern Railroad reaches 85 miles north of El Paso and enters a new town of tents and survey stakes called Alamo Gordo. Charles B. Eddy had planned to go on to White Oaks. However, the property values at White Oaks soared, so the rails went to Carrizozo and Capitan instead. White Oaks became a ghost town.

SEPTEMBER 8: El Pasoans recruited for the Spanish American War are discharged. They never left Galveston, and never fired a shot in anger.

NOVEMBER: A temporary Pest House is established in the Long Barracks at Old Fort Bliss. After the smelter bitterly complains about the Pest House, the building is abandoned. It was burned to prevent the spread of smallpox germs.

NOVEMBER 1: All El Pasoans must be vaccinated for smallpox. All citizens comply except the prostitutes. Most believe the serum will "make them frigid."

NOVEMBER 26: The police department enforces an order to vaccinate the prostitutes. A majority of the girls comply within a few weeks.

1899

There is a short-lived movement in the Texas legislature to create a separate state called "West Texas" or "Sacramento."

JANUARY: The Current Topics Club will hereafter be known as the Woman's Club of El Paso.

JANUARY: Otero County, named for Governor Miguel Otero of New Mexico, is organized from portions of Lincoln and Doña Ana counties. Alamogordo is the county seat. The county was created so that three fugitives from justice might surrender to a sheriff other than Pat Garrett of Doña Ana County. Garrett wanted Oliver Lee, Jim Gilliland and Bill McNew on charges of murdering Colonel Albert Jennings Fountain and his son, Henry. The wanted men prevailed upon their attorney, Albert B. Fall, to have the county created.

FEBRUARY 5: A Harry Block arrives from San Francisco and immediately tries to set up a territorial government with El Paso as the capital. The territory would include parts of West Texas, New Mexico and Arizona. Many El Pasoans agree, saying El Paso has gained nothing by being in Texas, and would lose nothing by getting out. New Mexico countered by trying to get El Paso freed from Texas and made a part of the Territory of New Mexico.

MARCH 1: The United States and Mexico reestablish international boundary commissions to solve border problems arising primarily from a meandering Rio Grande.

MARCH 16: A convention to create a separate state or territory is called in El Paso. Dozens of New Mexico and West Texas delegates arrive. However, the convention is torpedoed when Mayor Joseph Magoffin appoints El Paso convention delegates who are politicians opposed to separating from Texas.

MARCH 17: A cornerstone is laid for city hall.

APRIL 13: The Cordova Island levees are finally completed.

APRIL 19: The Forty-First District Court is created. It is the second district court established in El Paso.

APRIL 21: The Marlborough Club brothel mails over 1,500 engraved invitations for the grand opening.

JUNE 1: The mountain resort of Cloudcroft opens.

JUNE 20: A cornerstone is laid for the Jewish Temple of Mt. Sinai at the corner of Oregon and Idaho (Yandell).

JULY 14: A new church at Smeltertown is called San José, and it replaces the old St. Rosalia and St. Joseph Church.

JULY 19: A fire broke out in the El Paso Smelter. The El Paso Fire Department sent its equipment by railroad to the smelter, but the smelter had no facilities to unload the train.

AUGUST 24: The El Paso Coffin and Casket Company gets a contract from the city to bury paupers as well as smallpox victims.

SEPTEMBER 14: A Corporation Court takes the place of the Recorders Court, which took the place of the Mayor's Court.

SEPTEMBER 20: The Border Rifles, a state militia, is organized in El Paso. They assemble at the courthouse and drill by the light of the moon on the courthouse road.

SEPTEMBER 30: A carload of Tigua Indians left Ysleta for Dallas where they will appear in the World's Fair.

NOVEMBER 7: The El Paso (Towne) Smelter becomes ASARCO (The American Smelting and Refining Company).

DECEMBER 4: The El Paso Public Library, with its collection of 4,000 books owned by Mary I. Stanton and Fannie J. Clark, moves from the Sheldon Hotel to City Hall. The city hires a librarian and the library is open all day.

DECEMBER 7: The El Paso Chamber of Commerce organizes. It grew out of the Board of Trade and the Merchants and Shippers of El Paso.

1900

The town of Clint, Texas, is founded about this time. It was originally named Clinton, probably after the Clinton Collins family, prominent farmers in the area. When the post office found a prior Clinton in Texas, however, the local name was shortened to Clint.

Cloudcroft is platted in the Sacramento Mountains.

The City of El Paso has 15,906 residents, a 54 percent increase from 1890. El Paso County has 24,886, a 59 percent increase. Ciudad Juarez has 8,218 people, an 18.8 percent increase since 1895.

The United States Bureau of Reclamation builds the Montoya Drain to reclaim marshlands in the Upper Valley for farms and ranches. Other drains followed, as did flood control dams.

The Congregation B'nai Zion is organized.

The White House Department Store opens in El Paso at San Antonio and Oregon streets.

ANUARY 1: The El Paso Woman's Club kicks off its campaign for a headquarters building. It arrived 16 years later.

ANUARY 6: A double-header hanging takes place at the El Paso jail when officers legally hanged Geronimo Parra (who had murdered Texas Ranger Charles Fusselman), and Antonio Flores (who had murdered his girl friend). However, both men broke loose in the jail corridor and, armed with homemade knives, made a fight of it. No one was seriously hurt, and the executions, although botched, went off as scheduled.

EBRUARY 17: A squad of black soldiers from Fort Bliss attack the city jail on Overland Street in a vain attempt to free comrades. Police officer Newton Stewart, a former Rough Rider, is slain, as is one of the black soldiers.

EBRUARY 20: The local branch of the Woman's Christian Temperance Union says it will drive the dance halls out of business and reduce the size of the brothel area.

PRIL 5: Former United States Deputy Marshal George Scarborough, slayer of Constable John Selman in El Paso, has himself been shot and dies on the operating table in Deming, New Mexico. Burial is in Deming.

1AY: El Paso has become a big city. The police chief states that boys can no longer play baseball in the streets. Citizens fear accidentally running them down with horses and buggies.

UGUST 16: After years of being in court, the Santa Teresa Grant is finally certified as valid.

EPTEMBER 9: In 1881, Louis Sheldon, a doctor from Brooklyn, New York, bought property where the Plaza (former Hilton) Hotel now stands. He paid $15,000, and called it the Plaza Block because it fronted on Pioneer Plaza and the Public Square (San Jacinto). Initially (about 1887) he erected an office building with the first elevator in El Paso. On this date the building opened as the Sheldon Hotel, famous from 1906 to 1927 as the home of war correspondents covering the Mexican Revolution. It also housed soldiers of fortune as well as the Mexican and American equivalent of the CIA. For three decades the Sheldon was the most colorful, exciting, mysterious hotel in North America. In 1907 Sheldon sold the hotel to Alzina Orndorff DeGroff.

1901

ASARCO is revamped to handle low-grade copper ores. Until now the plant has chiefly refined gold and silver ores from Mexico.

The El Paso Chamber of Commerce wants Boer immigrants in the El Paso valley. South Africans can develop a farming potential.

The Cloudcroft Lodge is completed.

A grocery store on the northwest corner of El Paso and Overland streets is remodeled and becomes the first Popular Dry Goods Company.

JANUARY: The Midwinter Carnival starts, a predecessor to the Sun Carnival.

JANUARY 11: A. P. Coles, a developer, calls for cog-trains to haul tourists to the top of Mt. Franklin as well as to the top of the Juarez Mountains. Coles believed the view would make El Paso renowned as an international city.

APRIL 27: Pete Adams, former assistant collector of customs in El Paso, marries May Palmer, one of the Big Five madams. The Elks Club expelled Adams from its organization.

MAY 5: President William McKinley visits El Paso. The train came in from the west and steamed four blocks past the station where the crowd had gathered. The president reluctantly appeared, and by the time he did the day was hot and the crowd tremendous. Indians who had come to smoke the peace pipe with him couldn't find room, so that event was canceled. The president went to Trinity Methodist Church although he knew preparations had been made for him to attend services elsewhere. Finally, the president, Mayor B. F. Hammett and General Hernandez of

Mexico, led a two-mile-long parade through the city. It had been an astonishing day.

UNE 10: A fire nearly destroys ASARCO.

AUGUST 1: The recently built Santa Fe Power Station, the first in El Paso, is running at full capacity.

AUGUST 30: The El Paso Electric Railroad Company begins operation. In the beginning, the Electric Company put its emphasis on transportation, especially street railways. Not until 1920 did the sale of electricity become the more important part of the business.

SEPTEMBER 10: The Federal Smelter begins its operation in what is now the Manhattan Heights area. It processed copper ore from the company mines in Arizona and Mexico. Neighborhood streets still bear the names: Federal, Copper, Silver, Gold.

SEPTEMBER 14: President William McKinley dies in Washington from an assassin's bullet.

1902

The National Reclamation Act opens up the West to possibilities of irrigation.

A group of local doctors build Providence Hospital at Upson and North Santa Fe to get away from the noise and confusion of the city. The hospital was later torn down to make way for I-10 when Providence moved to North Oregon Street near the university.

A Christian Science Society is organized.

JANUARY: The *El Paso Herald* suggests this town needs a school of mines.

JANUARY: A county hospital is built on Smelter Road near Old Fort Bliss. Thirty-seven cents per day is allocated for food per patient. There are no full-time attendants, and people who die upstairs are lowered by rope from a window.

JANUARY: The eleventh annual convention of the Texas Livestock Association takes place. It is the first known livestock show in El Paso.

JANUARY 4: Four nurses graduate from Hotel Dieu Hospital. They are also the first to graduate from any nursing school in Texas.

JANUARY 6: The Senate confirms Pat Garrett's nomination by President Theodore Roosevelt as collector of customs in El Paso.

JANUARY 11: The electric streetcar puts Mandy the Mule out of business. In an elaborate ceremony, Mandy makes her last trip as a passenger, not as a worker. The final trip extended from Pioneer Plaza to Juarez. The mule-drawn streetcars had operated since the 1870s. Mandy was a generic name for all the mules.

JANUARY 13: The El Paso Bar Association holds its first annual banquet.

FEBRUARY: The El Paso grand jury finds that 600 professional gamblers in town make their living in 96 saloons. .

APRIL 12: The El Paso Council of the Knights of Columbus is established.

APRIL 24: An enlarged and modern ASARCO is rebuilt within ten months of the 1901 fire.

MAY 3: Mayor B. F. Hammett publishes a "gambling proclamation." Gambling must be taken out of saloons and moved upstairs or into the basement. All saloons must close on Sunday.

JUNE 19: Mayor Hammett tempers his proclamation by saying saloons must close only from 9 A.M. to 4 P.M. on Sunday.

JULY: Philip Bargman organizes the Bargman Shirt and Overall Company on South Mesa Street. This is the earliest recorded clothing plant in El Paso.

SEPTEMBER: The McGinty Band has played its final concert. An era has ended.

SEPTEMBER 17: The *Labor Advocate* begins publication. It concentrated on the struggles of labor, but carried some municipal news.

NOVEMBER 4: Texans approve a $2 poll tax for the privilege of voting. Although this is generally perceived as a racial tactic to deprive blacks and Hispanics from the ballot, the reasoning was just the opposite. Most citizens believed big business, especially the liquor business, controlled huge blocks of minority votes by bribery. The poll tax would make that control more difficult. (El Paso voted against the poll tax amendment, but Texas carried it.)

NOVEMBER 18: Articles of Incorporation are signed for the Toltec Club. The professional people in El Paso needed a club where dinner, balls and parties could be held.

NOVEMBER 22: El Paso becomes the second city in the United States to have a fully metered water supply. For a minimum monthly charge of 90 cents, one could use 4,500 gallons. Each additional gallon cost 20 cents. The International Water Company agreed to abandon the Rio Grande and get its water from underground supplies on the mesa north of Fort Bliss.

DECEMBER 13: El Paso policeman Dan Riley takes charge of the Secret Service Bureau, a fancy name for a first-time-ever city Detective Bureau in the Police Department.

1903

Henry C. Trost arrives in El Paso, and becomes the Southwest's foremost architect.

President Theodore Roosevelt briefly visits El Paso.

All public school female teachers who marry must resign as of the date of their marriage. This rule is in effect, initially, only through 1904. From then until 1920, no further economic notice is taken of married, female teachers.

The corner of Mesa and Mills (now the Roberts-Banner Building) during the early 1900s. Outdoor advertising wasn't necessarily art in those days, but then it hasn't changed much. (Aultman Collection. El Paso Public Library)

FEBRUARY 7: Carrie Nation visits El Paso on her way to California. She sells a few hatchets, jerks a cigar from one man's mouth, but makes no attempt to go on a local saloon crusade.

FEBRUARY 27: The Charity Union of El Paso is organized in the office of the *El Paso Herald*. The Union helps the needy find suitable charitable organizations. However, the idea died a quick death because most of its funds went for administrative expenses. The Woman's Charity Association replaced it.

MARCH 25: As of today, everyone who votes must first preregister. Heretofore, people simply went to the polls, signed a name and voted. All they needed was a poll tax. So Democrats and Republicans alike bought hundreds of $1 poll taxes, and herded voters to the station. Voters were paid after the polls closed.

APRIL 1: The *Herald* dubs the northwest corner of Oregon and San Antonio streets as "The Famous Fighting Corner." Three fist-fights occurred here today, all of them between lawyers and a *Herald* newspaperman.

APRIL 10: The Christian Science Church will build at the corner of Stanton and Montana streets. The church was not constructed until 1910.

MAY: The Excelsior Sanatorium, a hospital for non-contagious diseases and surgery, opens at 601 N. Oregon.

MAY 1: Immigration agents will now wear blue uniforms.

MAY 8: Customs Collector Pat F. Garrett brawls on San Antonio Street with former cattle appraiser, George M. Gaither. The *El Paso Evening News* described the fist fight as bordering on the comic opera.

MAY 23: A federal court in New Mexico cancels an English firm's option to build a dam at Engle, New Mexico.

JUNE 27: All Texas volunteer guard units are mustered into the Texas National Guard.

JULY 6: A new bull ring is nearing completion in Juarez.

SEPTEMBER: The Sisters of Loretto at the Foot of the Cross open the Sacred Heart School at Myrtle and St. Vrain streets.

1904

A church is built in Stormsville near Rim Road, and is called Nuestra Senora de la Luz.

The new channel for the Cordova cutoff is finished. The old bed of the Rio Grande formed a horseshoe curve around an area called Cordova. Because the water slowed at this point, the river flooded South El Paso. This new channel severed the neck, and turned Cordova into an "island" of Mexico protruding into the United States.

JANUARY 17: A Chinese Masonic Temple is dedicated on South Virginia Street.

APRIL: The chief of police announces that all slot machine operations will be closed if they cater to children.

APRIL 25: The first library building opens. Andrew Carnegie, a New York philanthropist, donates $35,000. The City Council votes a tax to support it. Buckler Square, the old cemetery, is the site. The name is changed to Carnegie Square to honor the donor. The library is built at a cost of $40,000.

MAY 19: The city informs the International Water Company that if the firm does not promptly build a sufficient water works using mesa water, its franchise will be canceled.

JULY 25: The First Christian Church holds its first meeting at 500 N. Oregon. Prior to this it had been at 107 Myrtle and in a paint shop.

OCTOBER: Lucy Houghton and Marion Farmer become the first graduating nurses of Providence Hospital.

OCTOBER: A contract is let to build Union Station. Since the area needed fill dirt, McGinty Hill, from which the famed McGinty Cannon had fired so many rounds, fell victim to the steam shovel. The hill was near the present City Hall/Convention Center complex.

SEPTEMBER 4: After the most thunderous meeting ever held locally, the Citizens League puts 1,400 names on a petition. The signers demand that Sheriff J. H. Boone enforce the Sunday Blue Laws and anti-gambling measures. .

OCTOBER: The commissioner-general of immigration assigns a group of mounted inspectors to patrol the Mexican border and curb the illegal entry of Orientals. These inspectors never numbered over 75 and were the beginning of the Border Patrol.

OCTOBER 26: Seventeen civic-minded El Pasoans offer a $500 reward for the arrest and conviction of any juror accepting a bribe or of any person offering a bribe.

NOVEMBER 10: When asked if gambling was going to be put upstairs and out of sight, Mayor Charles Morehead answered: "There are more liars in El Paso than any place I have ever seen. If all the liars were taken out of El Paso, there would not be a corporal's guard left."

NOVEMBER 15: The Irrigation Congress holds its convention in El Paso. It supports the creation of Elephant Butte Dam as well as an equal distribution of water between the United States and Mexico.

NOVEMBER 19: Sheriff J. H. Boone sets out to enforce the law, and 6,000 gamblers and prostitutes cross the Rio Grande into Juarez. The sheriff also tries to close the smelter, the streetcars, the candy and cigar stores, all for operating on Sunday in violation of the Blue Laws.

DECEMBER 11: The Blue Laws are challenged in court, and are not upheld. The saloons and dance halls reopen.

1905

El Paso's first Symphony Orchestra disbands.
Mexico goes on the gold standard.
The Partido Liberal Mexicano, *or PLM, a leftist revolutionary Mexican group led by Ricardo Flores Magón, establishes a cell in El Paso known as Club Liberal.*
The El Paso Electric Railway Company purchases the International Light and Power Company.
The present Trinity Methodist Church is built.
The streets are so bad in El Paso that wags have placed signs in the middle of the roads warning that boating is not permitted after heavy rains.

JANUARY 4: The Citizens League meets to plan another campaign against gamblers.

JANUARY 7: The Municipal Water Works League meets to select a slate of officers. The League wants the city to force the International Water Company to live up to its contract to supply El Paso with plentiful supplies of pure mesa water.

APRIL: El Paso Collector of Customs Pat Garrett meets with President Theodore Roosevelt in San Antonio, Texas, during a Rough Riders Convention. Garrett has taken Tom Powers, a notorious El Paso saloon owner, with him and introduced Powers as a "West Texas cattleman." Photos are taken of everybody, and Roosevelt is furious upon learning he has been misled.

APRIL 14: The Citizens League has talked its El Paso legislators into making it illegal to use any building for the purpose of gambling. After court tests, open gambling disappears from El Paso.

MAY 1: The St. Ignatius Church and school opens at Park and Second. By 1917, this was the largest parochial school in El Paso.

July 1: Mexico abolishes the *Zona Libre* (free zone) along the entire international border with the United States.

OCTOBER 19: The city passes its first automobile ordinance. All cars must display a city license, and have at least one light up front when driven at night. Speed laws of six miles per hour must be obeyed. (Many autoists use Montana Street for a speedway.)

NOVEMBER: The American Mining Congress holds its convention in El Paso.

NOVEMBER 4: The Myar Opera House is destroyed by fire. Thousands of people turn out to witness the death of a proud monument. This time the Myar did not rise from the ashes.

NOVEMBER 7: The Fire Department becomes fully professionalized, meaning everyone is now paid.

1906

Paving has taken place on Mesa Street in front of the Orndorff Hotel (Cortez Building).

The Southern Pacific builds a steel railroad bridge across the Rio Grande near ASARCO. This bridge replaces an iron one, which had replaced the wooden one of 1881.

The Southern Pacific Railroad Building is completed.

The W. W. Turney Home at 1205 Montana becomes the largest home designed by Henry Trost. When Turney died, his wife deeded the home to the City of El Paso. Turney was an attorney and state senator, a man of many civic responsibilities.

The Escobar brothers open La Escuela Particular de Agricultura. *The school was inaugurated by Chihuahua Governor Enrique C. Creel.*

Orogrande, New Mexico, is founded. The name means big (or lots of) gold.

JANUARY: Mark and Mary Price, who live at 1616 Wyoming Street, purchase a family cow. It is the beginning of Price's Creameries.

JANUARY 1: St. Mary's Church reopens as the Holy Family Chapel. It will later be destroyed by fire.

A paving machine in front of the Orndorff Hotel (Cortez Building) on Mills Street across from San Jacinto Plaza. The aldermen caused a scandal when all six of them went east to study street paving and charged their expenses to the city. (Jack Vowell)

ANUARY 2: President Theodore Roosevelt refuses to reappoint Pat Garrett as collector of customs in El Paso. The president's anger stems from the Tom Powers incident of last April in San Antonio. Garrett is now out of a job, and returns to his ranch in the San Andres Mountains near Las Cruces, New Mexico.

ANUARY 26: Attorney Albert Bacon Fall receives clear title to the Three Rivers Ranch in New Mexico.

EBRUARY 8: When the Civic Improvement League is unable to provide a name for a new park, the matter went to City Council. Alderman George Look suggested Cleveland Square, for the park west of the library, and Houston Park for the square on Montana Street. They were named for U.S. President Grover Cleveland and Texas President Sam Houston.

EBRUARY 3: Frank B. Cotton, a Boston man, finally gets title to his 400 acres on the east side of the city, an area bound by Cordova Island, Eleventh Street, Cotton Avenue and Kentucky Street.

EBRUARY 27: Union Station is completed at a cost of $260,000. Over 10,000 people attended the grand opening.

1AY 2: The United States and Mexico sign an agreement for an "Equitable Distribution of the Waters of the Rio Grande." When times are "normal," the Juarez Valley will receive 60,000 acre feet of water annually from Elephant Butte Dam.

1ARCH: The Grandview and Government Hill subdivisions are filed.

PRIL 25: Attorney Albert Bacon Fall commences construction on his El Paso mansion on Golden Hill Terrace (1725 Arizona Street). It costs an estimated $14,000.

1AY: The Airdrome Summer Theater opens on San Antonio Street. It reportedly seats 1,000 people and has a roof garden and bleachers.

UNE 1: Refinery workers go on strike at Cananea, Sonora. Although the strike is suppressed, most historians believe this is where the Mexican Revolution actually began.

JUNE 7: An El Paso Country Club is opened just west of Washington Park and extends from Alameda Street to near the Rio Grande. The Fort Bliss band played to 300 guests, and attendants fed the crowd by shooting duck and geese off the golf course.

SEPTEMBER: Ricardo Flores Magón and Juan Sarabia, radical Mexican intellectuals, issue their first call for revolt. Their El Paso proclamation calls for the overthrow of "the criminal despotism of the usurper Porfirio Díaz."

SEPTEMBER 29: The Crawford Theater on North Mesa opens. It is fully equipped with dressing rooms under the stage, stars' dressing rooms at stage level, stage rigging and two balconies, the top one for those who can afford only a dime. The Crawford was initially used for dramatic theater, but by 1913 musical comedy and vaudeville had taken over. Later it was converted into a movie theater, and then destroyed to make way for the Bataan Trainway.

SEPTEMBER 30: The Franklin Theater, known first as the Standard, then the Bijou, opens at Paisano and Oregon. It featured vaudeville and road show theater, and seated 800. But it had a corrugated tin roof and looked like a barn. Sarah Bernhardt played at the Franklin in *Camille*.

OCTOBER 19: Officials arrest Mexican anarchists implementing an attack upon Juarez from El Paso. They planned to blow up the Juarez army garrison, the police station, the national bank, and then take a train to Chihuahua City and capture it. However, most revolutionaries were quickly rounded up. Flores Magón fled to Los Angeles. An ineptly planned revolt had failed miserably.

LATE IN THE YEAR: The Lyric theater opens at 220 South El Paso Street.

DECEMBER 23: Lord Delaval James Beresford dies in a North Dakota train wreck. Lord Beresford, an Irishman, had a Mexican ranch

A trolley entering Pioneer Plaza about 1906. San Jacinto Plaza is directly behind. The Sheldon Hotel (where the Plaza Hotel is now) is on the right, and the Plaza Block (today's Centre Building and Plaza Theater) on the left. (Aultman Collection. El Paso Public Library)

near Casas Grandes, plus ranches in Canada, although he spent much of his time in El Paso. He allegedly had married Florida Wolfe, a black woman better known locally as Lady Flo.

1907

Severo G. González opens the Central Cafe in Juarez. If there was such a thing as a Cafe Society in those days, it most probably congregated in the Central. Until prohibition ended, the Central remained the best of the first-class cafes.

The Popular Dry Goods Company moves from the northeast corner of El Paso and Overland streets to the present downtown location at Mesa and San Antonio. The store takes over the old Masonic Lodge #130 building. Other than the railroads and the Times *and* Herald-Post, *the Popular is the oldest, continuously operated business in El Paso.*

International boundary markers are placed around Cordova Island.

Tom Powers, leader of the El Paso gambling world, converted his Wigwam Saloon and gambling hall into the Wigwam Theater. The Wigwam was El Paso's first movie palace. Ten cents paid for three reels of entertainment lasting 30 minutes. Later the Wigwam became the State Theater.

The Southwestern Portland Cement Plant opens near ASARCO. What had once been a narrow limestone Rio Grande gorge is ground into powder on the northeast bank.

JANUARY: The Protestant women of El Paso organize the Woman's Missionary Union. The women hired a matron to meet the trains and give assistance to female strangers.

FEBRUARY 11: The Texas Grand Theater is built at the corner of Campbell and Texas. In terms of vaudeville, it was "big time," and many of the better known stars performed there.

MARCH 15: The Civic Improvement League recently paved the sidewalk around San Jacinto Plaza, and then started a campaign to keep chickens, burros and other animals from having the freedom of the streets. The League fought against promiscuous expectorating, describing it as a dangerous health hazard. The League

Texas Grand Theater at corner of Campbell and Texas. Before it switched to movies, it featured "big time" vaudeville and many of the better-known stars performed here. (Aultman Collection. El Paso Public Library)

volunteered to furnish sanitary tissues and make them available in public places.

APRIL 23: Near the present intersection of Hondo Pass and Railroad Drive, in northeast El Paso, Frank R. Tobin divided the area into building sites, and established a post office and fire department. Altogether there were 1,200 owners of Nation's Tobin Park, but as a community it failed even though a steam railroad car connected it to the city. The proposed community was too far from anywhere.

APRIL 27: The first Music Festival is held at the Elks Club.

MAY: Robert and Mary Price purchase the Story Dairy at Alameda and Piedras Streets. They change the name to Price's Dairy.

MAY 1: The Albert Baldwin Health Resort, a large (19,000 square foot) sanatorium is constructed in the Highland Park Addition at the foot of Mt. Franklin. The elevation of 3,764 feet was considered ideal for consumptives.

MAY 14: Our Lady of Mount Carmel (Ysleta Mission) suffers a disastrous fire. Only the adobe walls remain.

MAY 19: A cornerstone is laid for the second location of the First Presbyterian Church, generally called the Yandell or Boulevard Church.

JUNE: St. Clement's Church lays its cornerstone. The building will be constructed on the southeast corner of Montana and Campbell streets.

JUNE 5: The 1905 Convention for the Elimination of Bancos (oxbow curves in the Rio Grande and Colorado rivers) is proclaimed. A straight line was drawn across each banco neck, and the bottleneck of severed land was presented to whichever country it protruded into. Dozens of bancos alone were straightened near El Paso.

JULY 11: Immigration agents will switch to olive drab uniforms.

NOVEMBER: The Church of Christ organizes in El Paso. Years will pass before a church building is constructed.

NOVEMBER 30: The Shalam Colony near Las Cruces locks its doors. The *Faithists* scattered around the world. Some are still active.

DECEMBER 16: Several hundred squatters have built more than 200 adobe shacks on the Cotton Estate and claimed it as part of the Chamizal area. The squatters are evicted.

1908

The El Paso Public Library starts a Spanish language collection of books.

The El Paso Auto Club organizes with 18 members. Most of its funds were spent for highway signs. The Chamber of Commerce absorbed this group in 1915.

The El Paso Mining Journal, a monthly magazine, begins publishing.

ANUARY 10: The Woman's Club of El Paso has served notice that it objects to the aggregation of idle men basking in the sun on the Oregon Street side of the Plaza. The men "take delight in surveying the women as they pass and making remarks about them."

EBRUARY 29: Pat Garrett, the famed lawman and slayer of Billy the Kid, is murdered in the sandhills north of Las Cruces, New Mexico. Garrett, accompanied by Carl Adamson, was driving a buckboard to Las Cruces to work out an agreement for the sale of Garrett's San Andres Ranch to James Miller. Wayne Brazel, a local cowboy, rode horseback alongside the buckboard, and shot Garrett in the back of the head after the buckboard stopped so that the occupants could urinate. Garrett left a wife and nine children.

1ARCH: The first YMCA building is completed at the corner of North Oregon and Missouri streets.

1ARCH 27: A mass meeting of church representatives, charity organizations and city and county officials is called at the courthouse to discuss the care and problems of sick and indigent people.

APRIL 20: The United El Paso Consumptive Relief Association is organized. The name soon changed to the Health League, and a clinic was opened in the courthouse. Forty-six patients were examined during the first two days.

JUNE 7: The Guardian Angel Church is blessed.

JULY 16: The restored Ysleta Mission is rededicated.

SEPTEMBER 3: The El Paso Military Institute opens with 38 students on 20 acres east of Fort Bliss, a half-mile from the main gate.

OCTOBER 25: Etta Clark, one of El Paso's Big Five madams, dies in Atlanta, Georgia. She is buried there.

DECEMBER 1: Because of crushing debts, the Federal Smelter is sold. The ruins of the old smelter will stand until 1912 when housing develops in the area.

DECEMBER 29: Mannen Clements, relative of John Wesley Hardin, and last of the Wild West gunmen, is mysteriously slain in the Coney Island Saloon (First National Bank Building). As he walked across the crowded barroom floor, someone shot him in the back of the head . . . and no one saw a thing.

1909

Policemen are now dressed in the latest New York fashions.
Architect Henry C. Trost designed his own home at 1013 W. Yandell,
although it wasn't built until one year later. It is an adaptation of the
Prairie House.

FEBRUARY 5: The Logan Heights subdivision is filed.

JANUARY: Tornillo, Texas is platted as a townsite, although Southern

Pacific records indicate that between 1896 and 1906, a siding station here was known as Tornillo. The name refers to the tornillo bush, a species of mesquite prevalent in the area.

JANUARY 16: A new El Paso Country Club opens just east of Dyer Street, near Fort Bliss.

APRIL 19: Wayne Brazel, the confessed slayer of Pat Garrett, is tried for murder in Las Cruces. It is the only time in Western history where one man confesses to shooting another in the back of the head while he is urinating, and then claims self defense. The jury buys it, and Brazel is acquitted on grounds of self defense. Within five years, Wayne Brazel has himself become a mystery. He disappears, and efforts to locate him have been futile.

AUGUST 13: The City of El Paso purchases the water company for $927,000 after a group of investors buy the *El Paso Times* to silence it on the water issue.

AUGUST 13: Logan Heights Addition starts.

AUGUST 16: The El Paso Police Department purchased its first motorcycle because the mounted patrol horses could not keep up with automobiles, some going 15 miles per hour. However, since no one knew how to drive the motorcycle, Mayor Joseph Sweeney gave patrolman Ed Mebus permission to take the machine home and learn to operate it.

SEPTEMBER 24: The El Paso Tin Mining and Smelting Company incorporates. This tin mine on the east flank of the Franklins will be the first and only tin mine in the United States. Within a few years it will close, as there wasn't enough tin, and enough profit, to pay out the cost.

OCTOBER: The Woman's Club raises sufficient funds to build a YWCA at the corner of Missouri and Davis streets.

OCTOBER 16: Presidents William Howard Taft and Porfirio Díaz meet in El Paso.

Charles Hamilton, the "Birdman," soars and cavalry horses get skittish at Washington Park. Upon landing, Hamilton dragged his feet to keep from crashing into a fence. (Aultman Collection. El Paso Public Library)

1910

The City of El Paso has 39,279 residents, a 149 percent increase since 1900. El Paso County has 52,599, a 111 percent increase. Ciudad Juarez has 10,621, a 29 percent increase.

The Southwestern Portland Cement Company starts shipping its first sacks of cement to customers.

ASARCO purchases the Santa Rita, New Mexico, copper pit to be assured of copper ore. Revolutionary Mexico is too unreliable.

The Albert Baldwin Health Resort becomes Homan Sanatorium.

The city gets its first "automobile fire engine."

The road between El Paso and Canutillo is graveled.

Morningside Heights, south of William Beaumont General Hospital starts developing and is oriented primarily for people employed at Fort Bliss.

Altura Park is filed for sub-division.

The Peyton Packing Company opens.

The El Paso Sanatorium is established at 1109-1111 North Cotton. In a few years it will be renamed the Annie Laurie Home.

The Roberts-Banner Building is constructed on the southwest corner of Mills and Mesa. It is one of the first concrete reinforced buildings.

El Paso ha 20 miles of paved streets.

FEBRUARY 23: Charles K. Hamilton, the "birdman", flew briefly above the cottonwood trees at Washington Park. He is the first man and machine ever to fly in El Paso.

APRIL 7: St. Louis Street is changed to Mills Street to honor Anson Mills who laid out the first street plat of El Paso. Mills is in town to tear down the old Mills Building and make way for an eight or ten story reinforced concrete building.

APRIL 22: Mark Twain died.

SUMMER: The Woman's Charity Association of El Paso sponsors a "Save the Babies" campaign. Its purpose was to educate mothers and reduce the infant mortality rate. A baby clinic opens in the basement of the El Paso Courthouse.

JUNE 7: Father Carlos Pinto builds the Sacred Heart Church. Monsignor Gavilan, the Bishop of Chihuahua, dedicates it.

JULY 4: Religion and patriotism blend during a massive open air meeting at Cleveland Square. All Protestant churches join in the Sunday night service.

AUGUST 14: Mayor W. F. Robinson is killed when a fire-weakened wall at Calisher's Dry Goods falls on him. City fireman Tod Ware also dies. Ware had been a fire fighter for 18 days, and was the first fatality on record in the El Paso Fire Department.

SEPTEMBER 15: The El Paso School for Girls opens with an enrollment of 18 young ladies. It was both a boarding and a day school.

OCTOBER 14: The Toltec Building is created on the ruins of the First Baptist Church at San Antonio and Magoffin streets. The Toltec was a first-class gentleman's club, and only prominent El Pasoans were members. The Toltec was the brightest spot of its time in the social life of El Paso.

SEPTEMBER 30: Porfirio Díaz is reelected president of Mexico for the eighth time.

OCTOBER 30: The first YWCA building is dedicated at 541 West Missouri. The YWCA had formerly been in rented rooms in the *El Paso Herald* building.

NOVEMBER 20: Francisco Madero issues his "Plan of San Luis Potosí." It is a call to arms against President Porfirio Díaz, the official beginning of the Mexican Revolution.

DECEMBER 29: A thunderous explosion rocks ASARCO. While slag was being removed, the dynamite charges prematurely exploded, trapping men beneath the slag dump. Several were dug out alive. Six bodies were recovered. An undetermined number were never found.

1911

Tony Lama opens his first shoe and boot repair shop.
Culberson County is formed from El Paso County.
Vado, New Mexico, gets a post office. The name means "ford." Early
Spaniards lived in the area. It was also a home for former black slaves after
the Civil War. It has been called Earlham and Center Valley.

JANUARY: Abraham González, of Chihuahua, arrives in El Paso and
establishes a Mexican revolutionary *junta* on the 5th floor of the
Caples Building. The Sheldon Hotel was another headquarters for
revolutionary leaders. Meetings of revolutionary groups are openly
held all over town, and two Spanish language newspapers were
published: *El Paso del Norte* and *La Reforma Social.*

JANUARY 24: Secretary of State Philander C. Knox states that any-
body can purchase guns in the United States and use them to
overthrow another country.

FEBRUARY: The Juarez banks, the post office, most government
offices, and many businesses begin transferring money and accounts to El Paso.

FEBRUARY 2: Pascual Orozco, Mexican revolutionary, approaches
Juarez by train with 1,500 fighting men. He announces an attack
upon Juarez within two days. Pancho Villa and his revolutionaries
join Orozco, as do dozens of mercenaries looking for a war. Hundreds of young Juarez men flee to El Paso, fearing impressment
into the Federal Army.

FEBRUARY 2: El Paso doctors Ira Bush and E. D. Sinks organize an
emergency hospital corps. Holding aloft a Red Cross flag, they start
for Pascual Orozco's camp. (The Red Cross has not yet been organized in El Paso.)

FEBRUARY 4: Dr. Ira Bush opens a hospital for wounded Mexican
revolutionaries at 410 South Campbell Street.

Mexican revolutionaries steam toward El Paso. These men believed they were the toughest fighters in the world, and they probably were. (Aultman Collection. El Paso Public Library)

FEBRUARY 10: Charles K. Hamilton, a "birdman" barnstorming the country and currently in El Paso, flies over Juarez "on the first scouting flight ever attempted over a fortified city in time of actual warfare." Hamilton was in the air 19 minutes and flew 22 miles.

FEBRUARY 14: Francisco Madero, recently arriving in El Paso, assumes personal command of Mexican revolutionary forces.

FEBRUARY 20: War correspondents from around the world gather in El Paso, most of them staying at the Sheldon Hotel.

MARCH 15: Ex-President Theodore Roosevelt visits El Paso and in Cleveland Square makes what will forevermore be known in the media as his Baby Speech. ". . . of all the splendid crops produced in the great Valley of the Rio Grande, I like the baby crop the best, for I see it as right, not only in quantity but in quality."

APRIL 10: Tillie Howard, last of El Paso's "Big Five" madams, dies in El Paso. Buried in Evergreen.

APRIL 21: For the first time, the name Pancho Villa is mentioned with Orozco and Madero. Villa is described only as a major.

APRIL 23: An armistice is declared by Federals and Revolutionaries so that daily talks can take place in Peace Grove, a collection of cottonwoods across the Rio Grande from today's Hacienda Cafe.

APRIL 27: Alongside International Boundary Marker No. 1, before a vast multitude, Francisco Madero promotes Pancho Villa to colonel, and Pascual Orozco to brigadier general. Giuseppe Garibaldi, an Italian soldier of fortune and grandson of the Italian liberator, is commissioned a colonel in the revolutionary forces.

MAY 8: The First Battle of Juarez commences. The Mexican Revolution is underway. Six El Paso civilians will be slain and fifteen wounded by bullets falling in the city.

MAY 10: At 12:35 P.M., General Juan J. Navarro, the Federal commander, surrenders Juarez to Giuseppe Garibaldi, the Italian soldier of fortune.

MAY 11: Giuseppe Garibaldi sits in a tub at El Paso's Sheldon Hotel. As war correspondents cluster around the bathroom, Garibaldi explains how he conquered Juarez and accepted the surrender.

MAY 11: Ciudad Juarez is named the provisional capital of Mexico.

MAY 14: Madero releases Federal General Juan Navarro. Navarro flees to El Paso, spends three days in the chinaware department in the basement of the downtown Popular Dry Goods store, and then is smuggled into Hotel Dieu Hospital. At that point, he disappears.

MAY 15: The Chamizal Arbitration Commission begins its deliberations in the El Paso Federal Courthouse. The commission ends by finding for Mexico, a decision the United States rejects.

MAY 21: The Treaty of Ciudad Juarez is signed in the glare of automobile headlights outside the Juarez customs building.

MAY 25: President Porfirio Díaz resigns and agrees to enter exile. Mexico will have free elections.

JUNE 14: A Baby Sanatorium opens in Cloudcroft. It operates during the summer months when baby health care is such a problem in the heat of El Paso.

SEPTEMBER 16: The Elite Theater opens with *Romeo and Juliet*. Admission is 15 cents.

OCTOBER 2: The first session of the Eighth Court of Civil Appeals opens for business. It has jurisdiction over 22 West Texas counties.

OCTOBER 10: The El Paso chapter of the American Red Cross is officially chartered.

NOVEMBER: Fort Bliss officially becomes a cavalry post. Until now, Fort Bliss had always been infantry, although cavalry has briefly paused there in times past.

1912

The B'nai Zion Synagogue is erected at 902 North El Paso Street.

JANUARY: The Woman's Club of El Paso raises $123,000 for a new YWCA.

JANUARY 6: The Territory of New Mexico becomes a state. President William Howard Taft signs the proclamation.

JANUARY 14: Federal troops in Juarez mutiny. They disarm their superior officers, imprison the police in the city jails and turn loose 200 prisoners. Railroad bridges are destroyed, businesses looted and burned, and court records destroyed. More American troops reach the border.

FEBRUARY 1: The Juarez Post Office and two banks move their assets into El Paso.

MARCH: The Taft administration announces an arms embargo toward Mexico.

MARCH: The White House Department Store opens between Pioneer Plaza and San Jacinto Plaza.

MARCH 4: Father Carlos Pinto is seized by army officers in Juarez and held for ransom as he leaves Our Lady of Guadalupe Church and heads for the Sacred Heart Rectory in El Paso. The officers demanded $3,000, then reduce the amount to $2,000, then to $500, and finally to $100, which Pinto agrees to pay. Meanwhile, El Paso's Mayor Charles Kelly hotly demands Pinto's release, and he finally achieves it. Nevertheless, after returning home, Pinto writes out a check for $100 to Colonel Antonio Rojas, and it is duly delivered to the officer.

APRIL 23: By some accounts, three-fourths of the Juarez population has moved to El Paso to escape the revolutionists.

JUNE: Fort Bliss becomes a regimental post for the first time.

JUNE 5: General Victoriano Huerta orders Pancho Villa executed. As Villa is being stood against a wall, Madero intervenes and saves Villa's life. Villa is sent to the penitentiary in Chihuahua City.

JULY: The Rose Gregory Houchen Settlement is founded at 5th and Tays Street, teaching English, hygiene, cooking, and child care.

JULY: English, German, Spanish, and French refugees are fleeing Chihuahua and entering El Paso. One German said, "We are all Americans in Chihuahua City," a reference to anti-Americanism sweeping northern Mexico.

JULY 25: Over 2,000 Mormons from the vicinity of Casas Grandes, Chihuahua, abandon their homes and flee to El Paso. The *El Paso Herald* compares the onslaught to the flight of Jews leaving Egypt. Over 500 Mormons accept temporary quarters in a lumber shed on Magoffin Avenue. The rest are scattered in tenements around the city, or with relatives. One of the arrivals is George W. Romney, five-year-old nephew of Junius Romney, president of the Juarez Stake of the Church of Jesus Christ of Latter Day Saints. After spending most of the year in El Paso, the family moved to Los Angeles and then east. George eventually became president of American Motors, Governor of Michigan, and a candidate for president of the United States.

SEPTEMBER 12: Pancho Villa bribes his way out of the Chihuahua City prison. He flees to El Paso.

OCTOBER 14: The Franklin Irrigation Company sells the Franklin Canal and all of its assets to the United States Government. However, until the opening of Elephant Butte Dam, few farmers in the Lower Valley receive any irrigation because the natural flow of the river is insufficient.

THANKSGIVING DAY: Zach White opens the Hotel Paso del Norte on the site of the old Happy Hour Theatre, El Paso's vaudeville house. Before that, the site was the Manning Saloon and the Ben Dowell Saloon.

The Franklin Canal as it lazily rippled through El Paso on its way to valley cottonfields. Area residents treated it almost as a recreational asset, but it held dangers for the young and unwary. (Aultman Collection. El Paso Public Library)

NOVEMBER 28: Tom Lea, acting as grand master for Masonic Lodge No. 130, lays the cornerstone for the new Masonic Temple on Missouri Street. Construction costs will be $111,750, and Trost and Trost are the architects.

1913

The Gunning-Casteel Drug chain starts as the first store opens at the corner of Copia and Hueco streets.

Mills Building constructed. At the time, it is the largest concrete monolith building in the world.

The Lydia Patterson Institute opens as a two-story brick building to train preachers for Mexico. It also included 70 or 80 boys from Juarez and the Mexican interior whose parents wanted them to learn English and live in an atmosphere of stability.

An El Paso Masonic Lodge is constructed on Missouri Street. It will be torn down in 1969 to make room for the Holiday Inn.

Clint, Texas becomes the cradle of cotton production in the El Paso valley.

FEBRUARY 15: Fort Bliss now has the 22nd Infantry Regiment, the 2nd and 13th Cavalry Regiments, a battery of artillery and a company of Signal Corps. Bliss is still converting into a full regimental cavalry post.

FEBRUARY 21: Mexican President Francisco Madero is assassinated. Victoriano Huerta assumes control in Mexico City. American arms embargo lifted.

MARCH 7: Pancho Villa and six followers leave El Paso.

APRIL: Venustiano Carranza leads a Rebel army south from Coahuila. Alvaro Obregón drives south from Sonora. Pancho Villa gathers an army for an invasion of Mexico. Within days he has captured Torreon, and by late June has flattened Zacatecas. The armies call themselves "Constitutionalists," and although Carranza was the titular head, Villa's forces are the hardest-striking and the most feared. However, Villa still spends much of his time in the north, and around El Paso.

APRIL: General Leonard Wood, Army chief of staff, visits Fort Bliss and confers with Mexican Federal officers detained in a wooden barracks.

APRIL 16: The Texas legislature creates the State School of Mines and Metallurgy at El Paso.

APRIL: The remnants of Geronimo's Chiricahua Apaches (187 people), after years of exile in Florida and Fort Sill, Oklahoma, are shipped in boxcars to the Mescalero Reservation in New Mexico. Geronimo has already died, but some of his descendants make the trip.

MAY: The El Paso Military Institute at Fort Bliss closes.

MAY 17: Pancho Villa is named "Supreme Commander of Chihuahua for the Constitutionalist Forces." Villa now has the rank of brigadier general.

JUNE 9: Morningside Heights subdivision is filed.

JULY 14: The *El Paso Times* begins printing a full page of news and advertisements in Spanish.

JULY 19: Nine prostitutes who thought they were as good as anyone went swimming in the Washington Park pool, the only municipal pool in town. The police had to drag them out, and all nine women were jailed.

AUGUST: Mexican refugees stream across the international line at Columbus, New Mexico, and make their way to El Paso.

AUGUST 13: The Rio Grande Valley Traction Company constructs and operates the first interurban street car to Ysleta. The trip takes 40 minutes. There are separate smoking compartments.

Mexican revolutionaries skirmish on the outskirts of Juarez. (Aultman Collection. El Paso Public Library)

NOVEMBER 15: Pancho Villa, protecting his back trail, captures a train, orders the engineer to steam backwards into Juarez, and the revolutionaries capture it at 2:30 A.M. Juarez changes hands for the fourth time in less than three years. The second battle for Ciudad Juarez has abruptly begun and ended. El Paso doctors and nurses convert the Juarez Tivoli Gambling Casino into a hospital.

NOVEMBER 16: The Reverend Edward Barry, S. J., starts raising funds for a proposed new Catholic Church, the new cathedral in El Paso. But the response is sluggish. So he announced that whoever gave the largest single donation would get the honor of naming the church after their favorite saint. Mrs. Delia Lane sent a check for $10,000, the largest amount donated, and requested that the privilege be given to the Daughters of Erin. The Daughters chose St. Patrick's.

NOVEMBER 25: Villa fights a brutal battle on the southern outskirts of Juarez. He captures three trains, all the Federal artillery and 700 prisoners.

NOVEMBER-DECEMBER: Villa's execution squads are working overtime as groups are marched to a cemetery in the barren foothills. Old scores are settled.

DECEMBER 8: The Lydia Patterson Institute opens its doors. The school was a memorial to Lydia Patterson who, as a member of Trinity Methodist Church, did missionary work in El Paso's Second Ward, *El Segundo Barrio.*

DECEMBER 9: The fighting in Juarez panics Chihuahua City. Throngs of citizens, including the well-to-do, plus thousands of Federal soldiers flee toward Ojinaga. The *El Paso Herald* calls it "a spectacle of despair" as refugees spend eight days walking the 185 miles of desert to the international border where they cross the Rio Grande into Presidio, Texas.

1914

Portions of the 13th Cavalry are camped in Washington Park.
The Circle Cross Ranch organizes, and before it vanished during the
Great Depression, its one million plus acres stretched from Mescalero to
Ysleta. Alamogordo rancher Oliver Lee managed it.

JANUARY: Nearly 3,000 Mexican refugees at Presidio are taken by
train to El Paso and incarcerated by the United States Army. The
government calls them prisoners-of-war. Governor and General
Luís Terrazas, his family and entourage, who were also refugees,
take over an entire floor of the downtown Paso del Norte Hotel.
Terrazas brought out 20 wagons of treasure, so he could afford the
amenities.

JANUARY: General José Ynez Salazar, a revolutionary constituent of
former Mexican president Victoriano Huerta, is arrested in
Sanderson, Texas, and held at the Fort Bliss detention center. In
November the Army transferred him to Fort Wingate, New
Mexico, and from there to Albuquerque, where he escaped jail and
disappeared into Mexico.

JANUARY 4: Lew Vidal dies after being shot seven times by a holdup
man. The London born Vidal had moved to El Paso in 1893, and
for over twenty years owned several saloons as well as two-thirds
of all brothels in the city. He was a vice lord. Buried in Concordia.

JANUARY 15: The Texas legislature creates the Sixty-Fifth Judicial
District for El Paso.

FEBRUARY 1: St. Mary's Chapel, on North Oregon between
Wyoming and Boulevard (today's Yandell), is reopened to
provide Catholic Church services for Mexican refugees.

FEBRUARY 12: The Army discovers over 400 horses and military
equipment at Ysleta, all of it hidden by former Federal soldiers
waiting to make an assault on Juarez.

FEBRUARY 16: William S. Benton, a British subject who ranched in Chihuahua, is murdered by Mexican forces. Villa is now getting bad press in the United States.

APRIL: The Army has a full division at Fort Bliss. Two regiments are placed near the downtown area.

APRIL 3: The Diocese of El Paso is created. Due to the death of Pope Pius X, however, the new diocese remains vacant for 18 months.

APRIL: General John J. Pershing assumes command at Fort Bliss, and the base becomes the largest cavalry post in the United States. More troops are stationed here than at any site since the Civil War.

APRIL: Camp Cotton is established east of Cotton Street between Paisano and 11th Street. It contains the Georgia National Guard, the 16th Infantry.

APRIL: The Board of Regents of the University of Texas authorize the State School of Mines and Metallurgy.

APRIL 17: The Rebel consulate in El Paso moves from the Alberta Hotel to the Mills Building.

APRIL 24: With the Mexican Revolution threatening El Paso, over 500 citizens volunteer their services to Chief of Police I. N. Davis. Fifty are armed with shotguns and rifles and assigned to patrol the south end of town.

APRIL 28: The State School of Mines and Metallurgy is established in the El Paso Military Institute on Fort Bliss. The first class started last fall.

MAY 4: Nearly 5,000 Mexican prisoners-of-war are moved from Fort Bliss to Fort Wingate, New Mexico. El Paso residents feared that the prisoners might break out, or be turned loose on the city streets and overwhelm the community with their impoverishment.

JUNE: Doctors Charles Hendricks and R. D. Harvey build the Hendricks Sanatorium in Mesa Heights. It contains 53 private rooms.

AUGUST 1: The Alhambra Theater opened at 209 South El Paso Street. It was later renamed the Palace. The Texas Grand and the Alhambra were the leading theaters in the El Paso Southwest.

AUGUST 14: The San Lorenzo Mission at Clint, Texas is dedicated.

AUGUST 26: General Pershing escorts Pancho Villa across the Santa Fe International Bridge for a personal review at Fort Bliss and a reception at the Country Club as well as in Quarters No. 1 (the Pershing House).

FALL: A football team is organized at the School of Mines. It won two games and lost three during its first year.

OCTOBER 9: As an inducement for a proposed Scenic Drive, thousands of El Pasoans turn out for a "big feed" on the mesa overlooking the town. Six thousand loaves of bread, 4,000 pounds of barbecue and four barrels of pickles are consumed. Two Fort Bliss bands play as citizens take a look at El Paso in the dark, its hundreds of lights deliberately turned on and blazing from houses, businesses and streets.

NOVEMBER 21: The Kern Place subdivision starts.

NOVEMBER 26: The Woman's Rescue Home Association deed a building and lot at 3918 Bliss Avenue to the Salvation Army. Five girls and one abandoned child became the first residents. Within two years there were 38 children under ten years of age living in the home, nine of them having been born there. During these years the Salvation Army Home was more of an orphanage than a maternity refuge, although the unwed mother was the motive for establishing it.

DECEMBER: The architectural firm of Trost and Trost gets a contract for construction of El Paso High School.

Coney Island Saloon (ca. 1915) on Oregon Street. First National Building is at left. El Paso Collector of Customs Pat Garrett was a regular. Revolver that killed Billy the Kid once hung behind bar. The last gunfighter in Texas, Mannen Clements, slain here in 1909. (Aultman Collection. El Paso Public Library)

DECEMBER 6: Pancho Villa and Emiliano Zapata enter Mexico City with 50,000 revolutionaries. For a glorious few days, Villa is even president.

1915

Elizabeth Garrett, the blind daughter of the famous sheriff, Pat Garrett, copyrights her song, "O Fair New Mexico." It remains the state song to this day.

Cotton is first planted in the Upper Valley.

The Peak Undertaking Company purchases the first motor-driven ambulance in El Paso County.

Four additional stories are added to the Mills Building, giving it a total of twelve.

The Rio Grande Irrigated Land Company plats Alamo Alto (Tall Cottonwood), alongside the Rio Grande, five miles southeast of Tornillo, Texas. During the Mexican Revolution, several Mexican families moved across the river and lived here.

JANUARY 9: General Hugh Scott and Pancho Villa meet at the customs house in Juarez and walk to the International Bridge.

JANUARY 20: The Reverend John J. Brown, S.J. of Denver, Colorado is appointed the first Catholic bishop of the Diocese of El Paso. However, Brown turned down the position.

JANUARY 26: The El Paso General Hospital opens east of Washington Park. Its three stories cost $40,000 and had a capacity of 100 beds. One doctor and one nurse operated it. The manageably insane were locked in the basement. Tubercular patients sweltered in stifling, unventilated wooden shacks on the hospital periphery. The greatest single hospital expense was alfalfa for the cattle herds.

JANUARY 31: The celebrated New Mexico attorney, politician and gunman, Elfego Baca, shoots and kills Mexican revolutionary Celestino Otero on the streets of downtown El Paso. A jury calls it self-defense.

FEBRUARY 15: A chapter of the American Association of University Women is founded in El Paso.

MARCH 4: Police arrest a soldier in the red light district, and his friends try to free him. A mob of several hundred soldiers gather before military and civilian police establish control.

SPRING: A School of Mines publication, the *Prospector* is founded.

MAY: Pershing's men from Fort Bliss assist in a series of campaigns to improve South El Paso (Little Chihuahua). Some buildings are torn down, the streets are hosed and the refuse and dead animals are buried or burned. General Pershing placed his entire medical corps, officers and enlisted men at the disposal of the city.

JUNE 3: The El Paso City Council passes ordinances against the public sale of narcotics and marijuana.

JUNE 3: The city provides street name signs for the first time.

JUNE 18: Anthony J. Schuler, S. J., is appointed the first Catholic Bishop of El Paso, and he accepts it. The Immaculate Conception Church is designated as the Cathedral until Saint Patrick's is ready.

JUNE 27: Former Mexican president Victoriano Huerta and Mexican revolutionary chieftain, Pascual Orozco, meet at Newman, New Mexico/Texas, when Huerta steps off the Southern Pacific. Also in the crowd are Department of Justice federal agents and federal troops. Huerta and Orozco are charged with violation of the neutrality laws. Both men are placed under house arrest in El Paso.

JULY 3: Orozco escapes house arrest in El Paso. Huerta is placed under barracks arrest at Fort Bliss.

JULY 4: The Church of Christ opens.

AUGUST 10: Pancho Villa and General Hugh Scott meet in the residence of Joseph F. Williams at 323 West Rio Grande Street in El Paso.

AUGUST 27: Mrs. John J. Pershing and her four children die in a fire at the San Francisco Presidio. They had planned to join General John Pershing at Fort Bliss in one week. Norman Walker, an El Paso correspondent for the Associated Press, telephoned General Pershing at Bliss and broke the news to him. "There was silence on the other end of the line," Walker later wrote, "then General Pershing said 'Thank you,' and hung up."

AUGUST 30: Pascual Orozco and four of his companions are shot to death in Green River Canyon, Culberson County, Texas (near Sierra Blanca) by a posse of federal marshals, deputy sheriffs, Texas Rangers and troops of the 13th Cavalry. Orozco's remains were draped in a Mexican flag and interred in a vault at Concordia Cemetery.

SEPTEMBER 16: The Associated Charities replaces the Woman's Charity Association.

SEPTEMBER 23: The county accepts the plans of Trost and Trost for a new courthouse.

SEPTEMBER 25: Mexican Jesuit Fathers take charge of the Ysleta Mission.

OCTOBER: Rodolfo Fierro, in charge of Pancho Villa's executions, a man known as "The Butcher," reportedly drowns near Villa Ahumada. Other accounts say he was executed.

OCTOBER 15: President Woodrow Wilson formally recognizes Venustiano Carranza as president of Mexico.

OCTOBER 25: El Paso police officers get life insurance for the first time.

NOVEMBER: County commissioners agree on a municipal auditorium combined with the new County Courthouse. By December the proposed facility had been named Liberty Hall after the statue of the Goddess of Liberty.

NOVEMBER: Liberty Bell tours El Paso.

NOVEMBER 4: The county grand jury gave the following report about El Paso's voting practices: "The names of men long dead, boys 18 to 20, foreigners who have never attempted to become citizens; men from other parts of our country, who are not residents of El Paso, and fictitious names by the score are found on our polling lists."

NOVEMBER 5 - 6: William F. Cody, better known to the world as Buffalo Bill, is in El Paso with the Sells-Floto Circus. Mayor Tom Lea and a host of dignitaries met him at the train. A military band cranked out "For He's A Jolly Good Fellow," and "There'll Be A Hot Time in the Old Town Tonight." But this wasn't the Buffalo Bill of old. The 69-year-old Cody suffered from prostate trouble, as well as rheumatism and neuritis. When he rode into the area, he had to be helped on and off his horse. Bill went from El Paso to Albuquerque and then into retirement. He died a year and two months later.

NOVEMBER 22: The El Paso Police Department is now using fingerprints as a method of identification. Up until now the department utilized the Bertillion System of photographs plus facial measurements.

NOVEMBER 29: Pancho Villa's Rebel agency in El Paso, called the *Consulado de Mexico*, has closed its doors. Since the United States has recognized Venustiano Carranza as the legitimate Mexican president, there is no further need for a Villa headquarters in El Paso, or anywhere else.

DECEMBER 15: The Texas Supreme Court rules that El Paso vice (brothels) could not be segregated. In other words, the Tenderloin where the girls had to live was illegal.

DECEMBER 15: Mayor Tom Lea and General John J. Pershing agree that "all soldiers of Villa's command and other persons from Juarez who were considered undesirable were to be given six hours to leave town."

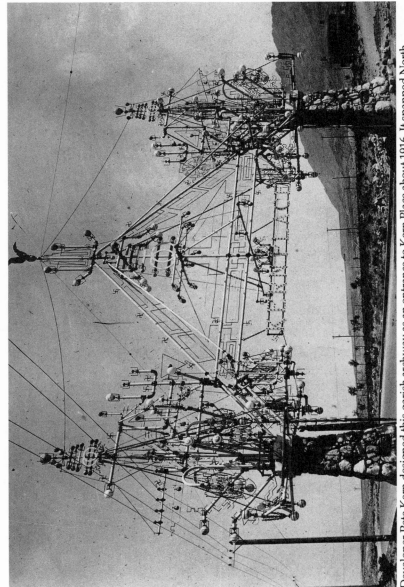

Developer Pete Kern designed this garish archway as an entrance to Kern Place about 1916. It spanned North Kansas Street at today's Robinson intersection. (Aultman Collection. El Paso Public Library)

DECEMBER 18: Texas Governor James Ferguson, over strenuous opposition of Sheriff Peyton Edwards, permits Carranza forces to cross El Paso County in route to attack Villista forces. In revenge, Villa partisans sack Juarez during a savage pre-Christmas raid.

DECEMBER 31: Alvaro Obregón, a co-revolutionary along with President Carranza, comes to El Paso and has his headquarters in the Paso del Norte Hotel. Obregón will become one of Mexico's greatest heroes, as well as president.

1916

The El Paso Country Club moves to near Fort Bliss.
The El Paso Mining Journal, *a monthly, ceases operation.*
John J. McCloskey organizes the Rio Grande Baseball League.
McClosky took baseball out of the amateur status in Washington Park and established Rio Grande Park, which was across Wyoming Street from today's KDBC-TV.

JANUARY 8: Chihuahua Governor and General Luis Terrazas and his wife, now refugees from the Mexican Revolution, rent the A. B. Fall mansion at 1725 Arizona Street. Their servants live in the basement and attic.

JANUARY 10: Pancho Villa's troops remove 16 American mining engineers from a train near Santa Ysabel, Chihuahua, and execute them. When the bodies arrived by train in El Paso, a huge mob attacked Hispanics in South El Paso. Mayor Tom Lea managed to contain the mob south of Overland Street. Order was finally restored after Pershing sent two companies of troops to impose martial law.

JANUARY 16: Victoriano Huerta, former president of Mexico, dies of cirrhosis in El Paso at 415 West Boulevard (West Yandell).

JANUARY 16: The girls in the Tenderloin are given six weeks to find new places to live. It doesn't happen.

JANUARY 29: Chinese along the Mexican border, fearing massacres from Carranza and Villa forces, ask special permission to enter the United States.

SPRING: The School of Mines organizes a baseball team.

MARCH 5: Twenty-seven jail prisoners bathing with gasoline to ward off typhus, burn to death when H. Cross, better known as "Hop Head," strikes a match. Ten others died shortly afterwards.

MARCH 9: Pancho Villa raids Columbus, New Mexico.

MARCH 12: The 1st Aero Squadron, the first of its kind in the United States Army, joins the Punitive Expedition.

MARCH 15: The Punitive Expedition led by General John J. "Black Jack" Pershing enters Chihuahua. Two separate columns of 4,000 men cross the border into Chihuahua near Columbus. The entire regular army of the United States, with the exception of a regiment of cavalry and some of the coast artillery, are now either on the border or with the Expedition. The Red Cross recruits 200 El Paso civilians to make bandages for presumed American and Mexican casualties.

MARCH 16: The 1st Aero Squadron makes its first reconnaissance flight into Mexico, doing so from Columbus.

MARCH 16: At Montana and Oregon streets, a new Temple Mt. Sinai is opened.

MARCH 17: Elements of the American Army occupy Colonia Dublan, Chihuahua.

APRIL 10: The Hotel Dieu Training School for Nurses is chartered.

APRIL 12-13: The American Army skirmishes with citizens and Federal forces at Parral. Two soldiers are slain.

APRIL 29: General Pershing divides Chihuahua into five military districts.

MAY 2: Generals Hugh Scott and Alvaro Obregón meet at the Paso del Norte Hotel and plan the American withdrawal from Mexico. Scott dismissed the meeting, saying "We evidently came prepared to discuss one question, Obregón another."

MAY 2: The El Paso Country Club near Fort Bliss is destroyed by fire.

MAY 5: Mayor Tom Lea ends the practice of collecting fines from prostitutes.

MAY 5: American forces ambush and kill 61 Mexican Villistas at Ojos Azules, Chihuahua.

MAY 9: The state militias (National Guard) of Texas, New Mexico, and Arizona are mobilized into service, as are units from other states.

MAY 25: Colonel Candelario Cervantes, who actually commanded the Columbus raid by Villa forces, is slain by American units during a running battle.

JUNE: Nearly 2,000 destitute Mexican refugees are waiting in Juarez, camped along the river bank and seeking entry into the United States.

JUNE-AUGUST: Streets are graded and dozens of hovels are razed in South El Paso. Hundreds of Hispanics move to Juarez, which already has horrible housing problems.

JUNE: St. James Church is dedicated in Van Horn.

JUNE: St. Gertrude's Church is dedicated in Sierra Blanca, Texas.

JUNE: Camp Cotton is moved from near Cotton Street to slightly west of what would become Peyton Packing Company.

Amid all the revolutionary disruptions on both sides of the border, El Pasoans still found time to drink a beer and support their baseball teams. These are the El Paso Mavericks. Left to right: Gray, unidentified, Kane, Schultz, Keifer, Nellis, Wooten, Jackson, Gurtz. (Aultman Collection. El Paso Public Library)

Camp Stewart, with regular Army and National Guard units, is established west of the railroad and is between today's Fred Wilson Road and Sunrise Shopping Center.

Camp Owen Bierne is established on both sides of today's Fred Wilson Road, and west of the airport road. The balloon hangar was located at Camp Owen Bierne.

Camp Boyd was established on Fort Bliss north of Tompkins Street, but between the Southern Pacific tracks and the top of the mesa.

Camp Pershing was on both sides of Dyer from Tyler to Fort Boulevard and from Memphis to Fort Boulevard.

Camp Courchesne was established on both sides of the Rio Grande near present-day ASARCO and the Southwestern Portland Cement plant. A pontoon bridge crossed the river.

JUNE 4: A *Soldiers Comfort Guild* is published for Company K by El Paso women.

JUNE 14: Twenty-five thousand soldiers and thousands of El Paso citizens march through town on Flag Day. A sham battle takes place in Washington Park.

JUNE 16: Juarez organizes a Chamber of Commerce. It promptly announces a boycott against El Paso merchants.

JUNE 21: American forces suffer a debacle at Carrizal, Chihuahua. The Army has 44 casualties.

JUNE 24: Construction starts on the Hoover House, although it is built for Richard Dudley at 711 Cincinnati. Dudley organized the First Bank and Trust Company, and served in Texas politics before becoming mayor of El Paso in 1923. After Dudley's death, Robert Hoover acquired the mansion, deeding it in 1965 to UT El Paso, where it has remained a home for university presidents.

JUNE 27: Harry T. Ponsford and Sons build the Rolston Hospital in what is now Five Points (Piedras and Montana).

JUNE 29: The first of two streetcar strikes take place. Rampaging rioters and sympathizers derail cars in the center of town. They smash windows and beat motormen. Mayor Tom Lea and former Mayor Charles Kelly climb aboard overturned trolleys and try to calm the crowd.

JUNE 30: Several captured Mexican raiders of Columbus, New Mexico, are publicly hanged in Deming.

JULY 13: Mayor Tom Lea, at a political rally in Alta Vista School, insists Pancho Villa has "bought" the *El Paso Times* because the newspaper is busy magnifying "little fights into great battles" in order to "make a national hero of the man."

JULY 19: The *El Paso Herald* publishes a paid political advertisement consisting of two pictures. One is a check draft directing Pedro Maese, Villa's collector of customs in Juarez, to pay $10,000 to Wyche Greer, manager of the *El Paso Morning Times*. The second photo is a receipt from Wyche Greer, accepting the $10,000. Greer denied receiving any money.

AUGUST 16: ASARCO workers strike for an eight-hour day. Six deaths result, directly and indirectly, from the violence. The International Workers of the World (IWW) sends in Mother Jones, a labor agitator from Colorado, and she harangued 1,500 ASARCO workers in Cleveland Square. She exhorted the workers to fight for their rights, and they roared back, "You tell 'em, Mother." The strike lasted two weeks, and black men, who had been brought in as strike breakers, returned home.

SEPTEMBER: Thousands of people, mostly women, march through downtown El Paso on Preparedness Day. They were prepared to make whatever sacrifices were necessary to defeat Germany.

SEPTEMBER: Lew Gasser died on Labor Day. The popular sportsman was digging a 40-foot cesspool when a helper cried out that he was being overcome by gasses. As bystanders looked on helplessly, Gasser lowered himself down with a rope, tied it to his employee, and the man was hauled up. When the rope dropped back down, Gasser was too weak to tie it about himself. He died, but the man he had sent up, lived.

SEPTEMBER 4: A second streetcar riot rips El Paso. Burning streetcars litter the downtown. Sympathetic police do not arrest the rowdies, and Mayor Tom Lea threatens to dismiss the officers.

SEPTEMBER 17: Holy Family Church at 900 West Missouri is dedicated with a high mass. The church was created to provide services for Mexican refugees.

SEPTEMBER 18: El Paso High School opens at 800 E. Schuster. This four story structure of classic architectural proportions remains a marvel to this day.

SEPTEMBER 20: Twenty-six thousand regulars and guardsmen march through El Paso. They and the high school bands form a line 20 miles long.

SEPTEMBER 21: Texas Ranger W. B. Sands is unruly in the Coney Island Saloon (where the old First National Building is now). Sands shot and killed Army Sergeant Owen Bierne.

OCTOBER 29: A fire at Fort Bliss destroys the Texas School of Mines and Metallurgy.

OCTOBER 10: Piedmont Addition starts.

OCTOBER 20: Dedication ceremonies are held at Elephant Butte Dam.

NOVEMBER 8: The Woman's Club of El Paso opens its clubhouse on North Mesa Street.

NOVEMBER 12: The cornerstone for St. Patrick's Cathedral is laid.

DECEMBER 25: St. Joseph's Church on Travis and Hueco is blessed by the bishop.

The Paddy Wagon, plus three unidentified El Paso policemen and two detectives. Ca. 1917. (Aultman Collection. El Paso Public Library)

1917

Peyton Packing Company is established.

Until this year, Mexican immigration into the United States was unrestricted except for the handicapped, beggars, prostitutes, criminals and anarchists.

The El Paso Board of Realtors is organized.

A Bhutanese style of architecture is adopted for the new School of Mines on the mesa north of El Paso.

Hudspeth County is formed from El Paso County.

The landmark now known as Mt. Cristo Rey is identified on U.S. topographic maps as Rodadero Peak. In local parlance, it is also Cerro de Muleros, *which means Mule Drivers Mountain, or Mule Mountain.*

The El Paso Council of Jewish Women is organized with 52 charter members. This group will be eventually responsible for the Lighthouse for the Blind, the Memorial Park School for Retarded Children, and the Drive-A-Meal project.

The Fire Department becomes fully motorized. Fire wagons are no longer pulled by horses.

JANUARY-FEBRUARY: The Punitive Expedition withdraws from Mexico through Columbus, and Pershing will take it to Europe to fight World War I. The withdrawal column extends five miles and includes 10,690 soldiers and 2,749 refugees. The latter comprised 2,030 Mexicans, 197 Mormons, 533 Chinese, and thousands of animals. Over 300 wagons, trucks and private cars form the procession. Mothers protected their babies against bitter winds and sands by draping serapes over their heads. Upon reaching Columbus, immigration officials began processing everybody. Those self-sufficient or with relatives left first, and that included most of the Mormons. Agents for railroads, ranches and farms took the Mexicans. By the end of the first week, only the Chinese were left. Most of them remained until early June when a special train carried them to Fort Sam Houston where they worked for the Army's Quartermaster Department.

FEBRUARY: Twenty-one thousand Mexican nationals will be bathed and their clothes fumigated this month at the Santa Fe Street

Bridge. This is probably a record because of so many people entering the country due to unsettled conditions in Mexico. The practice started about 1910, and continued for several more years.

FEBRUARY 7: General Pershing enters El Paso to a tumultuous welcome. At Fort Bliss, he changed the name of Camp Pershing to Camp Baker in honor of Secretary of War Newton D. Baker.

FEBRUARY 2: St. Rosalia Church is dedicated in Fabens.

FEBRUARY 10: General John J. Pershing assumes temporary command in San Antonio of the Southern Department, following the death of Major General Frederick Funston.

MARCH 24: El Paso National Guardsmen are mustered out of federal service. They march through decorated streets to Cleveland Square where speeches and presentations are made. (No El Paso guardsmen were slain in Mexico during the Punitive Expedition.)

MARCH 31: Mayor Tom Lea proclaims Loyalty Day. President Woodrow Wilson orders the mobilization of the Texas National Guard for duty in World War I. El Pasoans had been mustered out for just one week. Since no one had orders about where to report, the El Paso Chamber of Commerce turned its offices into a barracks for several days.

APRIL 1: The new County Courthouse is ready for occupancy. Total costs, including furniture and fixtures, is $760,000.

APRIL 3: The El Paso National Guard has been ordered to Elephant Butte Dam. Because several Germans live in that vicinity, the Reclamation Service has requested dam protection.

APRIL 5: Two soldiers kidnap a bulldog from the back seat of a city detective's car.

APRIL 6: President Woodrow Wilson declares war on Germany. World War I starts for the United States.

MAY: The United States passes a conscription law and drafts young men into the armed forces. Mexican immigration slows.

JUNE: When El Paso pressed Washington for military training camps, Secretary of War Newton D. Baker stated that he abhorred liquor and prostitution, and both evils thrived at the Pass. He said soldiers would not be stationed in areas still maintaining segregated vice districts.

JUNE 22: The first County Court-at-Law is created.

JUNE 26: The I.W.W. (International Workers of the World) threatens the mines of Bisbee and southern Arizona with a labor strike unless demands are met for higher wages and shorter hours. When the demands were not met, the I.W.W. calls a strike.

JULY 12: Arizona Sheriff Harry Wheeler and a twelve hundred man posse, each with a white handkerchief tied around the arm for identification, begins arresting I.W.W. strikers, some on the picket line, others in their homes. Over 1,000 were taken into custody. They were marched to a ball park in Warren, Arizona, and placed on an empty train bound for Columbus, New Mexico.

JULY 20: Company A, a group of 121 El Pasoans assigned to the First Texas Infantry, laid claim to some interesting firsts: "First company, first battalion, first regiment, first brigade, and also the largest, from the largest city, in the largest county, in the largest state, of the largest nation involved in the largest war in the history of the world."

NOVEMBER 29: St. Patrick's Cathedral is dedicated. The rectory was built in 1955. St. Patrick's has since remained the cathedral or main church of the El Paso Diocese. While the architecture is often referred to as Gothic, it is more properly modified Byzantine. When the steeple was destroyed by lightning during the late 1980s, Orlando Fonseca, a county commissioner, claimed God was angry at the priests.

DECEMBER: The James McNary Home is completed in the Austin

Terrace Addition. The region was just sandhills, but McNary prevailed upon Fort Bliss to dump 5,000 loads of horse manure on the property. After being plowed under, the fertilizer converted four acres of desert into a gardener's paradise.

1918

Five Bhutanese style buildings have been constructed for the School of Mines.

JANUARY: Sewing rooms are in the White House Department Store, and in churches, houses and businesses all over the city. Volunteer ladies recruited by the Red Cross make hospital garments, surgical dressings, socks, scarves and items into the hundreds of thousands before the war ends.

JANUARY 6: *Revista Católica*, a Catholic newspaper printed in Spanish and published by the Jesuits, is moved to El Paso and blessed and inaugurated at 1407 E. Third Street. It had started in Las Vegas, New Mexico, around 1875.

JANUARY 27: El Paso churches are filled as religious leaders call for prohibition.

JANUARY 30: The city votes down prohibition. The Wets win by a narrow 246 votes.

FEBRUARY: A new YWCA arises at 315 E. Franklin.

FEBRUARY 14: The Guardian Angel Church is relinquished to Mexican exiled Catholic priests who belong to the Society of Jesus.

MARCH 3: Many El Pasoans, some of them prominent, recommend vigilance committees to combat prostitution and illegal liquor sales.

MARCH 5: The 18th Amendment (prohibition) is ratified in Congress.

MARCH 24: May Palmer, one of El Paso's Big Five madams, dies of cancer and is buried in Evergreen Cemetery.

APRIL 15: All saloons in Texas are closed due to the 18th Amendment ratification. As the closing hour of 10:30 P.M. approached, 250 saloons did a huge business as the Wets had their farewell libation. Meanwhile, requests for barrels of beer and casks of whiskey went unfilled. Strangely, there were no reported deaths that day: John Barleycorn died alone.

APRIL 17: Liberty Hall opens with its first public gathering, a patriotic one with Secretary of the Treasury William G. McAdoo as speaker.

JUNE 22: Ike Alderete, a popular Mexican-American philanthropist, was shot and killed by a Mexican national stoned on drugs. Within days, another Mexican high on drugs shot and killed a woman, her two children, two bystanders and an El Paso policeman. Both killers were slain by policemen, the first by gunfire, the second by dynamite after he had taken refuge in an outhouse.

JULY 15: Juan Hart dies. He is interred in the family tomb near the old homestead.

MAY 2: The College of the City of El Paso (not the Mines) is incorporated.

AUGUST 12: El Paso military units arrive at Brest, France. Within six weeks they are fighting the German Army.

SEPTEMBER: Juarez starts paving three main thoroughfares: Lerdo Avenue, Juarez Avenue and Comercio (16th of September) Street. The job isn't completed until October 1921.

SEPTEMBER 30: Local newspapers ran a minor story of influenza circulating in El Paso. Within a week, nearly a thousand people had the Spanish flu. Before the flu epidemic ran its course two months later, nearly 600 citizens had died, schools, churches and movie houses closed, public meetings banned. The hospitals overflowed and even the streetcars emptied.

OCTOBER 8: El Paso had two nationally decorated heroes during World War I: Private Marcelino Serna and Sergeant Sam Dreben, the latter better known as the "Fighting Jew." Dreben led 30 volunteers in an assault upon a German machine gun nest near the junction of the American and French lines. Dreben captured four guns, killed over 40 German soldiers, and captured two. Dreben, who already had the Distinguished Service Cross, now received the French Medaille Militaire and the French Croix-de-Guerre with Palm. The Croix-de-Guerre with Palm is the highest grade of that particular decoration. The Palm signifies that Sergeant Dreben's deeds have been cited to his entire division. The Medaille Militaire is the highest award in the French Army, and corresponds to the American Congressional Medal of Honor. The Medaille Militaire meant that the attention of the whole army was called to the recipient. Marcelino Serna picked up the U.S. Distinguished Service Cross, Purple Heart, Italian Cross of Merit, French Croix de Guerre, French Croix de Guerre with Palm, French Medaille Militare, British Honor Medal, WW I Victory Medal with five stars, French Commemorative Medal, St. Mihiel Medal, and the Verdun Medal.

OCTOBER 16: The 28-room Aoy School is converted into an emergency hospital for influenza victims in South El Paso.

NOVEMBER 9: With 17 new flu cases in the city, and three people a day still dying, the newspapers declare the epidemic over. Schools, amusement places and churches reopen. However, Fort Bliss still has 2,000 cases, and the post remains under strict quarantine.

NOVEMBER 9: The Ellanay theater opens. The movie is *Stolen Orders*, with Kitty Gordon and Carlyle Black. The theater is named for the initials of two El Pasoans named Louis and Andreas.

NOVEMBER 11: World War I ends at about 1 A.M., El Paso time. Police rush into the street and blow whistles, and are joined by hundreds of residents, half-clad and screaming with joy. Fort Bliss troops march into town at 9 A.M. with thousands of still-crazed civilians falling in behind. Churches are packed. The downtown fills with honking cars. Hundreds of guns are fired into the air. Restaurants stay open until late. Nobody wants to go home.

NOVEMBER 30: The *El Paso Herald* quoted an army officer of accusing American soldiers guarding the international bridges of smuggling liquor out of Juarez and into El Paso. Brigadier General James J. Hornbrook, commander of Fort Bliss, demanded the officers's name . . . and the *Herald* declined to furnish it. Hornbrook then refused to provide any more military information to the *Herald*, and the *Herald* accused the general of exercising "a military dictatorship over an American newspaper."

1919

A civil service commission will govern fire and police departments. Mann Overall Company starts producing clothing and moves to 394 Chihuahua Street.

JANUARY 16: The 18th Amendment, Prohibition, becomes the law of the land. Cabarets and saloons run wide open in Juarez.

MARCH 11: The El Paso Chamber of Commerce forms a Convention and Tourist Committee.

APRIL 25: Highland Park Addition is filed.

MAY 8: Guadalupano Day Nursery opens. It aids poor Mexican children.

JUNE: World War I heroes arrive back in El Paso. Among these were:
Maj. Richard F. Burges: French Croix-de-Guerre with Gilt Star.
Capt. Frank A. Loftus: French Croix-de-Guerre with Gilt Star.
Capt. Warren W. Windham: French Croix-de Guerre with Gilt Star.
Ist. Lt. Claude H. Mason: French Legion d'Honneur (Chevalier)
    French Croix-de-Guerre with Palm.
    Distinguished Service Cross.
1st Lt. Wollford Swanson: French Croix-de Guerre with Gilt Star.
2d Lt. Edmond E. Behr: French Croix-de-Guerre with Gilt Star.
Cpl. Morris Price: French Croix-de-Guerre with Bronze Star.
Cpl. Dionicies Roumeliotis: French Croix-de-Guerre with Palm.
Pvt. Guy C. Mercer: French Croix-de-Guerre with Gilt Star.

The awards of Sergeant Sam Dreben and Private Marcelino Serna are found on October 8, 1918. These two men were the most highly decorated Americans in Texas.

JUNE 15: Pancho Villa again attacks Juarez. Fort Bliss shells Juarez with downtown cannon, then invades Juarez with infantry across the Paso del Norte Bridge. Three units of cavalry cross the river in the lower valley. All units engage the revolutionaries, drive them back and return to El Paso by daylight the following day.

JUNE 17: The Army Border Air Patrol is activated. Originally it is called the 1st Bombardment Group, then the 1st Surveillance Group. The landing area was an infantry drill field.

JUNE 17: The school up on the mesa is now called the State School of Mines and Metallurgy. It is a branch of the University of Texas.

JUNE 17: Camp Chigas is established between Santa Fe and Stanton streets, between 11th Street and the Rio Grande.

JUNE 17: The first El Paso airport is a Fort Bliss cavalry and artillery drill field.

JUNE 18: Thousands of people jam the streets of El Paso for the first Corpus Christi Procession. It was a marvelous tribute of Catholic faith.

JUNE 18: The first border reconnaissance patrol flight takes place. The DH-4 left Fort Bliss and flew to Fort Hancock. After that, the aircraft flew to Presidio, then went north to the airdrome at Marfa. The trip back was just a reversal of the trip down. The maximum flying time was one hour because that's how long the gas lasted.

AUGUST 10: A military airplane on reconnaissance duty out of Fort Bliss and near Presidio, mistakes the Rio Conchos for the Rio Grande and crashes several miles deep into Mexico. Mexican bandits captured the two airmen and demanded $15,000 in ransom. An international ground and air search took place before the men were dramatically rescued by cavalry units.

SEPTEMBER: Classes in vocational training start in several area schools.

SEPTEMBER 21: St. Margaret's (Catholic) Orphanage opens. J. E. Morgan, an El Paso builder, purchased the home of J. D. Ponder for the orphanage, plus an eleven acre farm surrounding it in the El Paso lower valley. St. Margaret's Orphanage was named in honor of the donor's wife, the deceased Margaret Morgan.

NOVEMBER: The Colon theater opened with *Rigoletto*, by an Italian Company. Gypsy Rose Lee performed there in 1925. The Colon later featured Mexican movies.

NOVEMBER 3: A great road race takes place between El Paso and Phoenix. There was practically no pavement, and Hugh B. Miller of Phoenix won with an average speed of 41.9 miles per hour. During this race, John T. Hutchings of Alamogordo was shot in the back of the head and killed by a mental patient who claimed he was target practicing. The mechanic for Hutchings, who rode along, was Oliver Lee, famous Dog Canyon rancher. Two El Pasoans, driver S. O. Bottorff and his mechanic, Lloyd Brown, were killed in an accident near Vail, which was close to Tucson.

NOVEMBER 5: Father Carlos Pinto, the Catholic Apostle of El Paso, dies. Burial was in Concordia Cemetery.

NOVEMBER 7: The El Paso Symphony Orchestra gave its first concert in Liberty Hall. The Hall remained the home of the Symphony Orchestra until the Civic Center Theater was constructed.

NOVEMBER 15: General Felipe Angeles, an artillery genius fighting for Pancho Villa, is captured by President Venustiano Carranza's forces.

NOVEMBER 17: The Blimp Hangar, later called the Tow Target Hanger, is constructed at Fort Bliss on Camp Owen Beirne. The blimp made occasional flights over El Paso, but it was never assigned to patrol duty as was originally intended.

NOVEMBER 26: General Felipe Angeles is executed by Carranza's army despite protests before and after the execution.

DECEMBER 4: The Five Points Masonic Lodge No. 1137 is chartered.

1920

Mennonite colonists, mostly of Russian and German descent, pour into Chihuahua during this decade. The largest group settled in Chihuahua. Cuauhtemoc, Chihuahua, became a Mennonite commercial center.

Lieutenant Ulrick Bouquet tested the first parachute over Fort Bliss, jumping from 1,500 feet. He plunged head first, counted three, and said later that the "damn parachute nearly snapped my boots off."

The City of El Paso has 77,560 residents, a 98 percent increase since 1910. El Paso County has 101,877, a 94 percent increase.

The book collection of the El Paso Public Library is moved to the courthouse while a second story is added to the library building.

The Hicks-Hayward Clothing Company organizes.

JANUARY 16: 18th Amendment ratified.

JANUARY 16: Female, married, El Paso Public School teachers are notified of pending layoffs. Money is short. Single females are considered family wage earners, whereas married women have working husbands.

FEBRUARY 10: The Sacred Heart Orphanage for dependent girls opens in El Paso.

MARCH: The initiation of freshmen at the School of Mines on St. Patrick's Day begins its tradition. The ceremony was at the Palisades (the Rocks) along the Rio Grande. Afterwards it was held in a mine.

APRIL 24: A forty foot granite shaft is unveiled in the Masonic portion of Concordia Cemetery. This memorial monument was dedicated to Masons who died in action during World War I.

MAY 1: Zach White and C. B. and Horace Stevens donate 11.6 acres of land in the Upper Valley to the Boy Scouts of America.

JUNE 8: Memorial Park is established on the site of the old Federal Smelter.

JUNE 26: Construction starts on William Beaumont General Hospital.

AUGUST 9: Pancho Villa retires to his ranch, "El Canutillo," near Parral, Chihuahua.

SEPTEMBER: The Ysleta Parochial School (now Jesuit Hall) opens.

SEPTEMBER: The El Paso School Board establishes the El Paso Junior College on the top (4th) floor of El Paso High School. For a while the enrollment of the Junior College exceeded that of the School of Mines.

SEPTEMBER 21: The College of the City of El Paso closes its doors and merges with the State School of Mines and Metallurgy.

OCTOBER: Mansour Farah opens a manufacturing plant in El Paso. The Farah empire has started.

OCTOBER 6: Scenic Drive formally opens, although incomplete.

1921

Ciudad Juarez has 19,457 residents, an 83 percent increase since 1910. The First Cavalry Division is activated at Fort Bliss.

The home of the late Dr. Francis G. Gallagher on the southwest corner of Arizona and North Stanton was purchased and used as a home for nurses in training.

The El Paso Tennis Club is organized.

The Rose Gregory Houchen Settlement establishes a clinic in tenement style buildings.

The Point on Scenic Drive. The road was dirt and the drive still hazardous, but El Pasoans in convoy were willing to take the chance. (Aultman Collection. El Paso Public Library)

JANUARY 1: Burt Orndorff, president of the Sheldon Hotel Company, described 1920 as the best year ever for tourism in El Paso. The hotels were packed with conventions. Orndorff freely acknowledged, however, that much of this convention activity stemmed from the proximity of Juarez watering holes.

JANUARY 26: El Paso appoints its first city water board to survey water possibilities in the El Paso Southwest. When that survey (known as the Lippincott Report) was completed, the board disbanded.

SPRING: With a new El Paso Public School Board in power, married female teachers are again employed.

MARCH 4: West Texas is placed on Central Standard Time. However, El Paso ignored it and continued on, as it does today, with Mountain Standard Time.

MAY: Due to the lack of a copper market, ASARCO closes for six months.

MAY 11: General Billy Mitchell believed that air power could sink a battleship. So the Army ran bombing tests. Lieutenant Stacy Hinkle, and other Fort Bliss pilots, practiced with 25, 50 and 100 pound bombs. Hinkle and three other pilots left Fort Bliss for Langley Field. In June and July, using aerial bombs, they sank three former German ships—a destroyer, a cruiser and a battleship—belonging to American forces as a result of World War I. That experience changed warfare.

JUNE 14: Police Captain Harry Phoenix and Sergeant Houston are seriously wounded when fired upon by whiskey smugglers.

JUNE 18: Little Phil Alguin, bootlegger, gambler and armed robber, killed Detective John J. Fitzgerald in Los Angeles. Alguin then fled to Juarez. El Paso police officers and war hero Sam Dreben talked a Juarez physician into putting Little Phil under chloroform until the officers could snatch and smuggle him into El Paso. Unfortunately, Alguin awoke, screamed for help, and the police officers went to jail. Mexico then said it was deporting Alguin to Guatemala, but the ship took him to California where he was arrested and sent to prison.

JULY: Frontier Klan No. 11, Knights of the Ku Klux Klan of the City of El Paso, is organized. Crosses burn on Mt. Franklin.

JULY 1: William Beaumont Army General Hospital is opened on 120 acres once used as a Fort Bliss firing range. The hospital principally catered to tuberculars.

SUMMER: Nearly 10,000 motor vehicles travel around the city's 85 miles of paved streets.

AUGUST: The Southern Baptist Sanatorium, formerly a country club, is established.

SEPTEMBER 23: The Klan announces that it will parade through town with its members sheeted and masked. Chief of Police Peyton Edwards and Sheriff Seth Orndorff threaten to jail anyone who participates. The parade is called off.

OCTOBER: Gloria Swanson arrives in El Paso to make a movie entitled, *Her Husband's Trademark*. It wasn't much of a movie, but it played at the Palace Theater on March 26, 1922.

OCTOBER 7: The Women's Pioneer Association is formed.

OCTOBER 21: A cornerstone is laid for the Scottish Rite Cathedral at its new location at the corner of Missouri, Santa Fe and Upson streets. The Scottish Rite Temple was built by R. E. McKee. Its two stone lions out front were the largest ever carved from one stone.

NOVEMBER 4: The aggregate worth of Ku Klux Klan members in El Paso is estimated at $16 million dollars.

NOVEMBER 26: The Pan-American Round Table is organized in El Paso. It is the third such organization in Texas.

1922

The present Highway 54 is laid out between El Paso and Alamogordo, New Mexico. The previous road was dirt and lay alongside the railroad tracks. It was the Newman Road.

A 10th floor ballroom is placed on the Paso del Norte Hotel, originally a nine-story building.

The McKelligon Canyon Road is built by prison labor.

JANUARY 7: The El Paso Country Club, having moved from near Fort Bliss, reopens in the upper valley.

FEBRUARY: The B'Nai Brith, a national Jewish organization, becomes the first known national organization to hold a convention in El Paso. This was also the first national meeting of B'Nai Brith.

FEBRUARY 24: El Paso Masonic Lodge No. 130 announces that it will purchase the old Rolston Hospital property at Five Points and turn it into a Masonic Hospital.

MARCH 10: One thousand Klansmen in white hoods and robes initiate 300 men during a gathering near modern-day Kern Place. Afterwards, six Klansmen drove to the parking area on Scenic Point where they erected and burned a wooden cross. However, they were frightened away by an armed man parked nearby.

MARCH 22: The Auxiliary of the El Paso County Medical Society is organized.

APRIL: The Ku Klux Klan gains control of El Paso School Board.

EASTER SUNDAY: The first Easter Sunrise Service is held in the El Paso High School Stadium.

MAY 8: The El Paso School Board changes school names to honor Texas heroes: Manhattan Heights School became Crockett. Highland Park School became Fannin. Grandview School became Rusk.

El Paso High School is renamed Sam Houston High School. New schools under construction became Austin, Bowie, and Burleson.

MAY 20: Fifteen prohibition agents, firing from behind sand bag emplacements, rout a gang of smugglers crossing from Juarez to the foot of Eighth Street.

JUNE 2: Ben Jenkins, an El Paso aviator in World War I, is killed when his JN-4 plane crashes on Mount Franklin.

SEPTEMBER: The first unit for Bowie Grammar School opens at Cotton and 7th Street. A second unit opened in 1925.

SEPTEMBER 12: The town of Newman on the Texas/New Mexico state line is filed for subdivision.

OCTOBER 27: W. H. Fryer, a fiery lawyer and Catholic layman, files a petition in 65th District Court which names four democratic nominees in the November elections as swearing allegiance to the Invisible Empire (Ku Klux Klan). When the case went to court, he dismissed his own action, saying that he just wanted to get their names before the public.

DECEMBER: The Masonic Order of Rainbow Girls is organized in El Paso.

1923

Sam Houston High School resumes its former name of El Paso High School. The name Houston was later given to an elementary school.

A streetcar line is built from downtown to William Beaumont Army General Hospital.

The City Planning Commission is created.

Using Philippians 4:19 as collateral, the Reverend W. Hogg purchased a two story building for an orphanage. After two years, the New Mexico Conference of the Methodist Church, South, assumed control. In 1926, the institution became the El Paso Children's Home.

The road between El Paso and Las Cruces is paved.

FEBRUARY: The Big Kid's Palace Cafe opens in Juarez. The establishment is billed as "the home of aggravatin', syncopatin' jazz."

FEBRUARY 24: The Klan is soundly beaten at the ballot box when R. M. Dudley becomes mayor of El Paso.

FEBRUARY 24: Alzina DeGroff, better known as "Mama D," is appointed by Governor Pat M. Neff to the Board of Directors of Texas Technological College in Lubbock.

APRIL 14: Buena Vista addition starts.

MAY: The El Paso Chamber of Commerce launches a national publicity campaign to lure tourists to El Paso, and to entice them to return as permanent residents. Their slogan was "El Paso: Where Sunshine Spends the Winter."

MAY 13: The diocese dedicates the Community Center, plus its high and grade schools. The schools were placed under the supervision of the Sisters of Loretto at the Foot of the Cross.

MAY 28: The Santa Rita oil well blows in on West Texas property long regarded as worthless. The oil discovery led to the development of the Permian Basin empire, made El Pasoan Haymon Krupp rich, and made the University of Texas the wealthiest school in the United States, next to Harvard, perhaps.

JULY 21: Pancho Villa is assassinated in his touring car near Parral, Chihuahua.

SEPTEMBER 8: An academy for girls is opened in Austin Terrace by the Sisters of Loretto at the Foot of the Cross. The school struggles.

NOVEMBER 21: Company E, 141st Infantry of the National Guard is organized in El Paso. It is the only Spanish-American unit in the United States. Saul O. Paredes formed it. The unit quickly reached its full quota of 83 men, and there was always a waiting list.

1924

Dudley Field, the only adobe stadium in the nation, is built. Although initially called Athletic Park, the name was changed to honor R. M. "Dick" Dudley, a popular El Paso mayor who died in office on May 1, 1925, following abdominal surgery. The stadium was home to baseball for the next 66 years.

The Ysleta Woman's Club builds its first clubhouse.

Kate Moore Brown is the first woman to become a director of the El Paso Chamber of Commerce.

The Christian Brothers Cathedral High School is founded in El Paso.

All elementary schools in El Paso now have kindergartens.

The United States closes all border bridges at 9 P.M. for two years.

JANUARY 7: Rowena Robinson, a young girl in Smeltertown who attended El Paso High School, is brutally raped and murdered. It was the first recorded rape-murder case in El Paso County, and it was never solved.

MARCH 8: The Woman's Auxiliary of The State School of Mines is organized.

MARCH 18: Five bandits attempt to rob the G.H.& S.A. Railroad payroll in the yards at Octavia Street. William H. Meers, one of the guards, was slain, as was a bystander. Several people were wounded, including three of the bandits. Three were captured, but Alejo Minjárez and Manuel Villareal escaped to Mexico where they were unextraditable. One bandit died in jail, but Agapito Rueda and José Carrasco went on trial for murder. Both were convicted. Meanwhile, Jeff Meers, son of the slain officer, began a nine-year vengeance hunt for Minjárez and Villareal.

MAY 28: The United States Border Patrol is officially established. Previous mounted patrol inspectors searched primarily for Oriental entries.

JUNE: The Woman's Department of the Chamber of Commerce is formed.

UNE 2: By Act of Congress, all Indians in the United States are declared citizens, and allowed to vote.

UNE 24: The El Paso Community Chest is established with 16 agencies.

ULY 26: Dr. Lawrence A. Nixon, a black physician, is turned away from the East El Paso Fire Station when he tries to vote. This sets in place a chain of legal challenges that do not end until they reach the United States Supreme Court.

EPTEMBER 20: Around-the-World flyers arrive in El Paso.

NOVEMBER 1: The Southern Pacific Company purchases the El Paso and Northeastern Railroad.

NOVEMBER 5: Anson Mills dies in Washington, D.C. He is buried in Arlington National Cemetery.

NOVEMBER 11: Construction begins on a modern concrete international bridge at the foot of Stanton Street.

1925

Southwestern General Hospital opens as a sanatorium.

Congressional appropriations provide for the creation of Biggs Field, Castner Range, and more assistance for William Beaumont Hospital. The first great expansion of Fort Bliss has started.

The El Paso Electric Railway Company changes its name to the El Paso Electric Company. It is also authorized to do business in New Mexico.

ANUARY 5: The Fort Bliss Air Terminal is named Biggs Field in honor of El Pasoan James Biggs who was killed in an airplane accident in France during World War I.

UNE 29: El Paso National Bank organizes. The first day deposits amount to $1,226,719.

SEPTEMBER: The El Paso Vocational School, the first of its kind in Texas, is built and opened at North Oregon and West Rio Grande streets.

SEPTEMBER: The Rio Grande overflows. Smeltertown is abandoned, as is South El Paso and portions of Ascarate.

SEPTEMBER 12: Nuns from the Perpetual Adoration of the Blessed Sacrament, founded first in Italy and then stationed in Jalisco, Mexico, are driven from Mexico and take refuge in El Paso, Texas. On this date, they founded a convent at 1001 Upson.

OCTOBER 3: City Council suspends Chief of Police J. D. Reeder because he went to the *El Paso Post* and punched a reporter whom Reeder accused of misquoting him.

NOVEMBER 7: President Plutarco Elías Calles meets with Juarez and El Paso Chamber of Commerce officials regarding Mexican immigration restrictions that prevent many United States tourists from visiting Juarez. The tourist identification card requirements were lifted the following year, and tourists started returning to the border.

DECEMBER 1: Catholic Bishop A. J. Schuler decides to send girls at the Community Center to the Loretto College and Academy, and to use the Community Center for boys. Meanwhile, the Brothers of the Christian Schools in Louisiana sent a staff to El Paso to assume control of the Community Center. The Center was thereafter known as the "Boys' High School," later Cathedral High School.

DECEMBER 5: Fred McClure, circulation manager for the *El Paso Times*, is sentenced to 25 years for the murder of his secretary. She was slain in March 1920 on the new Alamogordo Road (Dyer Street, Highway 54) near William Beaumont Army Hospital. His wife stuck by him, and he was released after a brief period. However, he was slain during an attempted bank holdup in Alto, Texas in 1934.

1926

The local baseball team, the El Paso Colts change their name to the El Paso Giants and move from the Frontier League to the Copper League. The Copper League is better known as the "Outlaw League" since it houses teams and players expelled from organized baseball for consorting with gamblers. While the El Paso Giants were not "outlaws," the City of El Paso was nationally known as a casino of gambling. The league lasted three years.

Harry Bailey acquired the old Fort Selden property, and donated ten acres, where the post was located, to the Doña Ana Historical Society.

Mesa Street is extended into the Country Club area and opened for traffic.

The Sisters of Jesus and Mary open a school in El Paso.

The El Paso Electric Company decides on a slow transition of streetcars to buses.

JANUARY 9: Agapito Rueda is executed at the Huntsville, Texas state penitentiary for his part in the abortive holdup-murders of the Galveston, Harrisburg & San Antonio railroad shops in El Paso on March 18, 1924. José Carrasco was also sentenced to die, but due to errors in his trial, he went back to court again and received a life sentence at Huntsville.

APRIL 10: Jack Dempsey drew a crowd of 8,000 at the Juarez Coliseum where on opening day he knocked out four opponents in a row.

APRIL: El Paso has a drawn-out campaign to close the bridge at 6 P.M. With prohibition in force, and legalized gambling (off and on) already a fact of life in Juarez, for the next 20 years either the Mexican or the Americans are closing, or threatening to close, the international bridges early. As a result, relations between El Paso and Juarez remain chaotic as no one ever really knows whether they can return from Juarez on any particular day.

JUNE 30: The Air Service Group at Fort Bliss is transferred to Kelly Field in San Antonio. Biggs Field is closed and returned to the cavalry.

Downtown El Paso in the 1930s. Old Engine No. 1 is now parked at the
Centennial Museum at UT El Paso. Streetcar heads north on Stanton Street
behind downtown Post Office and Hotel Hussmann, now the Cortez Building.
(Dick Mithoff Collection)

SEPTEMBER: The Orndorff Hotel (later Hussmann and now the Cortez Building) opens.

DECEMBER 29: John W. Parrott and Leon Gemoets, two border patrol officers, stopped a car in the upper valley with three men inside. Gemoets found contraband liquor. One occupant shot Gemoets in the spine, but before collapsing the officer returned seven shots. The driver then shot Parrott in the stomach, but the officer, while firing wildly, grabbed the driver and handcuffed him to the steering wheel before slumping unconscious. Two hours later a motorcycle policeman happened upon two cars blocking the road. He found the two unconscious officers, a dead man in the car, and a petrified driver still chained to the steering wheel. The other occupant fled. Gemoets survived but Parrott died a week later of influenza.

1927

The new B'nai Zion Synagogue is dedicated.
Liberal arts courses are added to the School of Mines.

JANUARY: Waterfill and Frazier Distilling Company of Louisville, Kentucky, moves its equipment and offices to Juarez, and begins manufacturing its famous bourbon whiskey in Mexico.

MARCH 7: The rights of Dr. Lawrence A. Nixon, a black physician, are vindicated at the United States Supreme Court. Unfortunately, Oliver Wendell Holmes, who wrote the decision, concentrated on "equal rights" and not "voting rights." So voting rights for blacks were flouted in Texas for a few more years.

MAY: The Junior College closes its doors.

AUGUST: The Sisters of St. Joseph at Concordia (from Indiana) take over St. Joseph's Sanatorium in El Paso.

AUGUST 16: The Hole-in-the-Wall, a saloon, dance hall and gambling parlor, opens on Cordova Island where the Chamizal National

Memorial is today. The Chamizal Island was a 1,200-acre strip of Mexican soil protruding north of the Rio Grande into El Paso.

SEPTEMBER: Elizabeth Garrett, daughter of famed Sheriff Pat Garrett, composed a song called *El Paso*. The song was published and copyrighted by the Woman's Club of El Paso.

SEPTEMBER: Bowie Grammar School becomes Bowie High School.

SEPTEMBER: Dr. Lucinda deLeftwich Templin takes over the El Paso School for Girls (Radford). She gives the institution a national reputation as one of the best, fully-accredited boarding schools in the Southwest.

SEPTEMBER 2: Nuns from the Monastery of Perpetual Adoration leave 1001 Upson Street and move to 1401 Magoffin Avenue.

SEPTEMBER 23: The board of directors at the El Paso Chamber of Commerce pass a resolution asking Washington to close the international bridge at 6 P.M. for as long as open gambling exists in Juarez. When open gambling ceases, the directors want the bridge closed at midnight. The town split on the issue, and the resolution came to naught.

SEPTEMBER 16: Ten aviators meet on the fifth floor of the Times-Herald building at 200 West San Francisco Street, and form the El Paso Aero Club. The main objective is to acquire a municipal airport for El Paso.

SEPTEMBER 24: Charles Lindbergh and the *Spirit of St. Louis* visit El Paso during a United States tour. The airplane is housed in the balloon hangar.

SEPTEMBER 24: Castner Range is acquired by Fort Bliss.

WINTER: A tradition ends as the last Mask Dance is performed by the Tiguas. Miguel Pedraza, Sr. and Salvador Granillo impersonate their ancestors. Originally, after the ceremony, the impersonators used their heads to break ice in the Rio Grande, a vital part of the ceremony. The river became polluted and often dry, and the dance was discontinued.

DECEMBER 5: The United States Supreme Court declared the 1850 Rio Grande boundary between New Mexico and Texas was a fixed boundary and did not change simply because the river changed channels. The court supported Texas, and ordered the original bed surveyed and marked.

1928

S. G. Gonzales opens the Central Cafe, later known as the Cafe del Camino Real. Within a decade the building became the Del Camino Motel, the second largest motel in the United States.

JANUARY 1: The parish of St. Ignatius Church is assigned by the Diocese to exiled Mexican Jesuits.

JANUARY 5: Dr. R. A. Wilson, former city health officer, asks to be reinstated to the position he held until January 1. When the request was denied, Wilson drew a revolver and fired at Mrs. Louise McKeon, the chief city nurse. Wilson missed, then committed suicide.

FEBRUARY 26: Famous Juarez Tivoli Gardens reopen.

JUNE 27: Mayor Jimmy Walker of New York visits El Paso. He and city officials spend the day dining in Juarez. They retire to a cabaret called the Bucket of Blood on 16th of September Street where Walker and a hostess danced the Black Bottom.

JULY: The Standard Oil (now Chevron Oil) refinery begins operation.

JULY 1: Planning begins for Rim Road development. Stormsville is destroyed and the church, Nuestra Senora de la Luz, is torn down. The residents have until today to evacuate. Over 400 people live in Stormsville. There is no water, no phones, no electricity, no gas, four toilets and no sewers.

JULY 17: Alvaro Obregón is elected president of Mexico, but he is assassinated in Mexico City before he can take office.

AUGUST 22: Restlawn Cemetery on Dyer Street has filed for subdivision.

SEPTEMBER: A pipeline route is surveyed 204 miles from Jal, New Mexico, to El Paso. Texas. It will be the first natural gas pipeline to enter El Paso.

SEPTEMBER 8: Mayor R. E. Thomason dedicates the El Paso municipal airport on 260 acres of city-donated scrub land located north of Fred Wilson Road on the east side of the municipal (Valdespino) Golf Course, later the Fort Bliss Golf Course. Over 10,000 El Pasoans turn out for the ceremony. So did the National Air Derby and 18 Curtiss-Falcon A-13 Army planes from Kelly Field in San Antonio. Amelia Earhart flew in the next day, and became the first woman to land at the El Paso Municipal Airport.

OCTOBER 8: Oil speculators Paul Kayser and H. G. Frost form the El Paso Gas Utilities and obtain a franchise to construct and maintain pipelines.

NOVEMBER 8: Scenic Airways of Chicago signs a contract to build a hangar, maintenance shops and offices at the municipal airport. A flying school and air taxi services are probable.

NOVEMBER 10: Major Ignacio Dosamontes, a Mexican federal narcotics agent on special assignment for the Mexican Secret Service, is shot dead on the steps of the El Paso police station. Dosamontes had been sent to the border to clean up the narcotics traffic in Juarez, only to learn that the Juarez police were part of the problem. Dosamontes was killed by El Paso Police Detective Juan Escontrías, a close friend of the Juarez police department. An El Paso jury found Escontrías "guilty of murder with malice aforethought." Judge W. D. Howe sentenced him to five years in prison. The detective returned to El Paso in seven months.

1929

Between 1929 and 1935, due primarily to the Great Depression, a half-million persons of Mexican origin are returned to Mexico as repatriados *(repatriates) and* deportados *(deportees).*

The city appoints its second water board. This time the board becomes a permanent fixture.

The El Paso Electric Company builds the Rio Grande Power Plant in the Upper Valley.

Nichols Copper Company, soon to be Phelps-Dodge Refining Corporation, begins operation on North Loop Road.

Construction starts on the Bassett Tower.

Cathedral High School, limited to Catholic boys, grades 9-12, opens.

Alex Gonzales builds and privately owns the Zaragosa bridge at Ysleta.

JANUARY 17: The Southern Union Gas Company is incorporated. The "Union" refers to the union of a number of companies operating in the South and Southwest.

FEBRUARY 1: The *El Paso Times* and the *El Paso Herald* have been sold to Dorrance D. Roderick and Lindsay Nunn.

FEBRUARY 4: Standard Air Lines, headquartered at the municipal airport, carries three passengers from El Paso to Los Angeles and thus becomes the first air passenger service.

MARCH 3: The Escobar Revolution starts in Mexico although most of the fighting takes place in Juarez.

MARCH 8: Rebels again take Juarez. The Federals hide behind the river bank so that bullets zip over their heads and enter El Paso. The Federal garrison surrendered not to the Rebels but to the Americans. The generals and their staff, over 300 troops, families, baggage, horses and in some cases motor cars, cross the Santa Fe Street Bridge into El Paso, check in with immigration and customs, and then board trucks for transportation to Fort Bliss. Within a brief time, all had been repatriated by the Southern Pacific into Sonora, which was still Federal country.

APRIL 9: The Sheldon Hotel burns. A landmark is gone.

APRIL 9: The Mexican Rebels retreat from Juarez.

MAY 31: José Marin shot dead an entire law firm today. He killed
El Paso attorneys Frank J. Lyons and Herbert D. Oppenheimer as
they worked in their offices in the First National. Marin claimed
self defense, then committed suicide in his cell.

JUNE 18: Natural gas makes its first entrance into the city as the El Paso
Natural Gas Company brings it by pipeline from Jal, New Mexico.
Mayor R. E. Thomason ignited a giant flare that flamed sixty feet
into the night sky.

AUGUST 22: The Tri-State Broadcasting Company's KTSM
(for Tri-State Music) goes on the air from the basement of the
Tri-State Music Company on El Paso Street. Karl Wyler,
a car insurance salesman, chucked his job and went to work as
an announcer. At night he was "Karl the Kowhand," his resonant
voice wailing, "Who's Gonna Wash Your Laundry When the
Chinamen Go to War."

AUGUST 28: The Grey Friars, a branch of the First Order of
Franciscans, come to the diocese of El Paso.

AUGUST 26: Sunrise Acres is filed for subdivision.

SEPTEMBER: Ysleta High School opens.

OCTOBER 5: Standard Air Lines wants its own airport. It builds
on 640 acres of unimproved desert alongside the Carlsbad
Highway, six miles from downtown El Paso. It is this airport,
and not the municipal airport, that will evolve into the El Paso
International Airport.

OCTOBER 24: The Stock Market crashes.

NOVEMBER 9: The School of Mines has its first homecoming. The
Miners played the Aggies of New Mexico A&M, and won 8 to 0.

The whole town turns out to watch the death of a landmark, the Sheldon Hotel. During the Mexican Revolution it housed what passed for the Mexican and American CIA, soldiers of fortune, scoundrels, and war correspondents from all over the globe. The Hilton (Plaza) Hotel replaced it. (Aultman Collection. El Paso Public Library)

Standard Airlines announces the opening of its airport that will usher in what is today the El Paso International Airport. (Aultman Collection. El Paso Public Library)

DECEMBER 28: Mary E. Peyton files for divorce against J. C. Peyton, founder and president of Peyton Packing Company. Before it ends, the case becomes one of the most sensational in El Paso's history.

1930

The City of El Paso has 102,421 residents a 32 percent increase since 1920. El Paso County has 131,597, a 29 percent increase. Ciudad Juarez has 39,669, a 104 percent increase.

City health officer Dr. P. R. Outlaw says El Paso has the highest infant mortality rate of any city in the United States.

The Bassett Tower is completed. During an era when it was fashionable to ignore the back side of a structure, the Bassett Tower was designed as a completely finished building.

The International Museum of Art (now El Paso Museum of Art) is organized.

MARCH 13: Clyde W. Tombaugh, an assistant at the Lowell Observatory, discovers the planet Pluto. The planet was named for the Greek god of the lower world. Tombaugh spent most of his later career as a New Mexico State University professor at Las Cruces, and a scientist at White Sands Missile Range.

APRIL 5: Zach White donates land in the upper valley, and Zach White School is built.

MAY 13: El Pasoan James McNary is informed that Congress will likely confirm his nomination as comptroller of the currency. He didn't get it.

JUNE 18: Jeff Meers shot and killed Antonio Visconti, a Juarez bartender, in the Owl Saloon in Juarez. Meers believed Visconti was one of the bandits who murdered his father during a railroad payroll holdup on March 18, 1924. Meers goes to prison in Chihuahua City.

SEPTEMBER 11: H. Ponsford & Sons build the Showplace of the Southwest, the Plaza Theater. The Plaza opened with *Follow*

Through, starring Buddy Rogers and Nancy Carroll. The lobby, halls and stairs were ornate and furnished with art objects including a carved horse and rider, an oil painting of a Spanish woman and a bronze statue. "Homemade" clouds floated across the ceiling. The Wurlitzer Company installed a pipe organ costing $60,000. It rose out of the orchestra pit to stage level.

SEPTEMBER: Stephen F. Austin High School opens. This is one of the most modern schools in Texas.

OCTOBER 15: The first air mail flight reaches El Paso with 17,000 letters and cards weighing 246 pounds. Over 15,000 El Pasoans turn out to celebrate Air Mail Day. One plane was christened "Miss El Paso," and a bottle of Rio Grande water was broken across its nose.

OCTOBER 23: The Site for La Tuna prison is selected. It will hold 500 prisoners, and will be the first federal short-term prison ever built. Construction will take place on 635 acres.

NOVEMBER 5: The Hilton Hotel (now the Plaza) formally opens. It cost a million dollars, was designed by Trost and Trost and built by R. E. McKee. Fifteen thousand people attended the grand opening.

1931

As an economy measure, El Paso Public School teachers who are female and married will have their salaries cut 15 percent.
Mexico abandons the gold standard.

JANUARY: The Hole-in-the-Wall saloon on Cordova is closed. From 1929 to 1931, there had been 17 gunfights between inspectors and smugglers, resulting in one inspector and eight smugglers dead. Thirty people received serious wounds.

JANUARY: A free venereal disease clinic is established on South El Paso Street.

The Texaco service station at Grant and Elm streets. Houston Elementary School is across the street. The service station structure remains intact into modern times. (Darst-IrelandPhotography)

FEBRUARY: El Paso Natural Gas starts constructing a pipeline west from El Paso to Bisbee and Douglas, Arizona, as well as Cananea, Sonora.

APRIL 2: The *Amarillo News and Globe* has taken control of the *El Paso Herald* and the *El Paso Times*. The *El Paso Herald* is then sold to Scripps Howard and merged with the *El Paso Post* to become the *El Paso Herald-Post*. Then the *Times* is resold to Dorrance Roderick, who becomes owner and publisher.

APRIL 20: The El Paso Symphony Orchestra becomes a permanent organization.

MAY 18: The El Paso School for Girls becomes the Radford School for Girls.

MAY 23: The El Paso Children's Home becomes the Southwestern Children's Home.

MAY 24: The Church of Jesus Christ of Latter Day Saints (Mormon Church) is dedicated at Douglas and Alta streets.

JUNE 24: The "Bonus Army" of 800 men, on their way from Southern California by train to Washington, DC, spent a brief period in El Paso. Although city authorities were nervous, the Army caused no trouble.

JULY 31: Albert Bacon Fall leaves for prison. He traveled in an ambulance and his cell was a prison hospital.

SEPTEMBER: The School of Mines becomes a four-year college, and for the first time has a president, John G. Barry, instead of a dean.

SEPTEMBER 4: The Great Depression hits El Paso. James McNary's First National Bank goes under, and it is the largest bank in the city.

OCTOBER: The first livestock show in modern times gets underway in El Paso. It was called the Southwestern Baby Beef Show.

1932

The La Tuna Federal Prison is built in the Upper Valley on the site of La Tuna (present-day Anthony).

The Southern Pacific starts using air-conditioned dining cars, and quickly extends the air conditioning to lounge cars as well as sleepers.

As a further economy measure, the salaries of married female school teachers will be reduced to that of substitutes.

MARCH 6: President Franklin D. Roosevelt declares a Bank Holiday, and banks close all over the nation.

MARCH 14: Surviving banks in El Paso reopen.

JULY 17: The Claretian Fathers come to El Paso, and assume charge of the Guardian Angel Parish on Frutas Street. They replace the exiled Jesuits who arrived in January 1928.

FALL: W. G. Walz, the RCA Victor distributor, purchases KTSM radio and hires Karl Wyler to operate it. The station moves to the top floor of the Paso del Norte Hotel.

1933

As an experiment, 300 acres of bosque in the Mesilla Valley are put under irrigation and planted with pecan trees. Stahman Farms is born.

The White Sands of New Mexico becomes a national monument.

The W. R. Weaver Company opens shop in El Paso, and within a brief time is manufacturing 90 percent of all the rifle scopes made in this country.

The El Paso Boys Club opens under leadership of Harry A. Markham. It started in a Baptist Church at St. Vrain and Magoffin, then went to Lydia Patterson, then to Aoy School, and finally to Florence and Sixth streets. The club's original purpose was to rehabilitate boys from the reform schools, but the emphasis gradually shifted to programs for the prevention of delinquency.

JANUARY: The El Paso Police Department gets its first shortwave radio, as well as the first police radio patrol car.

FEBRUARY 1: The United States and Mexico approve the Rio Grande Rectification Treaty. The plan calls for a $6 million straightening of the Rio Grande channel from El Paso 90 miles downstream. This will permit the clearing of bosque and the creation of lower valley towns and farmlands. The river will be shortened from 155.2 miles to 85.6 miles.

FEBRUARY 19: Scenic Drive is reopened following the paving.

APRIL: The government starts stockpiling gold and silver.

APRIL 12: Beer sales are again legal in El Paso.

APRIL 20: Jeff Meers, in prison in Chihuahua City for killing the wrong man, is swapped at 3:30 in the morning for José Carrasco. The exchange (arranged by El Paso Sheriff Chris Fox) takes place between Texas and Mexican authorities in the middle of the Santa Fe Street Bridge. José Carrasco had been part of a band of outlaws who attempted to rob the Galveston, Harrisburg & San Antonio railroad shops, during which a guard, William Meers (father of Jeff), was slain.

MAY: Many married female teachers are dropped from the school system. Others resign.

NOVEMBER 3: Miner's Stadium is named Kidd Field in honor of Dean John W. Kidd.

NOVEMBER 7: Ground is broken for Harry Mitchell's Brewery.

DECEMBER 5: Prohibition ends.

1934

Eugene Cunningham writes Triggernometry: A Gallery of Gunfighters *while living in El Paso.*

*The El Paso School Board, for the first time, agrees not to discriminate
against married, female teachers. Merit will be the only criteria.*

*The U.S. Immigration and Naturalization Service starts rounding up
and deporting* Juarenses *who used local crossing cards to work in El
Paso. (A local crossing card permits one to visit or shop, but not work.)*

*People of Mexican origin are now considered "white" by the Bureau of
Census and other government organizations. In times past they had
frequently been labeled "foreigners" in spite of several generations of life
in the United States. Texas frequently described them as "nonwhites,"
and the Texas attorney general had once ruled that this minority class
should be recorded as "black," although he later changed it to "brown."*

JANUARY 1: Liquor sales reopen in El Paso. (Beer sales started
last April.)

JANUARY 20: The recently organized Family Welfare Association
holds its first meeting.

FEBRUARY 13: A 12-foot-high wooden Cross is erected on
Rodadero Peak (Mt. Cristo Rey), as thousands of people trek
up the mountain.

MARCH 24: An iron Cross, fashioned by ASARCO employees,
replaces the wooden Cross on Mt. Cristo Rey.

APRIL 10: Bishop Anthony J. Schuler decrees that the Catholic Boys'
High School will hereafter be known as the Boys Cathedral
High School. The word "Boys" is gradually dropped in
popular parlance.

APRIL 29: White Sands National Monument in southern New Mexico
is opened to the public. About 4,000 people attend dedication
ceremonies.

Flappers join male customers in saloon. The women's styles would indicate a date of the late 1920s or early 1930s. Note slot machines on right. (Aultman Collection. El Paso Public Library)

JUNE 27: Eugene Manlove Rhodes, the Bard of the Tularosa, dies and is buried at Rhodes Pass in the San Andres Mountains. A huge red boulder is his tombstone.

JULY 23: John Dillinger spent an hour at Air Mail Field (Municipal Airport) in El Paso. He had just left Tucson and was being taken to Indiana. Dillinger complained that he wanted to go to Wisconsin because it had no death penalty.

JULY 29: Tigua Indians at Ysleta are permitted to vote without a poll tax.

DECEMBER 3: The City Water Board advises that some of the city wells are saline and unfit for further use.

1935

The Civil Service Commission will govern all city employees including police and firemen.

The American Folklore and Ethnological Society reports that the Tiguas no longer exist.

JANUARY 1: The first Sun Bowl football game is played in the El Paso High School stadium. The El Paso Kiwanis brought a Ranger, Texas, high school team and matched it against a composite of El Paso high school players. El Paso won.

MARCH 24: Fire severely damages the San Elizario Church. The beams are replaced by pressed tin.

APRIL 27: Social Security laws go into effect.

MAY: Bowie School began as a grammar school, but as it relieved overcrowding from Aoy and Alamo, the grades kept increasing until this year Bowie graduated its first high school class, the students having gone through all grades.

1936

JANUARY 1: The first Sun Carnival Pageant winds through the business section of downtown. New Mexico State College and Hardin-Simmons fought to a 14-14 tie in the second Sun Bowl game.

MARCH 1: Bishop Anthony Schuler blesses fourteen stations of the Cross leading to the peak of Rodadero Mountain (Mt. Cristo Rey).

MARCH 16: Fort Bliss acquires another 4,000 acres, doubling the size of the post to 9,000 acres. The post had requested 50,000 acres.

MAY 12: The Santa Fe Railroad took delivery of the Super Chief, the first diesel locomotive.

JUNE: The Canalization Project straightens the Rio Grande channel from El Paso north to Caballo Dam in New Mexico.

JUNE 12: The Tiguas make President Franklin D. Roosevelt an "Honorary Chief" during the Dallas Centennial Exposition in the Cotton Bowl. Mrs. Roosevelt becomes an "Honorary Squaw."

JULY 15: Continental Airlines organizes at El Paso.

AUGUST 30: The Newspaper Printing Corporation is formed. The printing, sale, advertising and distribution of both El Paso newspapers will be handled through the corporation. Editorial departments will remain separate. The move strengthens the *Times* as well as the *Herald-Post*.

SEPTEMBER 13: The first night baseball game is played at Dudley Field.

SEPTEMBER 16: Standard Air Lines sells its 640 acre airport to the city. Air Mail Field, the municipal airport, transfers there and the future El Paso International Airport is assured.

Even in the 1930s, El Pasoans realized they had something going for them in terms of history, views, two cultures, and an international theme. (Aultman Collection. El Paso Public Library)

NOVEMBER 11: Armistice Day. Fort Bliss National Cemetery dedicated.

NOVEMBER 13: The El Paso Sheriff's Posse organizes. It is the second such organization in the country.

NOVEMBER 30: The old Federal Courthouse will be razed next year at Oregon and Mills to make way for a Kress store.

DECEMBER 27: R. E. McKee finishes the new United States Courthouse on San Antonio Street.

1937

The El Paso Pioneer Society donates 12 acres of land in the Upper Valley to the Girl Scouts of America.

The clinic at the Rose Gregory Houchen Settlement gives way to the Newark Hospital and Freeman Clinic.

Under the supervision of Albert Horwitz, the Hortex Manufacturing Company begins operations on South Oregon Street. Billy the Kid becomes a trade name for jeans.

JANUARY 21: El Paso Masonic Lodge No. 130 is the largest in Texas.

JANUARY: A new Doña Ana County, New Mexico, courthouse is built in Las Cruces.

JANUARY 25: Homan Sanatorium becomes Southwestern General Hospital.

FEBRUARY: A United States Geological Survey reports that El Paso is running out of water on the mesa. The city should start negotiations to secure supplies from the Rio Grande.

MARCH: The First Cavalry at Fort Bliss sponsors a 150-mile endurance horse race into New Mexico. Lieutenant Charles P. Walker won in 20 hours, 17 minutes and 20 seconds. He averaged 7.42 miles per hour.

MARCH: This is the last year for the city's controlled red-light district.

MARCH: The city establishes its first Housing Authority.

APRIL 23: The Centennial Museum at the College of Mines opens.

JULY: A campaign is launched to finance and build the Monastery of Perpetual Adoration, better known perhaps as The Shrine to Christ the King at 145 North Cotton Street.

JULY 7: The American Smelting and Refining Company (ASARCO) gives the College of Mines 150 acres.

SEPTEMBER 17: The Right Reverend A. J. Schuler dedicates Our Lady of Guadalupe Church at 2709 Alabama Street.

OCTOBER 8: Bishop Anthony Schuler informs Father Lourdes F. Costa, pastor of the Smeltertown Church, that the Diocese will support the Sierra de Cristo Rey project. However, instead of just a Cross, the monument will include Christ upon that Cross.

OCTOBER 31: Urbici Soler is retained by the El Paso Diocese to sculpt the statue for Mt. Cristo Rey. A fund raising campaign starts.

NOVEMBER 9: The Cotton Estate goes to the College of Mines. Frank B. Cotton lived in Boston but owned land in El Paso. Upon his death in 1907, the property was sold and the proceeds granted to the school by virtue of an endowment.

NOVEMBER 24: Henry Lorenz and Harry Dwyer, two boys in their twenties, board a Southern Pacific train leaving El Paso. That night in New Mexico, they rob the passengers and kill one man. Both are captured. It is the last Wild West train robbery.

1938

The Baptist Spanish Publishing House and Seminary occupies the old Southern Baptist Sanatorium.

Mexico expropriates American oil holdings. The Mexican peso, long valued at two pesos for one dollar drops to more than five to a dollar by 1940. Inflation ravages the country, especially along the border.

MARCH 30: Mrs. Hazel Frome and her unmarried daughter, Nancy, stepped out of the Hotel Cortez and into their new Packard and headed east toward North Carolina. Their car and bodies were found four days later near Van Horn, Texas, the two women being the victims of a bestial slaying. The murder was one of the Southwest's most sensational and revolting, but it was never solved.

MARCH 30: KTSM becomes an affiliate of NBC. The first national "live" radio comes to El Paso.

JUNE 12: Center Chapel One at Fort Bliss is dedicated. The old South Theater of the 7th Cavalry has been converted over for the 1st Cavalry Division.

SEPTEMBER 23: In the future, Tigua Indians must pay a poll tax to vote.

1939

La Posta in Mesilla, New Mexico, becomes a restaurant.

FEBRUARY: The Roosevelt Day Nursery for black children is organized. In 1946, it becomes the McCall Day Nursery.

APRIL 6: The city abolishes the police vice squad.

AUGUST 23: The first no-hitter is played at Dudley Field. The Albuquerque Cardinals thumped the El Paso Texans 10 to 0.

OCTOBER 29: The 42.5 foot monument of Christ reigning from the
Cross (from Mt. Cristo Rey) is completed for the first annual
pilgrimage for the Feast of Christ the King.

1940

*The City of El Paso has 96,810 residents, a five percent drop from 1930.
El Paso County has 131,067, a less than one percent drop from 1930.
Ciudad Juarez has 48,881, a 23 percent increase. During this decade,
Chihuahuita in particular will be overrun by pachuco gangs, sometimes
called "boogies" or "zoot-suiters." They roamed the streets armed with
chains that hung from the belt to the pocket in a long loop.*

*Until this year, most Mexican-Americans living in El Paso were
born in Mexico.*

El Paso's second radio station, KROD, goes on the air.

*The Alamito Project opens with 349 units, a neighborhood park and a
branch library. Average rent is $23 a month.*

*Most trolley lines have been converted to busses with the exception of
Fort Bliss, Washington Park and Juarez.*

*Mrs. W. W. Turney donates her family home at 1211 Montana Avenue
to the City of El Paso. The home will become the El Paso Museum of Art
in 1959.*

FEBRUARY 17: Southwest Air Rangers organize.

FEBRUARY 13: The Mexican government is fencing Cordova Island,
a boot-shaped wedge of land that belongs to Mexico. There will be
four miles of fence, six feet high on concrete posts.

MARCH: Should the name of Rodadero Mountain be changed?
Ballots containing six possibilities are circulated among residents
of Smeltertown and Anapra. The landslide vote favored Sierra de
Cristo Rey (the Mountain of Christ the King).

MAY 19: The Christian Science Church moves to Elm and
San Diego streets.

JUNE: Fort Bliss begins acquisitions for 52,000 additional acres.
Four people own 40,000 acres, but the other 12,000 are owned
by 2,000 people.

AUGUST: The Tenderloin is reorganized by the city under tough new
rules. Seven brothels reopen: the Mansion House at 306 West
Overland, the Cozy Rooms at 421 South El Paso, the Elite Hotel at
410 South El Paso, the Ramona Hotel at 417 South El Paso, the
Popular Rooms at 408 South El Paso, Betty Austin's Topeka Rooms
at 212 South Oregon, and the Stag Hotel at 401 South El Paso.

SEPTEMBER: The new Bowie High School opens. Trost and Trost
were the architects, but Bowie was not their finest hour. The
bathrooms had plumbing but dirt floors. The walls were partly
insulated with corncobs.

OCTOBER 17: A Pontifical High Mass celebrates Bishop Anthony
Schuler's 25th anniversary in office. High ranking church officials
attend, and thousands of faithful gather on Mt. Cristo Rey.
Monsignor Fulton J. Sheen delivered the sermon in English.

NOVEMBER 25: El Paso National Guard units are called into service.

DECEMBER: El Paso Electric begins its Star on the Mountain
Christmas tradition. The star originally measured 50 feet by 50 feet,
but eventually it grew to 459 feet by 300 feet. By 1993 it had
459 100-watt bulbs.

1941

*Construction begins on the Juarez Cathedral alongside Our Lady of
Guadalupe Mission in Juarez.*
El Paso enacts an ordinance banning fireworks in the city.
Monte Montana rides his horse into the Paso del Norte Hotel grand

ballroom during breakfast with the Sheriff's Posse. He stood on his saddle and performed trick roping.

ANUARY 22: The Lincoln Theater, with a capacity for 200, becomes the first theater for black people.

EBRUARY 20: The Fort Bliss movie theater opens on Dyer Street.

PRIL 3: The Tays Housing Project opens with 311 units. They were quickly rented.

PRIL 7: El Paso holds its first blackout.

UMMER: Due to heavy rains, artificial lakes surround many Upper Valley homes.

JNE: The College of Mines offers Master of Art degrees.

EPTEMBER 1: The United States Public Health Service notifies all military oriented cities that any community allowing zones of prostitution within ten miles of the base will no longer receive federal health funds.

EPTEMBER 9: A jury has been selected with as many blacks as white people. This is a first for El Paso.

ECEMBER 7: The Japanese attack Pearl Harbor. World War II starts for the United States. Juarez is immediately placed off limits to all soldiers.

1942

Fort Bliss now contains over 100,000 acres, with another 364,000 acres under lease.

EBRUARY 28: The War Department lifts its restrictions about military personnel in Juarez. But soldiers must submit to "pro treatments" upon reentering the country.

MARCH 19: St. Joseph's Maternity Hospital is dedicated.

APRIL 1: Dr. Wolfgang Ebell, naturalized in El Paso in 1939, has his citizenship revoked in El Paso after allegations surface that he is a German spy. He and several others are tried in Hartford, Connecticut, where Ebell pleads guilty of espionage and is sentenced to seven years.

APRIL 9: General Wainwright surrenders to the Japanese. The Bataan Death March commences, and New Mexico soldiers are a large part of it.

MAY 30: The El Paso County Coliseum is turned over to Commissioners Court by R. E. McKee, contractor. The facility was constructed primarily as a livestock and rodeo showplace.

JUNE 30: El Paso closes its Tenderloin District in compliance with the United States Public Health Service.

AUGUST: The first Bracero program goes into effect.

1943

The Chinese Exclusion Act is repealed. El Paso Chinese can now bring wives and children from China.

FEBRUARY: The First Cavalry Division is assigned to the Pacific.

FEBRUARY 15: Golden Glove exhibitions begin in El Paso at Fort Bliss.

JUNE: The Fort Bliss cavalry dismounts and becomes mechanized.

AUGUST: A thousand Italian prisoners-of-war arrive in El Paso from Lordsburg. They are housed in the El Paso Coliseum for six months, and spent most of their time picking cotton on Lower Valley farms. They drew the prevailing wage of $1.50 per hundred pounds of short staple cotton. German POW's join them a year later.

SEPTEMBER 21: The bloody battle of Salerno, Italy, ends. El Paso soldiers have proven their mettle. Only the mud and mountains remain to be overcome by Texas troops during a brutal winter campaign.

OCTOBER 24: By a vote of 2,475 to 651, El Pasoans have rejected the city's ambitions for purchasing the El Paso Electric Company.

1944

Dr. Lawrence Nixon, a black physician, in a landmark case, wins the right to vote in the El Paso Democratic primary.

JANUARY 20: El Paso soldiers of companies E and H (36th Division, better known as the Texas Division) fight their way across the Rapido River in Italy.

JANUARY 26: Southern Union Gas acquires the Lone Star Gas Company distribution facilities and moves into El Paso.

MARCH: A B-24 bomber takes off from Biggs Army Air Field and crashes in the Franklin Mountains Red Rock Canyon. No survivors.

AUGUST 3: An Antiaircraft Artillery School arrives at Fort Bliss from North Carolina.

1945

A second branch public library is opened, this one at the Tays Housing Project.

The Masonic Hospital at Five Points is sold to make way for a Sears store.

On a lazy afternoon, neither the alligators nor the viewers are showing much energy in San Jacinto Plaza. (Aultman Collection. El Paso Public Library)

MAY 5: The German Army in Austria surrenders to the Texas 36th Division. One captive is Field Marshal Hermann Goering. Twelve concentration camps are liberated.

MAY 8: The free world celebrates this date as V-E (Victory in Europe) Day.

JUNE 7: The Pleasant View Home for the elderly is established.

JULY 9: White Sands Proving Ground is established.

JULY 16: Fat Man, the world's first atomic bomb, is detonated at Trinity Site, White Sands Proving Ground.

AUGUST 6: The atomic bomb falls on Hiroshima, Japan.

AUGUST 14: World War II ends and San Jacinto Plaza is jammed with joyful people. Gas rationing ends the next day.

SEPTEMBER 26: The Tiny Tim sounding rocket is the first missile launched at White Sands.

1946

The San José del Rio Church in Smeltertown is destroyed by fire.
Following the wartime shutdown of minor leagues, the El Paso Texans join the Mexican National League. The League lasted one year.
The Loretto Shopping Center opens. By comparison it is a small, strip center but a forerunner of things to come.

FEBRUARY 6: The Texas National Guard is released from active military service.

JANUARY 19: A special three-cent commemorative stamp will celebrate the Texas Centennial.

FEBRUARY 24: General Dwight D. Eisenhower visits El Paso. He took a suite in the Hilton Hotel and conferred with dignitaries all day. Between chain smoking, he consumed a large Mexican meal.

APRIL 15: The El Paso Masonic Hospital closes at Five Points. The 65-bed hospital had been unable to expand, and was sold a year earlier.

APRIL 16: Wernher von Braun, German rocket genius, watches as the first V-2 rocket launches from White Sands Proving Ground.

JULY: Fort Bliss becomes the United States Army Anti-Aircraft and Guided Missile Center.

JULY 23: Milagro Acres (Hills) is filed for subdivision.

AUGUST 30: The El Paso Chapter of the National Society of Arts and Letters is organized.

SEPTEMBER: An avalanche of students enroll at the College of Mines as former soldiers attend college on the G.I. Bill of Rights. Vet Village rises on the southwest corner of the campus.

DECEMBER 7: El Paso is considering the annexation of Ascarate.

1947

Biggs Army Air Field officially becomes Biggs Air Force Base, and attached to the Strategic Air Command.
The Fabens Cotton Festival begins.
The El Paso Texans are a farm team for the Boston Red Sox.
Hacienda Heights Addition begins. It is located on an escarpment just above the valley agricultural area. The Heights was developed with government loans for returning World War II veterans.
The area south of William Beaumont Army General Hospital is annexed into the city.

MAY 29: An experimental V-2 rocket fired from White Sands Proving Ground becomes erratic and lands near Juarez, Mexico. Someone had wired a gyroscope backwards.

JULY 14: The Southwest National Bank opens at 305 Mills.

OCTOBER 10: Ysleta votes to incorporate, arguing that the City of El Paso is getting too close.

OCTOBER 17: Parkland filed for subdivision.

NOVEMBER: The Woman's Auxiliary of the El Paso Bar Association is organized.

DECEMBER: The first Bracero Program ends.

DECEMBER 2: Ysleta votes to disincorporate because it has no funds for police service or road repair.

1948

Harry Truman visits El Paso while stumping for president of the United States.
The peso devalues from 4.76 to 8.65 pesos to the dollar.

FEBRUARY: Sunshine Day Nursery organized.

FEBRUARY: Construction begins on Paisano Drive over protests that the city will never need that wide a street. Almost the entire length of the project will be built on condemned land. The street was designed to speed traffic on Highway 80 by routing it around the downtown section.

FEBRUARY: Karl Wyler and KTSM begin their expansion at 801 N. Oregon Street.

FEBRUARY: An El Paso Committee for the Border Project is formed, and the Border Patrol changed the way it handled children who had crossed into El Paso from Juarez to attend school. The children formerly had been held in detention. Under a new policy, they were returned to the Mexican side of the Rio Grande.

FEBRUARY 12: Ashley Classen and Associates issue the Classen Report to City Council. The report recommends a water storage reservoir in the Upper Valley. The dam would hopefully hold 11,800 acre feet of water annually.

FEBRUARY 17: Alamogordo Air Force Base becomes Holloman Air Force Base. The Alamogordo base had been constructed during the 1940s so the British could practice their B-24 bombing runs.

SPRING: The San José de Cristo Rey Church in Smeltertown is rebuilt and dedicated by the Most Reverend Sidney M. Metzger. It replaced the San José del Rio Church which burned in 1946.

SEPTEMBER: Fort Bliss grade schools are now on post. The children had attended El Paso schools, being transported by mule-drawn Daugherty wagons, then streetcars or buses. The teachers are hired, paid and supervised by the El Paso Independent School System.

SEPTEMBER 28: The *Revista Católica* newspaper moves to the late Senator A. B. Fall's house at 1725 Arizona. The residence becomes the Canisius House.

OCTOBER: Large numbers of labor migrants gathered on the Mexican bank of the Rio Grande across from El Paso and awaited entry into Texas. In Texas, cotton growers waited with trucks to transport them to the fields. However, Mexico refused to release the workers pending a settlement of wage rates. At this point, Border Patrolmen stood at the river and encouraged the "illegals" to cross. Upon arrival they were "arrested" and quickly "paroled" to the farmers. An international uproar ensued, and Mexico temporarily halted the Bracero Program, a system that had been on-again, off-again for years.

NOVEMBER 8: El Paso celebrates the centennial of Fort Bliss. The city builds a Fort Bliss Replica based on 1850 buildings at Magoffinsville. The Fort Bliss Replica Museum is today called the Fort Bliss Museum.

1949

Two large, federally financed, housing projects replace some of the El Paso slums.

A concrete bridge is built across the Rio Grande at Cordova Island. Only cattle are crossing.

The Lydia Patterson Institute includes an accredited high school.

EBRUARY 20: The Church of Christ moves to 3101 Montana and opens its first service.

EBRUARY 28: Ascarate votes to continue its incorporation.

UNE 1: The Texas College of Mines and Metallurgy becomes Texas Western College. Carl Hertzog and José Cisneros, world famous illustrators, design the college seal with its Pass of the North, wreaths of achievement, and Latin expressions. This name change reflected a shift in emphasis away from mining and engineering and toward the arts, a shift that started in 1931.

EPTEMBER: Jefferson High School opens. Jefferson took over the old Burleson Elementary School, and added on. Burleson Elementary moved across the street.

CTOBER 1: El Paso's four aldermen break with Mayor Dan Duke and demand that gambling and rumored payoffs be stopped. The aldermen want senior police officers dismissed or retired.

1950

The Pan American Road Races commence annually from Guatemala to Juarez. Tommy Deal of El Paso, who owned Deal Motor Company, won the first one by running from Juarez to the Guatemala border. On alternating years, the races will run in the other direction.

El Paso enters its greatest growth period. The city's population is 130,485 residents, a 35 percent increase since 1940. El Paso County has 194,968 people, an increase of 49 percent. Ciudad Juarez has 122,566, a 150.7 percent increase in ten years. During the 1940s, much of the Juarez

*growth was fueled by the fact that Juarez became an entertainment center
for thousands of military personnel stationed in the El Paso area.*

Fort Bliss becomes the largest single employer in the area.

*The El Paso Natural Gas Company becomes the largest natural gas
transporter in the world.*

The area north of William Beaumont starts developing.

*The Memorial Park Branch of the El Paso Public Library is opened to
serve East El Paso.*

MARCH 31: Hot Springs, New Mexico (originally established around
1905), changes its name to Truth or Consequences. Ralph Edwards,
master of ceremonies for the famous radio/TV program, in exchange for the name switch, agrees to hold a yearly fiesta in the
community. Most people refer to the town as "T or C."

APRIL 20: Clinton B. Jencks, president of the International Union
of Mine, Mill and Smelter Workers, signs an affidavit swearing
he is not a Communist. An El Paso grand jury indicts him, and
after a sensational trial, Judge R. E. Thomason sentences him to
five years in prison.

JUNE 25: The El Paso County Juvenile Detention Home is dedicated.

AUGUST 21: Since the city has no memorial commemorating the New
Mexico and West Texas soldiers who died during the Bataan Death
March in World War II, the Bataan Memorial Trainway is so
dedicated. The first train to pass through was the Sunset Limited,
operated by Mayor Dan Duke, a former locomotive engineer.

NOVEMBER: ASARCO completes the world's tallest smokestack.

NOVEMBER 7: La Calavera (Skull Canyon) originated before the turn
of the century on 8.52 acres of ASARCO land. Smelter employees
had squatted there since the company opened. As the plant ex-
panded however, so did the number of squatters. The company
hesitated to evict them, so it charged each family $2 rent a year. In
order to prevent further squatter expansion, the company surveyed
the land for the record, and on this date deeded the property to the
squatters and their heirs.

1951

The New York Yankees with Mickey Mantle beat the El Paso Texans 16 to 10 at Dudley Field. Mantle hit a homer and two singles, but is remembered best for the announcement that he was unfit for military duty (the Korean War was on) because of a chronic knee condition.

The Westminster Presbyterian Church at 915 North Florence is remodeled into the St. George Orthodox Church, the first Syrian church in El Paso.

Fred Hervey opens the first of his Circle K (called Kays) stores.

SEPTEMBER: The Fort Bliss School is moved from White Acres, and other locations, to 1823 Austin Road on Fort Bliss.

OCTOBER 13: El Paso voters defeat a water bond proposal calling for the purchase of water rights and the construction of a new water treatment plant.

DECEMBER 5: The Victor B. Gilbert Annex is established at the City-County Hospital. Insane people will no longer be lodged in the County Jail.

DECEMBER 23: A new Baptist Chinese Mission opens at 2030 Grant Avenue.

1952

Father Harold J. Rahm arrives in El Paso. He channeled the energies of boys into productive activities.

Carl Hertzog starts Texas Western Press, and a heritage of fine printing begins.

By international agreement, El Paso will hereafter spray Juarez as well as El Paso for mosquitoes.

The Mission Hills subdivision starts, although it is outside the city limits.

Anthony, Texas, is incorporated. (Anthony, New Mexico, is not.) Anthony used to be called La Tuna.

The city's water system is reorganized and refinanced. The Public Service Board is again created.

JANUARY: The first service is held in the First Christian Church at 901 Arizona Street.

JANUARY 14: Providence Memorial Hospital opens at its present location, Blacker and Oregon streets.

SEPTEMBER 14: For the first time in its history, the *El Paso Times* supports a Republican for president: Dwight Eisenhower over Adlai Stevenson.

DECEMBER 4: Ysleta Masonic Lodge No. 1333 receives its charter.

DECEMBER 14: KROD-TV (Channel 4) becomes the first El Paso television station on the air. Until now it and KTSM had been showing test patterns or snow, but on this day a viewer could watch 7 1/2 hours of programming. Some of the local celebrities were Bernie Bracher, Lois Kibbee and Red Brown and Anna Lee.

DECEMBER: Professor Howard E. Quinn at Texas Western College opened his office door and found an alligator from San Jacinto Plaza with a toothy grin. A large crew from the El Paso Parks Department wrestled the reptile back to the park.

DECEMBER: Ascarate is annexed into the City of El Paso.

1953

The Aztec Calendar (a Stone of the Sun replica) is presented to the city by Petroleos Mexicanos (Pemex)

JANUARY: KTSM TV is on the air. It would become the first to transmit in color, the first with an aerial tramway, and the first in stereo.

FEBRUARY 25: Fire destroys most of downtown Clint, Texas.

El Paso Street on a quiet afternoon in the 1950s. The photo is taken from the same location as earlier El Paso Street scenes. The Ellanay Theater was a popular movie house for many years. The original Paso del Norte Hotel is in back right. (Cleofas Calleros Collection)

APRIL 8: Mountain View filed for subdivision.

JULY: Three-quarters of Juarez lacks drinking water and sewage facilities.

SEPTEMBER 25: A group of El Paso women, the Association for Legalized Domestics, wants a blanket waiver under the McCarran-Walters Immigration Act. A survey indicates that domestics cannot be found on the local labor market, so the Association believes domestics (maids) should be legally admitted to the country.

OCTOBER 1: Our Lady's Youth Center opens in the Sacred Heart Schoolyard at Mesa and Fifth streets. Father Harold J. Rahm provides the leadership.

NOVEMBER: The Schellenger Research Laboratories get underway at Texas Western College.

1954

The city annexes 25 square miles in the Upper Valley.

JANUARY 6: Miss Beverly Pack, who won the Fabens Cotton Festival, becomes the first El Paso girl chosen Maid of Cotton.

JANUARY 19: The El Paso County Historical Society is formed by the Women's Division of the El Paso Chamber of Commerce.

APRIL 17: The peso sinks to 12.5 to the dollar, and Mexico launches a "Buy Mexican" campaign.

MAY 15: The El Paso Medical Center (Pill Hill) is opened.

MAY 30: A new City charter is soundly defeated at the polls.

JUNE: Operation Wetback starts. Over a million Mexican deportations take place.

SEPTEMBER 12: A new library opens on the same site as the old
   Carnegie Library.

1955

This is the last year for the Pan American Road Races. Too many
drivers are killing themselves. Too many drivers are also killing too many
pedestrians and too many chickens.
   The blimp hangar, usually called the Tow Target Hangar, at Fort Bliss
is torn down.
   W. T. "Mike" Misenhimer is elected mayor of El Paso and never serves
a day because of a nervous stomach.
   Crown Point and Coronado Hills subdivisions come into being.

JANUARY: German army officers arrive at Fort Bliss for air defense
   training.

MARCH 4: The 18-story El Paso Natural Gas Company Building at
   Texas and Stanton streets has its grand opening.

MARCH 13: Ysleta incorporates by a vote of 2,754 to 637.

MARCH 16: Forty-four square miles of Lower Valley, including
   Ysleta, are annexed into El Paso. The case went to the United States
   Supreme Court, and was decided in 1958 in favor of El Paso. El
   Paso becomes the oldest town in Texas by annexing Ysleta.

MARCH 24: A B-47 bomber crashes near a civilian housing area.
   All three crewmen die.

MAY: Douglass School, the school for blacks, closes as the black
   students start integrating into formerly all white schools. During
   its past years, Douglass graduated 484 students during exercises
   held in the courthouse. A few graduates were Henry Thomas, who
   acted in such films as *Lady from Louisiana*, *Road to Zanzibar*, and
   Gone With the Wind. Giels Bundy Grimes was a principal in the
   Gadsden School District for 17 years. Frances Grundy Hills was
   "Civil Servant of the Year" in 1970 and "Woman of the Year" in

1978. William Roseborough played professional basketball for the Harlem Globetrotters. Nolan Richardson attended Douglass, became coach at Tulsa University and guided its basketball team to the NIT championship in 1981.

JULY: John Prather cradles his rifle and refuses to be evicted by the Army from his ranch on White Sands Proving Ground.

JULY 2: Remodeling starts on the County Courthouse and Liberty Hall.

SEPTEMBER: Burges High School opens.

SEPTEMBER: St. Patrick's Parochial School opens.

SEPTEMBER: Thelma White is admitted to Texas Western College, and is the first black woman in Texas to gain admission to a state school. She had filed suit in April to gain entrance, but the Board of Regents admitted her before the case went to court.

NOVEMBER 14: Park Foothills filed for subdivision.

1956

Congress confirms agreements signed a year earlier by the Army and City of El Paso. The city gives up Valdespino Golf Course, and gets 1,170 acres east of the International Airport for runway extension. The city also acquires water rights to four square miles in the Castner Range area. Sunrise Shopping Center opens.

JANUARY 17: Mountain Park files for subdivision, and becomes the most unique such region in the city. The homes are beautifully spaced and integrated into the mountain scenery. Utilities are underground.

APRIL 26: Illegal immigrants into the United States are now subject to Operation Boatlift. The Mexican illegals are taken by ship to Veracruz and turned loose.

JUNE 14: El Pasoan José Cisneros becomes an "Honorary Tigua Artista."

1957

Construction is completed on the Cathedral alongside Our Lady of Guadalupe in Juarez.

MARCH 5: Husband and wife William D. and Margaret Patterson, owners of an El Paso photo supply house, disappear. Although numerous leads have turned up, no trace of them has ever been found. They have been declared legally dead.

MAY 2: Raymond Telles becomes the first El Paso Hispanic mayor. Telles was a former El Paso county clerk, and went on after serving as mayor to become ambassador to Costa Rica.

MARCH 13: Ridgecrest Addition starts.

MAY 7: Crestmont Addition starts.

JUNE 3: The conviction of Clinton E. Jencks in Federal Court for being a Communist is overturned. When FBI officers refuse to turn over investigative records, the case is dismissed.

JULY 1: Fort Bliss becomes the United States Army Air Defense Center.

JULY 21: A second addition is added to the Newark Hospital and Freeman Clinic.

AUGUST: The El Paso Texans are dropped from the Southwestern League. The Texans have nowhere to go, and are out of baseball until 1961.

AUGUST 6: A district judge orders New Mexico rancher John Prather evicted from his property. The government had been confiscating land for the expansion of White Sands Proving Ground, but

A trolley bearing José Cisneros art gliding down San Antonio Street. Behind the trolley (directly across from driver) is Lerner's Dress Shop, formerly the Acme Saloon. John Wesley Hardin was shot and killed here by Constable John Selman in August 1895. (Frank Mangan Photo)

Prather has successfully fended the government off at the point of
a rifle for almost two years.

SEPTEMBER: Bel Air High School opens.

OCTOBER: Ground is broken for the 20 mile I-10 section between
El Paso and Anthony. This is the first portion of I-10 locally
to be built.

DECEMBER: Illegal Mexican immigrants are now flown deep into
Mexico on a C-46 transport plane, and turned loose.

1958

JANUARY 8: Dolphin Terrace filed for subdivision.

MARCH 28: Sun Valley filed for subdivision.

MAY 13: Desert Hills filed for subdivision.

JULY 14: Terrace Hills filed for subdivision.

AUGUST 28: Two-way traffic moves through the Cordova Island port
of entry. The bridge is free, and open from 6 A.M. to 10 P.M.

SEPTEMBER: Bliss schools consolidate at 4401 Sheridan Road. The
Fort Bliss School was built by the El Paso Independent School
System on land leased by Fort Bliss.

DECEMBER 17: A Trans-Mountain Highway proposal is offered to
the Texas Highway Commission.

NOVEMBER: The voters of El Paso establish a hospital district.
Thomason Hospital will get sufficient funding.

DECEMBER 17: The Federal Reserve Bank Building is completed.

1959

B-24s, B-29s, and B-36s have retired from Biggs Air Force Base. The B-52 Strato-Fortresses replaced them.
The city annexes an additional four square miles of land in the Upper Valley.
White Sands Proving Ground becomes White Sands Missile Range.

JANUARY 28: Dr. Harold Eidinoff shot and killed Ted Andress at the International Airport. Andress was a prominent lawyer and president of the El Paso School Board. The two men were antagonists in sensational court cases whereby a nude photo of Eidinoff surfaced as part of the evidence. Eidinoff was judged insane. He later escaped from a mental hospital, and practiced medicine elsewhere.

APRIL 14: El Paso passes a charter amendment eliminating the City Democratic Primary. In the same election, the voters passed a $3.7 million bond issue for a new city-county hospital.

MARCH 22: The First Presbyterian Church moved from Yandell and Stanton streets to 1340 Murchison. The hall was dedicated on this date.

MAY 30: The City-County Building is dedicated.

JULY 30: The W. W. Turney mansion at 1205 Montana is remodeled into an El Paso Museum of Art which houses part of the famous Kress Collection.

SEPTEMBER: Irvin High School opens.

OCTOBER 9: Sunland Park Race Track opens.

NOVEMBER 23: Skyview filed for subdivision.

1960

During the 1960s, rail passenger service into El Paso all but ends.
The City of El Paso has 276,687 residents, a 112 percent increase since
1950. El Paso County has 314,070, a 61 percent increase. Ciudad Juarez
has 252,119 people, a 105.7 percent increase.
The first unit of the Newman Power Station in far northeast El Paso
is complete.

SPRING: The Northgate (now Northpark) Shopping Center opens.

JULY 7: Congress authorizes the Amistad Dam and Reservoir on the
Rio Grande near Del Rio.

NOVEMBER 8: Voters approve a bond issue for a new Sun Bowl, but
vote down a bond issue for a civic center.

1961

The Mexican government launches the Programa Nacional Fronterizo
(PRONAF), investing millions in commercial and cultural facilities.
The Santa Fe Power Station is retired and dismantled.
The Border Patrol Academy is moved from El Paso to Port Isabel,
Texas.
El Paso had been out of organized baseball for three years, so thanks to
John Phelan, sports announcer for KTSM as well as former general
manager for the El Paso Texans, the team reorganized as the El Paso Sun
Kings, an affiliate of the San Francisco Giants.

MARCH 1: President John F. Kennedy signs an executive order
bringing the Peace Corps into existence.

APRIL: Ranger Peak Aerial Tramway, owned by KTSM-TV, is opened
to the public. A three state, two country view is available.

APRIL 5: El Paso almost has its first woman mayor when Julia Breck loses a narrow, hard-fought runoff to Ralph Seitsinger. The new mayor was the first mayor to be elected from the Lower Valley (Ysleta).

MAY 5: El Pasoan Woodrow Bean offers himself in the Texas Democratic primary as a congressman-at-large, and it is widely anticipated that he will win. However, the news broke within days that he had not filed a federal income tax return since 1952. That "oversight" sank his chances for election.

JULY: A group of 30 Peace Corps volunteers arrive at Texas Western College for a six weeks course in road building and surveying. This will be the first Peace Corps class to graduate in the nation, and Sargent Shriver, director of the program, gave the commencement address. Before being sent to Tanganyika, the class visited with President John F. Kennedy in the White House Rose Garden.

JULY 15: El Paso judges have agreed to start wearing robes while sitting on the bench.

JULY 26: El Paso goes on an atomic bomb/fallout shelter construction spree. War with Russia seems certain.

AUGUST: Coach Don Haskins arrives on the Texas Western campus.

SEPTEMBER: Andress and Eastwood high school open.

OCTOBER: The first ever skyjacking has occurred, and it took place at the El Paso International Airport. Leon Bearden and his son, Cody, go on trial in federal court for aircraft hijacking. Cody is sentenced to a juvenile school in Colorado. His father received 20 years in Leavenworth.

DECEMBER 20: The Southern Pacific closes its line between Douglas, Arizona and Anapra, New Mexico. The last railroad built into El Paso became the first to be abandoned.

1962

*City Council makes it illegal to discriminate on the basis of sex or color.
The El Paso Sun Kings, still with the San Francisco Giants, join the
Texas League and win the championship. Nearly 149,000 spectators
attended the games, a team record.*

FEBRUARY 16: The third location of Temple Mt. Sinai opens at 4408
North Stanton Street.

MARCH: Bassett Center opens on 56 acres. This is the first mall-type
suburban shopping center in the city.

AUGUST: Rex Strickland becomes the college's first "research
professor." Dr. Strickland is a history professor.

SEPTEMBER: Parkland and Coronado high schools open.

OCTOBER 8: The Ladies Auxiliary of the El Paso Fire Fighters
is formed.

NOVEMBER 1: Rushfair Shopping Center opens.

DECEMBER 11: For the second time, voters fail to approve a bond
issue for a civic center.

1963

*Immediately south of Scenic Point is Murchison Park, developed by the
Woman's Department of the Chamber of Commerce. An American flag
flies day and night, a commemoration for First Lieutenant Chris P. Fox,
Jr., killed in France during World War II.*

*The Hilton Hotel is sold to the Kramer Hotel organization, and
changed to the Plaza Hotel.*

*A new City-County Hospital is dedicated and named R. E. Thomason
General Hospital.*

JANUARY: The El Paso National Bank Building is "put on the books," meaning it was ready to open. Its 19 floors made it the highest building in town.

APRIL: Billie Sol Estes is tried for mail fraud in Federal Court. Estes went to prison for 15 years. Judge R. E. Thomason described him as one of this country's biggest swindlers.

APRIL 12: Fusselman Dam in the Franklin Mountains is dedicated.

JUNE 1: R. E. Thomason retires as a federal judge in El Paso.

JULY 18: The Fiesta Hills Addition starts.

SEPTEMBER 28: The University of Texas Board of Regents formally abolishes Mining and Mining-Geology. The mining courses had dwindling enrollment, and Texas Western wanted to concentrate on other aspects of engineering.

OCTOBER 5: The new Sun Bowl is dedicated during half-time festivities of the Texas Western-New Mexico State University game. The college leased the land to El Paso County, which then constructed the stadium and leased the Sun Bowl back to the college for 99 years at $1 a year. The county reserved the right only to hold the annual Sun Bowl football game there.

NOVEMBER 22: President John F. Kennedy is assassinated in Dallas.

1964

Morehead School, the old El Paso High School building at the corner of Arizona and Campbell, falls to the demolition ball.

APRIL: El Paso and Juarez embark on a joint rabies eradication program.

MAY: Greyhound racing starts in Juarez.

MAY 18: The Southwest National Bank (now SunWest) moves to Stanton and Mills streets.

AUGUST 9: The Chinese Baptist Mission becomes the Chinese Baptist Church. Later it is the Grant Avenue Baptist Church.

SEPTEMBER 24: Presidents Lyndon B. Johnson and Adolfo López Mateos sign the Chamizal agreement.

NOVEMBER: Sun Towers Hospital opens.

DECEMBER: The second Bracero Program closes.

1965

The Border Industrial Program, better known as the maquiladora *or twin plant program, is established.*

The Magoffin Home is registered as a Texas Historical Landmark.

A tax collector foreclosing on houses because of nonpayment of taxes in El Barrio de los Indios, *discovers that the Tiguas still exist. Tom Diamond, an El Paso attorney, takes on the fight for recognition of the Tiguas as an Indian tribe.*

The Mills Building is sold to the Upper Valley Development Company.

MARCH 14: El Paso Mayor Judson Williams and Juarez Mayor Felipe Dávila Borunda launch a World Understanding Week. It had little significance and few paid any attention, but it set the stage for the Border Cities Association the following October.

MARCH 17: Mystic Heights filed for subdivision.

MAY 15: The El Paso Sun Kings and the Austin Senators engage in the most celebrated free-for-all in local sports history.

JUNE 12: Ann Landers, famous newspaper advice columnist, visits El Paso.

SEPTEMBER: Socorro High School opens.

SEPTEMBER: The new Clint High School opens.

SEPTEMBER 24: John Wesley Hardin's grave is marked with a headstone in Concordia Cemetery.

OCTOBER: A Border Cities Association is created for studying border problems.

1966

The German Air Force Training Activity is transferred from Aachen, Germany to Fort Bliss.

MAY 22: Tom Mays Park is dedicated on the west side of the Franklin Mountains near Transmountain Road.

MARCH 19: Coach Don Haskins leads his Texas Western College basketball team to the NCAA championship at College Park, Maryland. The Miners defeated the University of Kentucky 72-65 in a stunning upset. Texas Western fielded only two white players, this being the first time blacks had been the dominant majority on any major college or university team.

JUNE 30: The Chamizal National Memorial at El Paso is authorized by Congress.

JULY 1: Biggs Air Force Base is deactivated and becomes Biggs Army Air Field when the post is taken over by Fort Bliss.

JULY 30: An agreement has been reached between the United States and Mexico for the construction of port of entry facilities for Cordova Island.

OCTOBER: The Tiguas say they will pay no more city and county taxes.

1967

The Assistance League of El Paso is founded.
The El Paso Sports Association, having done its job by bringing professional baseball back to El Paso, sells the team to Gene Autry, who owns the California Angels, for one dollar.

JANUARY: A United States Commission for Border Development and Friendship is established in Washington, D.C.

MARCH 25: Mayor Judson Williams wins a third term as mayor. He defeated two candidates with the same name: Ed Lang.

APRIL 1: Daylight Savings Time is established for Texas and most of the nation.

MAY 23: Attorney Tom Diamond wins tribal status for Tigua Indians. The Tiguas are placed under the Texas Commission for Indian Affairs. A reservation is established.

SEPTEMBER 1: Texas Western College becomes the University of Texas at El Paso.

SEPTEMBER 1: A University Archives (more a historical manuscript collection) opens in the UT El Paso Library and quickly becomes one of the finest historical archives in Texas.

1968

The United States Special Olympics begin in El Paso and around the country. Children and adults with disabilities compete in local, national and international events.

JANUARY 27: There is considerable discussion about "green carders" taking American jobs. The Select Commission on Western Hemisphere Immigration meets in El Paso.

JANUARY 30: Commissioners Court discusses whether to turn Hueco Tanks over to the Tiguas.

APRIL 12: President Lyndon Johnson signs Public Law 90-287, recognizing the Tiguas as an American and Texas tribe. Three days later, the United States transfers responsibility for theTiguas to Texas.

JUNE: St. Anthony is the patron saint of the Tiguas, and the Feast of St. Anthony is celebrated in Ysleta each June. As per a centuries-old practice, a group of Tiguas take St. Anthony from house to house collecting funds for the feast. As usual, a shotgun is fired at the beginning of each street to let the people know that the procession is approaching. Anyway, Tigua Joe Sierra was arrested for firing a shotgun in the city limits. Attorney Tom Diamond rose for the defense, and the case was thrown out of court on religious grounds. Since then, however, shotgun blasts are no longer a required part of the Feast of St. Anthony ceremony.

JUNE 16: Lee Treviño wins the U.S. Open. El Paso celebrates.

JUNE 22: El Paso property owners approve a $15 million bond issue for a civic center.

OCTOBER 11: The McGinty cannon is dedicated at Eastwood High School. It had a long history of capture by Confederates at Valverde, New Mexico. It also roared from McGinty Hill, and was kidnapped from El Paso by Mexican revolutionaries during the early 1900s.

1969

City Council makes it illegal to discriminate in housing, whether buying or renting.

"Operation Intercept" begins as the Bureau of Immigration declares war against the Mexican drug traffic. Bridge traffic is tightened, and what once took minutes now takes hours to cross the bridge from Mexico into the United States. Trade between the two countries dips sharply.

MARCH 21: The Tigua Indians, through their attorney Tom Diamond, have filed suit to regain the Ysleta Land Grant consisting of 36 square miles in the Lower Valley. Tiguas have also laid claims to all lands in El Paso, Hudspeth, Culberson, Presidio and Jeff Davis counties.

JUNE: A bond issue creates El Paso Community College.

JUNE 12: The El Paso County Commissioners deed Hueco Tanks to the Texas Parks and Wild Life Commission.

JULY: Americans land on the moon.

SEPTEMBER: Riverside High School opens.

OCTOBER: Portions of the Chamizal land granted to Mexico, which includes part of Cordova Island, is slowly transformed into a forested showcase of monuments, parks and sports facilities.

1970

The City of El Paso has 322,261 residents, a 17 percent increase in 10 years. El Paso County has 359,291 people, a 14 percent increase. Ciudad Juarez has 424,135 people, a 68 percent increase in ten years. Juarez ranks sixth in size in Mexico, although if newspaper reports are correct, the population is close to a million. If true, Juarez would be fourth largest city in Mexico.

The Trans-Mountain Road is completed.

I-10 from El Paso county line to county line is finally open.

The modern-day Bell Telephone Company Building is completed although it would not be occupied until next year. (Site of old Central School.)

The Holiday Inn, now the Ramada, opens on Missouri Street. It is 17 stories high.

JANUARY 30: Ground breaking ceremonies begin for the State National Bank, its 22 stories will make it the tallest building in El Paso.

MAY: Hueco Tanks Historical Park officially opens to the public.

MAY 11: Josephine Clardy Fox dies and bequeaths $3 million to UT El Paso.

MAY 19: Texas passes liquor-by-the-drink and late-closing legislation. El Paso nightclubs subsequently open, and Juarez feels the economic crunch as nobody has to cross the Rio Grande to drink.

JULY: An Air Force Athena, a four-stage research missile, on its way by air from Green River, Utah, to White Sands Missile Range, landed near Torreon, Mexico. The missile contained two small vials of Cobalt 57 which upset the Mexicans because they didn't want to become radioactive—and they did not want the Americans conducting investigations on their land. After several yards of dirt were found to be radioactive, the Americans dug up 55 barrels of Mexican soil. The dirt is still in storage at White Sands.

DECEMBER 19: The Paso del Norte Hotel is sold for $600,000 by Zach White's daughters to the T.K.G. Investment Company.

1971

Our Lady of Guadalupe Mission in Juarez is restored.
Dolores Pellicano is the first Hispanic girl to be named Sun Queen.
The Farah Plant is completed on Gateway West.
Professional golfer Lee Treviño buys an interest in Santa Teresa.
The National Rail Passenger Corporation (AMTRAK) takes over the passenger responsibilities of a majority of the nation's railroads, including the three carriers serving El Paso.

MARCH 6: Mexico limits divorces to Mexicans and permanent resident aliens. For years, airline traffic known as "Divorce Runs" and "Freedom Riders' Special" have landed at El Paso International Airport. At least 250,000 divorce seekers have momentarily visited El Paso prior to slipping into Juarez for "quickie" divorces that substantially enhanced the Mexican economy.

EPTEMBER 20: The El Paso Community College opens with 901 students.

DECEMBER: The Chicano movement at UT El Paso staged a demonstration in front of the campus Administration Building.

DECEMBER: The Greyhound Bus Terminal is constructed.

DECEMBER: The Magoffin Home is placed on the National Register of Historic Sites.

DECEMBER: Mexico institutes a program of *Artículos Gancho,* which translates into the "hook" or "enticement." Specified American goods could cross the border duty free into Mexico and be sold. The aim was to keep Mexican purchasers in Mexico by removing a need to go to the United States.

1972

The United States Army Sergeants Major Academy is created at Biggs Army Air Field.

The Third Armored Cavalry Regiment is stationed at Fort Bliss.

The only streetcar left in town is the one operating between El Paso and Juarez.

A joint air quality monitoring activity is created along the international border.

Author-historian-publisher Frank Mangan suggests the stately palm trees for San Jacinto Plaza. A number of palms are hoisted into place.

ARCH 6: The *El Paso Times* becomes a part of the Gannett Newspaper chain.

AY: A thousand garment workers strike for two years at the Farah Manufacturing Plant in El Paso. The strike will have far-reaching repercussions, including a nation-wide Farah boycott.

LY 1: William Beaumont Army Medical Center is dedicated.

SEPTEMBER: The Sam Young Tower is completed at Providence Memorial Hospital.

SEPTEMBER: San Elizario High School opens.

NOVEMBER: The Exhibition Hall at the Civic Center is dedicated.

1973

A Texas Tech University Regional Academic Health Center is established in El Paso. Thomason is designated as the primary teaching hospital for the Center.

A Bullfighter Museum opens in the Del Camino Motel.

The El Paso Electric Company signs an agreement to participate in the Arizona Nuclear Power Project, better known as the Palo Verde Nuclear Generating Plant.

El Paso celebrates its centennial as a city. Another Great McGinty Band is organized and it flowers for the next decade.

AUGUST: A labor dispute halts streetcar operations between Juarez and El Paso. Juarez merchants then applied pressure to stop the streetcars altogether since they were delivering more Mexican citizens to El Paso stores than American purchasers to Juarez markets. The "transportation war" went on for several years, but the streetcars never ran to Juarez again.

SEPTEMBER: The first binational symposium on air pollution is held on the campus of UT El Paso. UT El Paso professors Howard T. Applegate and C. Richard Bath are major speakers.

SEPTEMBER: An organization called Discover El Paso is created.

SEPTEMBER: Bowie High School moves to a new high school at a different location, this one alongside the Chamizal National Memorial. Bowie came about largely because of the Chamizal Treaty settlement.

NOVEMBER 8: Judge R. E. Thomason dies in El Paso.

1974

UT El Paso offers its first doctoral program: geological science.
The UT El Paso track team wins the first of its four NCAA
indoor titles.

S. L. A. "Slam" Marshall, world famous military writer, donates his
3,000 volume collection of military books to the U.T. El Paso Library. It
becomes the "S. L. A. Marshall Military History Collection."

Jim Paul buys a part interest in the Sun Kings, and they become the
El Paso Diablos. The flamboyant, Brooklyn-born Paul Strelzin becomes
public announcer during the games, an act that offends some fans but
enriches others. Slowly the crowds swell.

EBRUARY 4: The Chamizal National Memorial is established in El
Paso. As a museum, showplace and park, it is unexcelled and the
only national memorial in town. The Chamizal National Memorial
commemorates the Chamizal history and settlement.

PRIL: Mexico abolishes the *Artículos Gancho* program. Its 1971 intent
was to keep Mexican shoppers in Mexico, and it wasn't working.

JLY 4: The Cavalry Museum is opened and dedicated by the City.
Former El Paso Mayor Fred Hervey created the El Paso Heritage
Foundation and gave it $75,000 to build the museum. Hervey
wanted it called the Black Jack Pershing Museum. His foundation
talked him out of it.

1975

Jim Paul assumes full ownership of the El Paso Diablos.
The UT El Paso track team wins the second of its four NCAA
indoor titles.

NUARY: Federal Judge William Sessions finds conditions deplor-
able in the El Paso County Jail. He orders the county to comply
with the Texas Jail Standards Act.

JANUARY: Charlie Crowder completes construction of Santa Teresa and sells the golf course to Lee Treviño Enterprises. The Federal Aviation Administration designates Santa Teresa as the site for a future Doña Ana County Airport.

JANUARY 7: La Fe Family Health Center dedicated.

NOVEMBER 8: W. R. Weaver, owner of the Weaver Scope Company, commits suicide. He had been ill for many years.

1976

The UT El Paso track team wins its third NCAA indoor track title.
Federal Judge William Sessions finds the El Paso Independent School District guilty of discriminating against Hispanic students. He orders a busing program and the redrawing of school boundaries for ethnic balance.
The Chihuahuita Improvement Association is established.

FEBRUARY 5: The pending arrival of women prison guards at the La Tuna Federal Correctional Institution is causing a stir among inmates.

FEBRUARY 6 & 7: Mayor Don Henderson hosts a conference of mayors in the civic center. The Mexican Border Regional Commission evolved.

FEBRUARY 21: Fort Selden, north of Las Cruces, is designated as a state historical site.

SEPTEMBER: Mexico deliberately devaluates the peso and allows it to "float." The peso exchange rate goes from 12 to $1 to 20 to $1.

SEPTEMBER 1: Mexico discovers that it has enormous oil reserves, black gold beneath its sands. Mexico then slipped into a dream world of more oil, higher oil productivity and sales, and ever higher oil prices. Oil destroyed the economy of Mexico.

1977

The City of El Paso annexes the Franklin Mountain range and starts condemnation proceedings against private owners.

The Southwest Border Regional Commission is created to study economic development.

The UT El Paso track team places second in NCAA indoor track.

The El Paso Electric Company forms a wholly owned subsidiary known as Franklin Land & Resources. While the original purpose was to acquire power plant sites, because of the forthcoming Economic Recovery Act, Franklin was able to purchase and restore the Cortez Building and the Paso del Norte Hotel.

UNE 23: A *Herald-Post* reporter, peering behind brick walls at the City-County Building, discovers 18,000 square feet of empty space extending upward for three stories.

'UMMER: The Mission Heritage Association is founded. By the late 1980s, it will evolve into the Mission Trail Association.

APRIL 22: District Judge Sam Callan swears in Ray Salazar as mayor of El Paso. Salazar becomes the second Hispanic mayor.

ULY: The Black Bridge (Puente Negro), owned by the Atchison, Topeka and Santa Fe Railroad Company, is closed. There have been too many violent deaths, too many illegal immigrants crossing. Now a railroad special agent opens and closes the gates for trains crossing the Rio Grande.

AUGUST 18: Bowie Kuhn, commissioner of baseball, visits El Paso.

OCTOBER 12: The Wilderness Park Museum opens at 2000 Transmountain Road after the Army sweeps 17 acres for unexploded artillery shells. Mayor Fred Hervey personally paid $75,000 to construct the building.

NOVEMBER 15: General Omar Bradley, the only living five-star general, comes to El Paso and resides near William Beaumont Army Medical Center.

1978

The UT El Paso track team wins its fourth NCAA indoor track championship.

Mike Sullivan leases a floor of the Plaza Hotel to house the overflow of jail inmates.

Judge William Sessions rules that employers could prohibit employees from speaking Spanish on the job.

JANUARY 23: Franklin Land & Resources purchase the Mills Building as headquarters for the El Paso Electric Company.

FEBRUARY 24: Federal Judge William Sessions finds Sheriff Mike Sullivan, County Judge Udell Moore and county commissioners Chuck Mattox, Richard Telles, Clyde Anderson and Rogelio Sanchez in contempt of court and sentences them for violations of the Texas Jail Standards Act.

MARCH: Dick Knapp, a local developer, purchases six square miles of land in the proposed Franklin Mountains Wilderness Park. It included North Franklin Peak and four springs. His plans called for major development, and he graded a road across the mountain.

JULY: A Wilderness Coalition is formed to fight Dick Knapp's development.

SEPTEMBER: The El Paso County Community College opens its Valle Verde and Transmountain campuses.

OCTOBER 18: The city annexes Dick Knapp's Franklin Mountain land.

NOVEMBER: Hanks High School opens.

DECEMBER 23: Prominent El Paso attorney Lee Chagra is shot and killed in his office.

1979

Lee Treviño Enterprises withdraws from Santa Teresa and sells the country club and golf courses back to Charlie Crowder.

1ARCH: A standoff occurs on the Paso del Norte bridge when immigration papers are examined closer than usual. Many Mexicans are deported back to Mexico. The bridge is blocked, and the American flag is torn down.

PRIL: The Wilderness Park Coalition, plus the El Paso Legislative Corps in Austin, passes House Bill 867 which commits Texas to purchase and develop the Franklins as a state park.

1AY 15: Mayor Ray Salazar dedicates the new City Hall before leaving office despite the fact that city employees cannot move in until at least July.

1AY 22: City Council passes a "ban the booze" ordinance for city parks.

ECEMBER: The Christmas Star on the Mountain lights up. Because of the Iran hostage crisis, the star continued shining for 444 days.

1980

The City of El Paso has 425,259 residents, an increase of 32 percent since 1970. El Paso County has 479,899, a 34 percent increase.

The University of Texas Board of Regents authorizes 20,000 more seats for the Sun Bowl.

During a rededication ceremony in honor of the 400th anniversary of the founding of El Paso del Norte (Juarez) and the 300th anniversary of Ysleta, the name of the Ysleta Mission is changed back to Mision San Antonio de los Tiguas.

PRIL: Family health clinic opens in northeast El Paso.

1AY: Mayor Tom Westfall sets up a Corruption Hot Line operating out of his assistant's office. El Paso citizens can dial that number and their identity will not be revealed. Nobody called.

JULY 13: The Cavalry Museum becomes the El Paso Museum of History.

AUGUST 27: The Texas legislature establishes a public defender program for counties in the state.

SEPTEMBER 5: El Paso Public Service Board files suit for a rightful portion of New Mexico's water.

SEPTEMBER 29: The Manhattan Heights District is placed in the National Register of Historic Places primarily through the efforts of Una Hill.

DECEMBER: The El Paso City Council creates the Tax Increment Financing District (TIF) composed of 88 blocks of downtown.

1981

The El Paso Diablo franchise switches to the Milwaukee Brewers.

JANUARY 21: The Iran hostage crisis being resolved, the Christmas Star turns off its light after 444 days.

APRIL 8: Omar Bradley, the nation's last five star general, dies in New York while visiting friends.

1982

JANUARY 26: Charles Harrelson and El Pasoans Joe, Patti, Jimmy and Elizabeth Chagra are tried for plotting and performing the assassination of Judge John Hill.

FEBRUARY: The economic structure of Mexico cracks as the Mexican Peso floats and finds its true value in the market place.

JULY 3: Franklin Land and Resources, a subsidiary of the El Paso Electric Company, announces plans to renovate the Cortez Building.

AUGUST: Ray Apodaca, a Tigua Indian who is the first from his tribe to have a post-graduate degree, is named executive director of the Texas Indian Commission.

SEPTEMBER 1: As Mexico suffers peso devaluations, President José Lopez Portillo nationalizes the Mexican banks. The Mexican economy staggers.

1983

APRIL 1: The Tiguas file an official land claim with the United States secretary of the interior that, if upheld, will give the tribe the right to sue every landowner in eastern El Paso County for the return of Tigua property.

1984

Mexican and American cattle raisers get permission to use Santa Teresa as an international crossing.

JANUARY 4: City officials at Sunland Park, New Mexico, start their first day of work. The mayor is a 24-year-old college student.

MAY: The W. R. Weaver Scope Company goes out of business. At one time its rifle scopes were sold all over the world.

1985

MAY 20: Mexico declares the Maquiladora Program industry a national priority. By the end of the year, nearly 800 plants are operating around the country, mostly along the United States border. They employ 200,000 people.

JUNE: The Mission Trail Association is organized with Sheldon Hall, director.

JULY 23: The Mexican Peso gradually drops to 381 to the dollar, but is stabilizing.

1986

The emergency room at R. E. Thomason Hospital is certified as a Level I Trauma Center.

New Mexico and Chihuahua officials snip the barbed wire fence at Santa Teresa during a ceremonial opening of an international border crossing point.

JUNE: The Westin Paso del Norte Hotel (the old Paso del Norte) with a new 17-story tower, opens in downtown El Paso.

JUNE 1: John Hancock Financial Services signs a three-year, $1.5 million contract to sponsor the Sun Bowl. The football game becomes the John Hancock Sun Bowl.

OCTOBER 10: El Paso voters approve a $6 million bond issue to build a new baseball stadium for the Diablos.

NOVEMBER: The Immigration Reform and Control Act is passed by Congress.

1987

The University of Texas Health Science Center at San Antonio develops a major affiliation with R. E. Thomason Hospital.

Hotel Dieu sells the hospital building between Arizona and Rio Grande streets.

Voters pass the most expensive bond issue in El Paso's history—a series of propositions worth $94 million.

An annual Carl Hertzog Award for excellence in book design is instituted by the UT El Paso Library.

Charlie Crowder announces his plan for an industrial village at Santa Teresa that will straddle the U.S.-Mexico border.

FEBRUARY 17: Dr. James Halligan, president of New Mexico State University, brings together a broad group of New Mexicans, and they hold their first meeting with regards to a Farm and Ranch Heritage Institute at NMSU. Tourists will get an opportunity to observe farming and ranching from prehistory into the future.

JULY 25: President Ronald Reagan nominates William Sessions as FBI director.

AUGUST 19: President Ronald Reagan signs a bill giving federal money to the Tigua Indians, ending a two-year congressional battle.

SEPTEMBER: Del Valle High School opens.

1988

A fire wipes out the cafe and Bullfighter Museum in the Del Camino Motel. The 100 units were thereafter converted into low-income housing.

APRIL 9: Syd Cohen, El Paso baseball great, dies after a struggle with cancer.

OCTOBER 29: Andy Cohen, brother of Syd and another El Paso baseball great, dies after a series of strokes.

1989

Suzanne Azar becomes the first woman mayor of El Paso.
Texas disbands the Texas Indian Commission because it singles out Indians for special consideration and assistance.
El Paso Electric discontinues all non-utility operations through Franklin Land.

MAY: El Paso Electric suspends dividends to its stockholders because of mounting financial problems.

JUNE: John Hancock renews its bowl sponsorship for five years, guaranteeing more than $1 million a year for a football game and a golf tournament. At John Hancock's insistence, El Paso's bowl game is renamed the John Hancock Bowl, dropping the word "Sun."

DECEMBER 3: The El Paso Diablos are named the Organization of the Decade in Class AA baseball.

1990

JANUARY 7: El Paso Electric sells its capital stock in Franklin Land.

JANUARY 31: Heritage Tourism Projects get underway.

JUNE 30: The Andy and Syd Cohen Center, the new home for the El Paso Diablos, is dedicated in northeast El Paso.

AUGUST 7: President George Bush orders deployment of United States troops, including those stationed at Fort Bliss, to the Persian Gulf.

AUGUST 23: Montwood High School opens.

DECEMBER: John Hancock Financial Services has, during this year, lent El Paso Electric $80 million.

1991

JANUARY 17: A United States led coalition launches a six-week war against Iraq to liberate Kuwait.

MARCH: Tom Diamond, attorney for the Tigua Indians, warns Texas Attorney General Jim Mattox that if the state sells any land claimed by the Tiguas, the state will be held accountable.

Completed in 1993, blue-mirrored El Paso County Court House adds a sparkle to the city's skyline. (Leon Metz)

APRIL: John Hancock Financial Services lends $27 million to the El Paso Refinery. The figure will grow to $31 million, with interest, within a year.

APRIL 1: KVIA-TV weather anchorman, Jim Gamble, predicts a heavy snow that will bury El Paso. Gamble called it an April Fool's joke, but some of the town took him seriously. One rancher claimed to have bought $9,000 worth of feed to weather the storm.

MAY: El Paso and New Mexico agree to a water settlement. Both sides will drop their lawsuits and form a commission to resolve the water problems.

AUGUST 21: The Christmas Star on the mountain shuts down after 263 days due to the Persian Gulf War.

1992

JANUARY: The El Paso Electric Company files Chapter 11 Bankruptcy.

JULY 24: The Tigua Tribal Council gives permission for a special committee to study casino style gambling for the Tigua Reservation. Governor Ray Apodaca protests the gambling proposals, and is removed as administrator of the tribe.

SEPTEMBER 26: Tigua women are warning Tribal Council that they will fight for the right to vote on tribal matters. They request seats on the Tribal Council.

OCTOBER: The El Paso Refinery (former Texaco Refinery) files for Chapter 11 bankruptcy.

NOVEMBER 11: Hueco Tanks closes due to vandalism (graffiti on pictographs). When it reopens in two weeks (November 25), park fees will have jumped from $3 to $25, thus eliminating the ordinary visitor as well as the vandals. (The problem was insufficient park staffing.)

NOVEMBER 20: Tigua Tribal Council removes roughly one hundred people from the tribal rolls, including the family of Ray Apodaca.

1993

JANUARY 12: The Santa Teresa port of entry opens between the states of New Mexico and Chihuahua. Only a trickle of automobiles pass through.

JANUARY 12: The historic Del Camino Motel is ordered condemned unless the owner makes needed repairs within 90 days.

JANUARY 12: One hundred and thirty soldiers from the 978th Military Police Company at Fort Bliss leave for Somalia as part of Operation Restore Hope.

JANUARY 31: The Heritage Tourism Project ends.

FEBRUARY 18: Hillcrest Junior High School burns. The structure was a Jesuit Seminary (1926) before becoming Jesuit High School in the late 1950s.

FEBRUARY 19: *El Paso Times* columnist John Laird walked 34.2 miles in six days from Tornillo, Texas to El Paso. He conducted Lower Valley town meetings along the way.

MARCH 1: The Westin Paso del Norte Hotel becomes the Camino Real Paso del Norte Hotel.

MARCH 4: The Border Steel Company files for Chapter 11 bankruptcy.

MARCH 8: County commissioners decree that no county money will be used to stage mock gunfights. A major blow has been struck for law and order in El Paso.

APRIL 1: The Texas Parks and Wildlife Service lowers entry fees at Hueco Tanks to $2.

APRIL 21: As of today, the Christmas Star on the mountain will shine every day of the year. Thanks to Jack Maxon, Chamber of Commerce president, the Chamber will pay the cost.

MAY 1: The Insights Science Museum opens in downtown El Paso.

REFERENCE MATTER

INDEX

EL PASO MAYORS

Ben S. Dowell 1873-75
Melton A. Jones 1875-76
Solomon Schutz 1880-81
Joseph Magoffin 1881-85R.
C. Lightbody 1885-89
Richard Caples 1889-93
W. H. Austin 1893-94
Adolph Solomon 1894
A. K. Albers 1894
Robert F. Johnson 1894
Robert Campbell 1895-97
Joseph Magoffin 1897-1901
Ben F. Hammett 1901-03
C. R. Morehead 1903-05
Charles Davis, Sr. 1905-07
Joseph U. Sweeney 1907-10
W. F. Robinson 1910
Charles E. Kelly 1910-15
Tom Lea 1915-17
Charles Davis, Jr. 1917-23
R. M. Dudley 1923-25
H. P. Jackson 1925-27
R. E. Thomason 1927-31
A. B. Poe 1931
R. E. Sherman 1931-37
M. A. Harlan 1937-39
J. E. Anderson 1938-47
Dan R. Ponder 1947-49
Dan L. P. Duke 1949-51
Fred Hervey 1951-55
W. T. Misenhimer 1955
Tom E. Rogers 1955-57
R. L. Telles, Jr. 1957-61
Ralph Seitsinger 1961-63
Judson F. Williams 1963-69
Ashley G. Classen 1969
Peter De Wetter 1969-71

Bert Williams 1971-73
Fred Hervey 1973-75
Don Henderson 1975-77
Ray Salazar 1977-79
Thomas D. Westfall 1979-81
Jonathan W. Rogers 1981-89
Suzanne S. Azar 1989-91
William S. Tilney 1991-93
Larry Francis 1993-

COUNTY JUDGES

C. A. Hoppin 1850
A. C. Hyde 1850-52
Simeon Hart 1852-54
A. C. Hyde 1854-56
Henry L. Dexter 1856-58
John L. McCarty 1858-60
Henry L. Gillett 1960-66
Albert H. French 1866-70
Maximo Aranda 1870-72
Telésforo Montes 1872-74
José M. Gonzales 1874-76
Joseph Magoffin 1876-77
G. M. García 1877-78
J. B. Leahy 1878-79
José M. Gonzales 1879-1880
Baptiste Mariany 1880
H. C. Cook 1880
José Baca 1880-82
E. J. Orn 1882
Marsh Rogers 1882-86
W. M. Chandler 1886-88
J. E. Townsend 1888-90
Allen I. Blacker 1890-92
F. E. Hunter 1892-96
James R. Harper 1896-02

Joseph Sweeney 1902-1908
A. S. J. Eylar 1908-1914
Adrian Pool 1914-1916
E. B. McClintock
Joseph McGill 1932-42
M. Scarborough 1942-46
Victor B. Gilbert 1946-52
Hugh McGovern, Jr. 1952-58
Woodrow W. Bean 1958-62

C. R. Schulte 1962
Glenn Woodard 1962-65
Travis Johnson 1965-66
Colbert Coldwell 1966-70
Udell Moore 1970-83
Pat O'Rourke 1983-87
Luther Jones 1987-91
Alicia Chacon 1991-

SHERIFFS

(incomplete)

William Ford 1852
William Wates 1859
Juan Armendariz 1870
Charles Ellis 1871
Charles Kerber 1874
Benito Gonzalez 1880
Batista Mariany 1880
Benito Gonzalez 1882
J. H. White 1883
H. R. Hildebrant 1890
F. B. Simmons 1892
J. H. Boone 1898
J. H. Comstock 1905
F. J. Hall 1908

Peyton J. Edwards 1910
Seth B. Orndorff 1916
Tom Armstrong 1929
Chris P. Fox 1933-42
W. W. Hawkins 1942
Allan Falby 1942-49
Joe Campbell 1949-51
W. O. Hix 1951-58
Bob Bailey 1958-64
Mike Sullivan 1965-1978
Ramon Montes 1978-1982
Michael Patrick Davis 1982-84
Leo Samaniego 1985-

FORT BLISS COMMANDERS

Major Jefferson Van Horne 1849-51
Lieut. Colonel E. B. Alexander 1855
Lieut. Colonel John B. Magruder 1855
Major James Longstreet 1855
Major John T. Sprague 1855
Major T. H. Holmes 1856
Lieut. Colonel Isaac V. D. Reeve 1857-59
Major T. H. Holmes 1859
Captain W. L. Elliot 1859
Captain E. G. Walker 1859
First Lieut. Thomas K. Jackson 1859-60
Captain Thomas G. Pitcher 1860
First Lieut. Thomas K. Jackson 1860-61
Lieut. Colonel Isaac V. D. Reeve 1861
Lieut. Colonel John R. Baylor (Texas) 1861
Brigadier General Henry H. Sibley (Confederacy) 1861-62
Brigadier General James H. Carleton (Union) 1862-63
Major William McMullen 1863
Colonel George W. Bowie 1864
Major Joseph Smith 1865
Captain David H. Brotherton 1865-66
Major William R. Gerhart 1866
Captain E. C. Mason 1866-68
Major H. C. Merriam 1869
Captain F. M. Crandall 1870
Captain C. Bentzoni 1871
Captain F. M. Cox 1872-74
Major Z. R. Bliss 1875-76
Major N. W. Osborne 1878-80
Captain H. R. Brinkerhoff 1881
Captain O. W. Bollock 1882
Major J. F. Fletcher 1883
Major H. S. Hawkins 1884-85
Captain Gregory Barrett 1886
Colonel M. M. Blunt 1887
Captain E. P. Ewers 1888
Colonel N. W. Osborne 1889-1890

Major J. Henton 1891-1892
Colonel H. M. Lazelle 1893
Captain W. H. McLaughlin 1893-94
Colonel D. Parker 1895
Colonel D. D. van Valzah 1896-98
Lieut. N. F. McClure 1898
Major Churchill Towles 1898
Captain Joseph F. Nichols 1898-99
Captain S. L. Woodward 1899
Captain H. R. H. Loughborough 1899-1901
Captain F. M. Caldwell 1901
Lieut. Colonel H. H. Adams 1901-02
Lieut. Colonel C. P. Terrett 1902
Lieut. Colonel H. L. Haskell 1902
Lieut. Colonel H. S. Foster 1903-04
Captain H. M. Dickman 1904
Major Ammon A. Augur 1904-06
Major J. M. T. Partello 1906
Colonel R. W. Hoyt 1906-07
Captain S. Burkhardt, Jr. 1907
Colonel J. F. Huston 1907-1910
Colonel A. C. Sharpe 1910
Colonel E. F. Glenn 1910-1912
Colonel E. Z Steever 1912
Colonel Frank West 1912-13
Colonel Joseph Gerrard 1914
Brigadier General Hugh Scott 1914
Brigadier General John J. Pershing 1914-16
Brigadier General George Bell 1916
Colonel John W. Heard 1917
Colonel William D. Beach 1917
Colonel George T. Langhorne 1917
Colonel Edward Anderson 1917-1918
Brigadier General Robert L. Howze 1918
Brigadier General James Hornbrook 1918
Major General Robert L. Howze 1918-1925
Brigadier General Joseph C. Castner 1925-1926
Brigadier General Edwin D. Winans 1926-27
Brigadier General George V. H. Mosley 1928-1929
Brigadier General George Barnhart 1930

Brigadier General Walker C. Short 1930-32
Major General Frank McCoy 1933
Brigadier General Walter C. Short 1930-32
Brigadier General Hamilton Hawkins 1936
Brigadier General Ben Lear 1937
Brigadier General Kenyon Joyce 1938
Brigadier General Robert C. Richardson, Jr. 1939-41
Major General Innis P. Swift 1941
Colonel Frederick D. Griffith 1941-42
Colonel Edgar B. Taulbee 1942
Colonel M. H. Tomlinson 1943
Colonel John K. Brown 1944-45
Colonel Frank L. Whittaker 1945
Colonel George J. Forster 1945
Colonel Robert H. Van Volkenburgh 1946
Major General John L. Homer 1946-50
Major General John T. Lewis 1950-52
Brigadier General F. L. Hayden 1952
Lieut. General Stanley R. Mickelsen 1952-54
Major General Paul W. Rutledge 1954-56
Major General Robert J. Wood 1956-57
Major General Sam C. Russell 1957-61
Major General Marshall S. Carter 1961-62
Brigadier General Stephen M. Mellnik 1962
Major General Tom V. Stayton 1962-65
Major General George T. Powers III 1965-67
Major General George V. Underwood, Jr. 1967-68
Major General Richard T. Cassidy 1968-71
Major General Raymond L. Shoemaker 1971-73
Major General C. J. LeVan 1973-76
Major General Robert J. Lunn 1976-77
Major General John J. Koehler, Jr. 1977-79
Major General John B. Oblinger, Jr. 1979-82
Major General James P. Maloney 1982-1985
Major General Donald R. Infante 1985-89
Brigadier General Jay Gardner 1989-89
Major General Donald M. Lionetti 1989-91
Major General John H. Little 1991-1993
Major General James J. Cravens 1993-

WHITE SANDS MISSILE RANGE COMMANDERS

Colonel Harold R. Turner 1945-47
Brigadier General Philip G. Blackmore 1947-1950
Brigadier General George G. Eddy 1950-54
Major General William L. Bell 1954-56
Major General Waldo E. Laidlaw 1956-60
Major General John G. Shinkle 1960-62
Major General J. Frederick Thorlin 1962-1965
Major General John M. Cone 1965-66
Major General Horace G. Davisson 1966-70
Major General Edward H. deSaussure 1970-72
Major General Arthur H. Sweeney 1972-74
Major General Robert J. Proudfoot 1974-75
Major General Orville L. Tobiason 1975-79
Major General Duard D. Ball 1979-80
Major General Alan A. Nord 1980-82
Major General Niles J. Fulwyler 1982-86
Major General Joe S. Owens 1986-87
Major General Thomas J. P. Jones 1987-90
Major General Ronald V. Hite 1990-91
Brigadier General Richard W. Wharton 1991-

EL PASO BOOKS I CONSIDER SPECIAL
(which are currently in print).

Braddy, Haldeen. *Pershing's Mission in Mexico*, 1916. Texas Western Press, UT El Paso, El Paso, TX., 79968.

Bryson, Conrey. *Down Went McGinty: El Paso in the Wonderful Nineties*. Texas Western Press, UT El Paso, El Paso, TX., 79968.

Cisneros, José. *Riders Across the Centuries: Horsemen of the Spanish Borderlands*. Texas Western Press, UT El Paso, El Paso, TX., 79968.

DeArment, Robert K. *George Scarborough: The Life and Death of A Lawman on the Closing Frontier*. University of Oklahoma Press: Norman, OK., 73019.

Egloff, Fred R. *El Paso Lawman: G. W. Campbell*. Creative Publishing, Box 9292, College Station, TX., 77840.

Frost, Gordon. *The Gentlemen's Club: The Story of Prostitution in El Paso*. Mangan Books, 6245 Snowheights, El Paso, TX, 79912.

Hamilton, Nancy. *UTEP: A Pictorial History of The University of Texas at El Paso*. Texas Western Press, UT El Paso, El Paso, TX., 79968.

Hooten, William J. *Fifty-Two Years a Newsman*. Texas Western Press, UT El Paso, El Paso, TX., 79968.

Hulse, J. F. *Revolutions and Railroads: The Story of Roy Hoard*. Mangan Books, 6245 Snowheights, El Paso, TX. 79912.

Latham, William I. *The Last Outpost of Texas: A History of the First Baptist Church*. Mangan Books, 6245 Snowheights, El Paso, TX., 79912.

Leach, Joseph. *Sun Country Banker*. Mangan Books, 6245 Snowheights, El Paso, TX., 79912.

Mangan, Frank. *El Paso in Pictures*. Mangan Books, 6245 Snowheights, El Paso, TX, 79912.

Sonnichsen, C. L. *Pass of the North: Four Centuries on the Rio Grande*. Two volumes. Texas Western Press, UT El Paso, 79968.

Timmons, W. H. *El Paso: A Borderlands History*. Texas Western Press, El Paso, TX., 79968

INDEX